Take Care of the Living

A NATION DIVIDED:
STUDIES IN THE CIVIL WAR ERA

Aaron Sheehan-Dean, *Editor*

TAKE CARE of THE LIVING

RECONSTRUCTING CONFEDERATE VETERAN FAMILIES IN VIRGINIA

Jeffrey W. McClurken

UNIVERSITY OF VIRGINIA PRESS

Charlottesville and London

University of Virginia Press
© 2009 by the Rector and Visitors of the University of Virginia
All rights reserved
Printed in the United States of America on acid-free paper

First published 2009

1 3 5 7 9 8 6 4 2

Library of Congress Cataloging-in-Publication Data
McClurken, Jeffrey W., 1973–
Take care of the living : reconstructing Confederate veteran families in Virginia /
Jeffrey W. McClurken.
p. cm. — (A nation divided : studies in the Civil War era)
Includes bibliographical references and index.
ISBN 978-0-8139-2813-5 (cloth : alk. paper) — ISBN 978-0-8139-2819-7 (e-book)
1. Reconstruction (U.S. history, 1865–1877)—Virginia—Pittsylvania County.
2. Veterans' families—Virginia—Pittsylvania County—History—19th century.
3. Reconstruction (U.S. history, 1865–1877)—Virginia—Danville.
4. Veterans' families—Virginia—Danville—History—19th century.
5. Veterans—Virginia—Pittsylvania County—Social conditions—19th century.
6. Veterans—Virginia—Danville—Social conditions—19th century.
7. Pittsylvania County (Va.)—Social conditions—19th century.
8. Danville (Va.)—Social conditions—19th century. 9. Virginia—History—Civil War,
1861–1865—Veterans. 10. United States—History—Civil War,
1861–1865—Veterans. I. Title.
F232.P7M337 2009
975.5'665041—dc22   2008048716

Contents

	List of Tables	vii
	Acknowledgments	ix
	Introduction	1
1.	The War Comes, 1860–1865	9
2.	Loss and Reconstruction: The Impact of the Civil War on Veteran Families and Their Postwar Rebuilding	44
3.	Local Support from Baptist Churches	72
4.	Appeals for Local Elite Assistance: The Case of William T. Sutherlin	99
5.	Veteran Families, Mental Illness, and the State: Dealing with the "Blue Devils"	118
6.	State Aid for Veteran Families: Artificial Limbs, Commutations, Pensions, and Confederate Homes	143
	Conclusion	173
	Appendix: A Note on Sources	175
	Notes	179
	Bibliography	215
	Index	235

Tables

1.1	Planters as part of the slaveholding population (1860)	11
1.2	Wartime disease deaths of county soldiers	18
1.3	Wartime infectious diseases among county soldiers	19
1.4	Battle casualties for county soldiers	24
1.5	Medical discharges for county soldiers	25
1.6	Wartime deaths for county soldiers	26
1.7	Wartime prices for food in county	32
1.8	Desertion rates for county soldiers	38
2.1	Economic impact of war for veteran families based on prewar slaveholding	47
2.2	Economic impact of various wartime experiences for county veteran families	48
3.1	Roanoke Baptist Association membership statistics, 1861–1865	76
3.2	Roanoke Baptist Association membership statistics, 1865–1880	92
5.1	Western Lunatic Asylum population, 1870–1900	138
6.1	Virginia's major Civil War pension laws	151

Acknowledgments

The creating of a scholarly work inevitably incurs significant debts from a number of people. This is my chance to thank them for their contribution to this work. Archivists and scholars at various institutions were extremely helpful in locating material and pointing me in the right direction for my research, including those at the Perkins Library at Duke University, at the Southern Historical Collection in Chapel Hill, and at Alderman Library at the University of Virginia. Darlene Slater at the Virginia Baptist Historical Society and Rick Wills at Western State Hospital were particularly helpful during my extended research visits at their institutions. The Virginia Historical Society awarded me a Mellon Fellowship for research in its archives. Francis Pollard, Nelson Lankford, and the rest of the terrific staff there offered useful advice and direction. Jack Bales and Carla Bailey at Mary Washington's Simpson Library deserve special recognition. An anonymous donor of a Summer Southern History Fellowship to the Department of History at Johns Hopkins funded the early stages of research for this project.

Parts of this project have been presented at the Veteran in America Conference at the University of Tennessee, the SIHC/Douglas Southall Freeman Civil War Conference, the Southern Historical Association Conference, the Virginia Forum, the SAWH Conference on Southern Women's History, and the SCWH Conference. I thank both the commentators and audiences for their critiques of my work, especially Jane Turner Censer, Steven Noll, Bob Kenzer, Susan Hamburger, and Nina Silber for their astute observations.

I am also indebted to a number of individual scholars and friends who have offered advice, constructive criticism, and encouragement during the years I have worked on this project. Bob Kenzer and Peter Bardaglio provided meals with their words of wisdom. LeeAnn Whites and Elna Green have offered sage advice and welcome support from the day I met each of them. Frank Levine answered all the questions of a database neophyte with humor, accuracy, and speed. Margaret Ray and Brad Hansen patiently explained wages and economic theories to a historian. Stephen Hanna put together the map. Ken Whitfield and Tobin W. Demsko provided an environment in which caffeinated final revisions were possible. Brad Wood, Ellen Pearson, Josh Rothman, Michelle LeMaster, Brian Gibney, Robyn Orr, Danielle Culpepper, Jason Davidson, and Sue Fernsebner provided friendship, advice, and more than a little motivation. I especially thank Ed Ayers for providing me the chance to learn some valuable skills and for always saying the right words at the right time.

Anne Sarah Rubin, Susanna Michele Lee, and Kara McClurken read versions of the complete manuscript. Their ideas and attention to detail greatly improved this project. Kara turned around the manuscript on a tight schedule despite her own array of projects. I will always owe her, a fact siblings tend to remember. I also thank Dick Holway and the reviewers for the University of Virginia Press, whose encouragement and recommendations made this a better book.

At the University of Mary Washington, the Department of History and American Studies gave me a start in the field of history, and now it is providing a home for my academic career, for which I am grateful. My colleagues' support, encouragement, and coffee have been essential to the completion of this project. That support included a Faculty Development Grant, which enabled key additions to several of the chapters.

I can only begin to thank the two men who served as my advisers, my mentors, and my friends. Those who know them will understand when I say that I have been truly lucky to work with two of the brightest scholars and teachers in the field of history. No young scholar could hope for better mentors. Among everything else, Ron Walters helped to broaden my perspective of the nineteenth and twentieth centuries in ways that not only made this work better but also improved my teaching and other scholarship. Many years ago, Michael Johnson took a chance by becoming my primary adviser. He has managed to steer me through the years with the same style, class, and penetrating observations that he brings to both academia and life.

My in-laws, Marilyn and Bob Orr, provided much-needed technical support, good meals and company, stimulating conversation, a welcome tolerance of their son-in-law's extended financial dependence on their daughter, and a willingness to spend lots of time with their granddaughters. My grandfather, Charles Wolfe, taught me long ago that history was important, interesting, and, like learning, an integral part of life. I hope that this work lives up to his impressive example. My parents, Laurel and Gene McClurken, provided me with a home that encouraged reading and intellectual pursuits and gave me the freedom and support to do both. They also created the ideal of a loving family that has greatly influenced both my life and this work. The arrival of my amazing daughters, Kate and Charlotte, undoubtedly delayed the completion of this project, but what wonderful delays they have been!

Finally, I thank my partner and spouse, Jennifer Orr. As I brought this project to its completion, she went well beyond what any spouse could be expected to do, and did so cheerfully and with great skill. Her love, support, patience, and perspective made this project both possible and better. For these and countless other reasons, this work is dedicated to her.

Take Care of the Living

Introduction

IN 1861 and 1862, James Redd, William Dix, and Joseph Miller enlisted in the Confederate Army from Pittsylvania County and Danville, Virginia. So too did George and James, the husbands of Barsheba Adams and Jane Smith. By the end of the war, Smith's and Adams's husbands were dead, Redd had been wounded, and Miller had lost his leg and spent a year as a Union prisoner of war. By 1870, Dix's family had lost 80 percent of their 1860 wealth, nearly $10,000. Beset with financial difficulties for many years, Dix attempted suicide. For these five soldiers and their families, the Civil War had brought significant consequences. Yet none of the members of these veteran families passively accepted their lot. They each employed strategies intended to maintain or reconstruct their families during and after the conflict. During the war, James Redd appealed for assistance to a member of the local elite, while Barsheba Adams and Jane Smith turned to their churches and families for emotional support. After the war, Mt. Hermon and Kentuck Baptist churches also provided the widows with financial assistance. In the aftermath of William Dix's suicide attempt, his family sent him to Virginia's Western Lunatic Asylum, from which he returned nineteen months later, apparently recovered. Joseph Miller turned to the state of Virginia for an artificial limb as well as for financial support, eventually gaining a pension in the later years of the nineteenth century. In the first years of the twentieth century, James Redd entered the Lee Camp Soldiers' Home, a state-supported home for disabled and elderly Confederate veterans. Like thousands of Pittsylvania's veteran families, these men and women looked for ways to cope with the consequences of the Civil War that often transcended the structure of their families.[1]

The goals of this study are twofold. First, it assesses the short- and long-term impact of the war on Confederate veteran families of all classes in Pittsylvania County and Danville, Virginia. Those families whose husbands, fathers, brothers, and sons served in the Confederate Army were affected demographically, economically, emotionally, and psychologically for the rest of their lives by what can be described as the human impact of the Civil War. Second, this book explores an array of strategies employed by those families to deal with the war's consequences, including reorganizing and reconstructing the household, turning to local churches for emotional and economic support, pleading with local elites for financial assistance or positions, sending psychologically damaged family members to a state-run asylum, and looking to the state for direct assistance in the form of replacement limbs for amputees, pensions, and even state-supported homes for old soldiers and widows. Although these strategies or institutions for reconstructing the family had their roots in previous practices, the extreme need of veteran families brought on by the scope and impact of the Civil War required an expansion beyond anything previously seen, eventually resulting in a wide-ranging state social-welfare system.

This work sits at the crossroads of three vibrant fields of scholarship: the social and cultural history of Civil War soldiers, the role of gender and family in the Civil War era, and the study of Southern social welfare. Scholars in the first area have described the difficult living and fighting conditions, debated the motivations of soldiers in enlisting, and catalogued the diseases, wounds, and deaths experienced. In studies of Civil War veterans, those historians have emphasized the roles of postwar organizations, military homes, and soldiers' pensions.[2] Historians examining the Southern household during the Civil War and Reconstruction have made clear that the conflict and emancipation significantly affected gender roles and relations—though these historians have debated the long-term effects of these events—and shaped a Southern transition from a potentially multiracial household to a more exclusive white family.[3] The final field has been defined in recent years by Elna Green's two edited volumes and her sweeping analysis of two hundred years of Richmond's welfare history. Green and other scholars have connected the history of Southern social welfare to the larger American narrative, arguing that the South's approach to assistance to the needy was uniquely Southern, though heavily influenced at times by trends in American society.[4]

In building on the scholarship and approaches of these three fields, this work contributes to the larger discussion in several key ways. First, given that families were the fundamental social and economic units in the nineteenth century, this work places Confederate veteran families, not just soldiers, at the center of analysis. The Civil War affected these families more than almost any other group. Although *family* and *household* are historically complex terms, I employ them here in a specific way; in this study, *veteran family* and *veteran household* refer to former Confederate soldiers and their relatives living in the same home.[5] (Based on a post-emancipation understanding of the Southern white family, this definition does not include those non-family-members, white or black, who lived at times in veteran households.) This study begins by asking how the war and its legacy affected Confederate veteran families and how families worked to deal with those consequences over the following decades. The Civil War destroyed some veteran families and deeply wounded others. The men and women and children in these families were affected during the war by shortages and by the realities of Civil War life and combat, by the death, wounding, or illness of their male family members. Ultimately these families suffered economically, emotionally, and physically. Those who survived confronted a postwar world with a different landscape with regard to the economy, race relations, and the interactions between men and women. Veteran families also had to cope with the legacy of their wartime sacrifices for decades after the war. Shared experiences strengthened some families' bonds, while others were weakened. This book argues that these veteran families turned, often as families, to numerous sources of social assistance to rebuild themselves in the aftermath of the war.

The second historiographic contribution of this work builds on the notion that Southern white masculinity, with its emphasis on independent household patriarchs, was challenged by the war and its aftermath. I argue that the attempts to deal with the consequences were shaped by the gendered frameworks within which the families operated. Sometimes familial strategies involved reinforcing previous gender roles, and sometimes those strategies—most notably women's efforts outside the home—challenged those gender roles; at other times, institutions outside the family stepped in to replace fathers and husbands as patriarchs.

Third, although many works on the Civil War era have focused on the experiences of the elite and middle class, this work explores the impact on and strategies of veteran families regardless of economic standing. Fourth, this book examines the way that as the years passed, as veterans and their families aged, they looked increasingly to the state for assistance. I argue that the state responded to the hole in soldiers' households that was created by the war with vastly expanded involvement in financial and institutional support, support typically reserved for whites. Much of this support was exclusively reserved for a subset of that group, the neediest of Confederate veteran families.[6] Finally, despite the extensive contemporary discussion and historical scholarship centered on emancipation and its effects, this work makes clear that the human impact of the war and the struggle to survive was at least as important to many Southern whites.[7]

This book is not a complete history of Confederate veteran families from 1860 to 1900. For example, it does not engage extensively with the growing literature on the construction of Civil War memory or explore in detail its role in the county, save for where it touches on the lives and strategies of veteran families.[8] Recent scholarship has demonstrated that the Confederate memorialization of the dead was a key part of the Southern white postbellum response to the war, but this book emphasizes that a strong current of white Southern life wanted "to take care of the living," as a minister from Danville told his audience after the war.[9]

I have chosen to study the impact of the war and its aftermath on Confederate veteran families in a specific place, Pittsylvania County, Virginia, and its largest town, Danville. Concentration on a particular county provides both precision and some continuity in the various documentary sources used.[10] Pittsylvania County is an ideal place to measure the human consequences of the war.[11] Nearly four-fifths of the county's men of military age served in front-line Confederate units, and one-fourth of those men died in service. Nearly half survived the war after being wounded, seriously ill, or imprisoned in Union jails. The area's high casualties and lack of property damage—the nearest battle was over fifty miles away—allows a focus on changes brought about by injuries to people rather than to property. Still, despite the narrow geographic focus, the experiences and strategies employed by the county's veteran families could probably be found in Confederate families throughout the South.[12]

The book is organized as a series of case studies based on the various people, places, and institutions to which Confederate veteran families turned during and after the Civil War. The case studies were chosen based on the availability of sources and on a desire to include a mix of familial, local, and state sources of assistance. Although not every possible source of aid is covered, those chosen highlight the breadth of survival strategies employed and the central role of the Civil War in the lives of these veteran families for decades afterward.[13]

Chapter 1 begins with a description of Pittsylvania County and Danville before the Civil War and then moves forward into the conflict itself. The chapter explores the wartime experiences of soldiers and their families, including the problems related to disease, wounding, death, separation from family, inflation, and mounting family debt. The strategies used by the women and men of the county's soldiers' families to deal with these problems foreshadowed the postwar efforts of veteran families to turn to extra-familial sources of aid.

The remaining chapters are structured around veteran families' survival strategies, starting in the household and moving outward, first to local assistance and then to the state of Virginia. Chapter 2 explores veteran families' attempts to deal with the impact of the war in their own households and in the homes of extended family members and friends. Primarily using manuscript census and military records, this chapter suggests that the war and its aftermath disproportionately affected the finances of veteran families, at least in the short term, though in different ways based on their soldiers' wartime experiences.[14] The chapter then describes a postwar support system grounded in the familial household and supplemented by other relatives and friends to which veteran families turned for emotional and financial assistance. Strategies included reconfiguring family household structures, trying to succeed in farming or other occupations through the labor of all family members, turning to the help of relatives and friends outside the home, and even leaving Pittsylvania County and Danville for a new start somewhere else. These strategies relied on the strength of the family, however, and the conflict and the postwar world sometimes weakened the bonds among members, resulting in familial strife, even violence. These problems made it difficult for some families to reconstruct themselves without outside assistance.

The failure of many veteran families to cope on their own with the consequences of the war led to their turning to other people and institutions for further assistance. In helping veteran families, these other people and institutions sometimes took over roles, if only temporarily, as provider and protector previously occupied by white male family heads. Chapters 3 and 4 examine two aspects of the local circle of assistance through an analysis of the aid provided by the Baptist churches of the area and by one member of Pittsylvania's elite. Part of a long-existing system of local aid, churches and elite men and women took on new importance and additional roles given the postwar needs of veterans and their families. As was the case for most people in need in the nineteenth century, veteran family members had to prove their worth and good character in order to receive any assistance from churches or elite men and women.[15]

Chapter 3 uses church records to detail the ways Pittsylvania's Baptist congregations provided their veteran family members with emotional, spiritual, and even limited financial and educational support during and after the Civil War. The procedure for distributing the churches' financial aid to their most needy members, typically the widows of veterans, took place within a gendered framework, in which the churches served as paternal replacements for men lost in the war. All church-based assistance, financial or otherwise, came at the price of conformity to the churches' behavioral standards. Some veteran family members were unable to conform and were expelled from their congregations, losing the support that the churches represented. Others abandoned their churches, angered or dissatisfied, with their emotional and economic needs unfulfilled.

As evidenced by growing membership during and after the war, however, many Pittsylvanians found some measure of solace and support, albeit limited financial aid, in the county's Baptist churches.

Another source of local aid to which veteran families turned was the wealthy members of their community. Appeals made to one of Pittsylvania County's wealthiest men, William T. Sutherlin, support the idea that an older system of perceived reciprocal obligations between the wealthy and the non-elite members of a community persisted in limited form in the postwar South.[16] Men and women wrote to Sutherlin, asking for his assistance in the form of money, jobs, or the use of his influence on their behalf. The petitioners all attempted to demonstrate to Sutherlin their need, their worthiness of assistance, and the ties of mutual obligation that they claimed bound Sutherlin to them. Analysis of the appeals to Sutherlin indicates that in deciding which of his needy petitioners to help, he favored veterans over non-veterans. Sutherlin's choices suggest that in the postwar world, needy veterans and their family members constituted a new category of worthiness for aid. The limited postwar assistance provided by Sutherlin and other members of Pittsylvania's upper class was not enough, however, even when added to the church support, to meet the needs of all of the county's veteran families.

The neediest veteran families turned to their state for assistance. Rarely in the antebellum period had the state of Virginia stepped in to help individual families. Such aid was perceived as the responsibility of the older network of relatives, friends, neighbors, churches, and members of the local upper class. The massive economic, physical, and psychological impact of the Civil War on Confederate veteran families caused the most needy to slip through the cracks of the older, local system. As other historians have described, the late nineteenth century was a time of expanded state and federal responsibility for individuals (especially for Civil War veterans and their family members). Whereas most of the scholarship that has been done in this area has focused on the growth of the federal government through its generous aid for Northern soldiers, in chapters 5 and 6, I explore Virginia's expanded role in assisting Confederate veterans and their families who slipped through the first two circles of aid.[17] These two chapters describe the needs and options for two specific groups of veteran families, those with mentally ill members and those that were impoverished or that had disabled soldiers.

Chapter 5 explores the links between the Civil War and mental problems and details the role that Virginia's Western Lunatic Asylum played in assisting veterans and their family members. This chapter adds to the literature on the psychological impact of the Civil War by focusing on Confederate veterans, their female relatives, and those whose mental illnesses were attributed to the war.[18] The asylum records for patients from Pittsylvania's veteran families and those admitted because of psychological problems attributed to "The War" indicate that many Virginians, including asylum doctors and the families of patients, believed that the Civil War and its aftermath caused mental illnesses. Although skepticism about adopting these nineteenth-century diagnoses is in order, it is also reasonable to accept that the political, economic, familial, and medical stresses placed on veteran family members had a significant mental impact. The chapter explores the effect that patients' mental illnesses and their status as "insane" had on the rest of their families. Ultimately, this chapter contends that through the asylum, the state of Virginia took on responsibilities that some veteran families or local support systems were unable to bear, caring for or even "curing" veteran family members.

Chapter 6 continues the discussion of expanded state support through an examination of the financial aid and homes provided by Virginia for the men and women of veteran families most physically and economically affected by the war. The first part of the chapter describes the evolution of Virginia's financial and housing assistance for certain veterans and their families, as seen in a series of acts passed by the Virginia General Assembly. Beginning with provisions for artificial limbs soon after the war ended, the legislators of Virginia gradually began to offer economic assistance to a wider range of the state's financially needy veterans, from amputees to those disabled during the war to those disabled by age, eventually making money available to impoverished widows of veterans. The aid came first in the form of artificial limbs, then cash commutations, annual pensions, and homes for elderly or disabled veterans and their widows or daughters. This chapter argues that Virginia's legislators responded to the human impact of the Civil War on veteran families by gradually creating a social-welfare system focused on the state's neediest and most deserving veterans and their widows. The second part of chapter 6 uses the application files for artificial limbs, commutations, pensions, and admission to the Lee Camp Soldiers' Home to argue for the economic and psychological significance of the state aid received by the veterans of Pittsylvania and Danville and their families. For those families with disabled or deceased veterans, this aid served both an obvious economic need and a less apparent, but not less important, desire for official recognition by the state of the sacrifices that soldiers and their families made in the war.

The financial assistance and homes made available to Confederate veterans and their widows never came close to the massive breadth and generosity of the federal pension system. The bulk of Virginia and other Southern states' assistance to their most needy veterans and veterans' widows came decades after the war's end and failed to satisfy completely all economic problems; the homes were limited in size, and the care was less than ideal at times. Nonetheless, the state's assistance and recognition were greatly appreciated and certainly needed. By helping these veteran families, the state took over some of the responsibilities previously handled by the families themselves, by their relatives and friends, or by their churches or local members of the upper class.

The Civil War was devastating for Southern veteran families, and it took time and help from a variety of sources to rebuild. Yet, beyond individual anecdotes, before now, historians have rarely examined systematically that impact or the process of rebuilding, nor have the stories been told from the point of view of a large number of veteran families. This study of Confederate veteran families in Pittsylvania County and Danville suggests that there were broader trends at work. When Confederate veterans and their families attempted to reconstruct their lives in the chaotic postwar world, they participated in and helped cause a gradual expansion from reliance on an older system of family, friends, churches, and local elites to the rise of a more state-based system of support. In the exploration of the people and institutions to which veteran families turned, it is possible to see the rise of a paternal state replacing some of the functions of individual families and their local support system.[19]

This work further argues that in the postwar period Pittsylvania's veteran families helped refine nineteenth-century understandings of what made one worthy of assistance. Impoverished Confederate veterans and their family members earned an honored place in the "worthy" category of the needy poor.[20] This shift was largely justified by the notion that their condition stemmed from the sacrifices they had made of themselves and their husbands and fathers to the Confederate cause, but it also grew out of the politics of the late nineteenth century. Due to the Civil War's array of consequences and the public reinforcement of veteran families' former Confederate status throughout the nineteenth and into the twentieth centuries, the conflict occupied a central role in many of these families' lives for decades after the war had ended. Ultimately, though the aid and support offered to Confederate veteran families in those postwar years were never as much as they might have wished and at times came with restrictive conditions, the various people and institutions discussed in the following pages offered some measure of substantive relief for the impact of the Civil War.

1

The War Comes, 1860–1865

> I live inhopes that I shall see you again.... I am inhopes that when we meet again it will be never to part again.
>
> —George Jones to Sarah Jones, his wife, January 6, 1864

PITTSYLVANIA COUNTY, Virginia's largest in area, has the rolling landscape typical of the foothills east of the Blue Ridge Mountains. The county is in the southern part of Virginia's Piedmont region, located on the North Carolina border. In 1860, as today, its largest community was Danville, a city located on the south bank of the Dan River and in the southern portion of the county. Economic growth, largely based on tobacco, had caused the city's population to more than double from 1850 to 1860, when it numbered over thirty-five hundred people. Although linked to western and northern Virginia, and northern North Carolina to the south, by road, canal, or river, on the eve of the Civil War the most important transportation route for Danville (and for all of Pittsylvania County) was the Richmond and Danville Railroad, completed in 1856, which connected the people of the area to Richmond, the economic and political capital of the state.

After Danville, the next largest concentration of people was at the county seat, called Pittsylvania Court House, although it was later named Chatham; in 1860, its population numbered about 350 people. Pittsylvania County had a number of other communities—Callands, Museville, Sandy Level, Whitmell, Cascade, Kentuck, Laurel Grove, and others—all largely rural farming towns of fewer than one hundred people. The county's total population, of over thirty-two thousand inhabitants, made it the third largest in the state in 1860. Almost entirely native born, the county's population was about 53 percent white. The remainder of the county's residents, almost fifteen thousand men and women, were black, the vast majority of them held in slavery and working on the region's ubiquitous tobacco farms.[1]

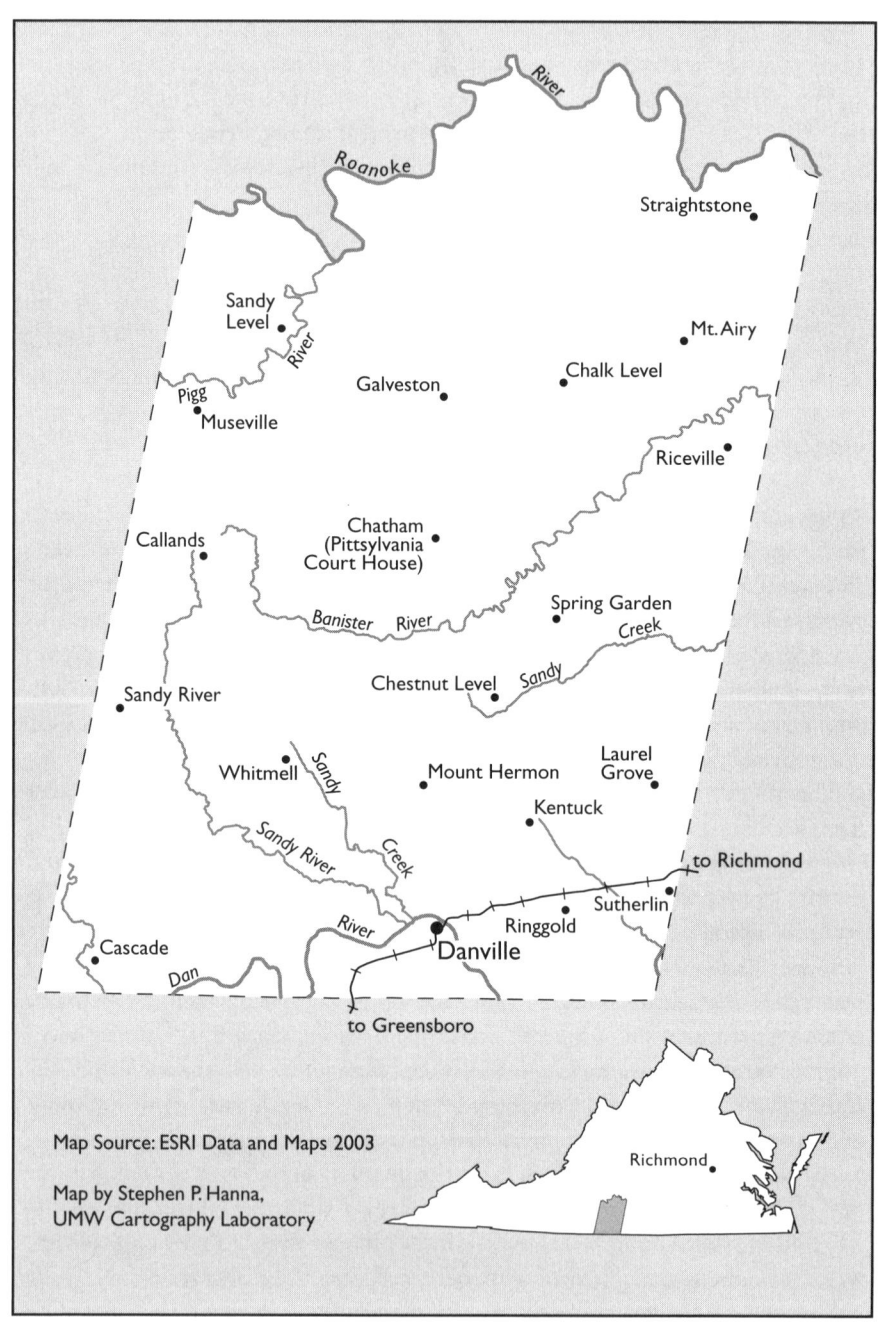

Pittsylvania County, Virginia

TABLE 1.1
PLANTERS AS PART OF THE SLAVEHOLDING POPULATION (1860)

	Total number of slaveholders	Total number of slaveholders who own twenty or more slaves	Percentage of slaveholders who own twenty or more slaves
Deep South totals	181,521	30,477	16.79
Upper South totals	212,446	17,094	8.05
Virginia	52,128	5,777	11.08
Pittsylvania/Danville	1,413	189	13.38

Source: ICPSR, *Historical Demographic, Economic, and Social Data*, 1860, as presented by the Historical Census Browser, http://fisher.lib.virginia.edu/collections/stats/histcensus/.

Some historians have argued that by 1860 the states of the Upper South had begun, for a variety of reasons, to reduce their investment in and commitment to slavery. Although this seems to have been true for certain regions in Virginia—the overall percentage of slaves in the state's population had fallen in the decade from 1850 to 1860, from 33 percent to 30 percent—Pittsylvania was not one of those regions. In that same decade, in Pittsylvania County, the number of slaves had increased, at the same rate as the increase in the white population.[2]

According to one historian, "Pittsylvania was not an area of large planters and poor whites, but an area of relative white equality." Indeed, slaveholding was fairly well distributed among the white population of the county. Although only about 25 percent of all Southern white households in 1860 owned slaves, about 40 percent of Pittsylvania County white households owned slaves. The county had a slightly larger percentage of planter households (those owning twenty or more slaves) among slaveholding households than the state had (see table 1.1), but its percentage was lower than for households in the Deep South states. Landownership was another indicator of the county's "relative white equality." Augusta County, a region described—both at the time and by historians today—as a county with good opportunities for middling people in 1860, had landownership rates of only 62 percent. Comparably, in 1860 roughly 65 percent of Pittsylvania's households owned land.[3]

Most of the land and slaves controlled by white Pittsylvanians were used to grow tobacco. The crop had been the dominant product of the county since its inception, and a recent boom in tobacco in the 1850s had merely increased Pittsylvania's commitment to it. Tobacco was central to the economy of all Pittsylvania farmers, in part because of a lack of alternatives. The county was too cold to grow cotton, too hot and humid for the grasses needed to raise large herds of cattle with great success, and its sandy soil, although perfect for tobacco, made raising grains difficult (although most farmers did grow corn for their own use). Partly for these reasons, Pittsylvania's farmers had not been able to embrace the diversified farming approach seen in many Virginia counties by 1860. Still, Pittsylvania County grew a great deal economically in the 1850s, largely because of the increasing popularity of a particular variant, bright-leaf tobacco, which grew well in the county's sandy soils, and because of the beginning of significant tobacco manufacturing in Danville. These two factors accounted for the county's focus on tobacco, obviating the need for the 70 percent of white rural households that were engaged in farming to try another style of agriculture.[4]

By 1860, one-third of the value of Virginia's manufacturing came from processing tobacco, and Danville (along with Pittsylvania County) was the state's third-largest producer of manufactured tobacco. Initially, tobacco processing just involved turning tobacco leaves into "plugs," or "twists," that Americans would chew after biting off a piece. Because such tobacco manufacturing was simple enough to be done on a small scale in individual households, it was not until 1850 that Danville's larger tobacco manufacturers produced more than the part-time operators in Pittsylvania County did. On the eve of the Civil War, although the focus of tobacco manufacturing was switching to the factories in Danville, some tobacco processing was still taking place in people's homes and in small processing factories in the county.[5]

The Coming of the War

In the momentous four-way 1860 presidential election, Pittsylvania County voted, by a plurality, for John Bell, the candidate of the newly created Constitutional Union Party. Danville also voted for Bell and did so overwhelmingly, giving him a sizable majority. Bell won Virginia as well, but the election went to Abraham Lincoln, and the process of secession began with South Carolina's withdrawal from the Union in December 1860. By February 1861, six other states had done the same, and the Confederacy was formed in Montgomery, Alabama.[6]

Like people in the rest of the Upper South, Pittsylvanians and Danvillians had varying points of view on whether their state should secede as well. The region had its "active and earnest advocate[s] of Secession" in the early months of 1861. When the election for delegates to the state's secession convention was held in early February 1861, however, the county and city elected, by wide majorities, William T. Sutherlin and William Tredway, both anti-secession men. Through February, March, and early April, although there were some dissident voices who spoke for secession—Sutherlin's brother, George, tried to convince the delegate that "Virginia is bound to go with the south"—most of the county and city waited with the majority of the Upper South to see what would happen with peace and reunification efforts, a stance that one historian has described as "conditional unionism." The majority of the people in Pittsylvania and Danville in early 1861 believed the crisis would be resolved in Washington or Richmond.[7]

Any hopes in Pittsylvania—or in the Upper South states as a whole—of a peaceful settlement were predicated on the notion that Lincoln and the Union would not take any military action against the seceded Southern states, a condition violated by the North's initial mobilization of seventy-five thousand soldiers to put down the rebellion in the Deep South states in the aftermath of the shelling of Fort Sumter in April 1865. William T. Sutherlin told the Virginia secession convention after reports of Lincoln's request were confirmed, "I have a Union constituency which elected me by a majority of one thousand, and I believe now that there are not ten Union men in that county to-day." As in the rest of Virginia, Tennessee, North Carolina, and Arkansas, Lincoln's call for troops swept Danville and Pittsylvania County into secession and war.[8]

Virginia's Confederate companies and regiments formed much the same way as they did throughout the North and the South for the Civil War. Although the Confederacy did eventually institute a military draft, the majority of its troops volunteered for service. A few units had been antebellum militia companies, but most were formed specifically for the war. Companies were typically formed from men of a particular city or village. Most communities held a rally with patriotic speeches, followed by men enlisting. The volunteers then elected their officers (often the rally organizers and almost always politically and economically prominent citizens). Many of Pittsylvania County's villages (Callands, Whitmell, Cascade, Kentuck, Laurel Grove) produced at least one company. The county's two largest settlements, Chatham and Danville, produced the most companies, three and five, respectively.

Because each company was formed from a single area, most of the men joined the army with their relatives, friends, and neighbors, people they had known their entire lives. Four of the Cousins brothers enlisted in the Pittsylvania Dragoons, a local cavalry company; George Jones and Isaac Dodson, who served together, lived near each other and were friends. This practice meant that Pittsylvania-Danville soldiers served with people who knew them and could provide support and camaraderie, but it also meant that their actions (or inactions) would be reported back to their homes.⁹

After a company or regiment was created, it was accorded a number of ceremonies and celebrations by members of the community. The experiences of two companies of the 18th Virginia Infantry as recorded by one resident of Danville in early 1861 were typical: "On Saturday there was a parade of the [Danville] Blues and Grays and the presentation of a Secession Flag by some persons of the [Danville Female] College." Several prominent townspeople made speeches praising the men of the units.¹⁰

There was also a ceremony, sometimes separate from the first one, to send off the men when they marched off to war. William Tredway, son of the secession convention delegate of the same name, later remembered the scene when his Chatham Grays left for Richmond. The whole town turned out, "vast crowds of men, women, and children assembled on the streets," to see them off. "Loving wives and children kissed husband, parent, brother, the sad good-bye; sweethearts parted with blessed promises of a more happy union when the cruel war should be over; friendly hands gave the parting grasp to the soldier in the line." The group marched out of Chatham to the railroad in Danville, where they received a warm welcome: "Champagne flowed freely and merry-making was the order of the night." The next morning they took the train to Richmond with some of the other area companies to join the Confederate forces forming there.¹¹

In May 1861, Powhatan B. Whittle, raising a company at Chatham, wrote to his brother, Lewis Whittle, "We are succeeding rather slowly. The men of this region do not seem to enlist as readily as persons in the South." Whittle's comment seems to indicate that after the first rush of volunteers, enlistment in the county may have slowed some. Eventually, however, men from Pittsylvania and Danville made up the majority of twenty-two companies in nine front-line Virginia regiments, including the 38th Virginia Infantry, known as the "Pittsylvania Regiment" for its seven companies from the county. A few more local men were scattered in other regiments, such as William Dame, who joined the Richmond Howitzers, or Chiswell Dabney, who joined a North Carolina cavalry unit.¹²

In fact, the vast majority of men of military age in the county served in the military in some capacity during the war. One historian has estimated that 61 percent of white Southern men of military age ("age 13 to 43 in 1860") served in the Confederate Army. About 79 percent (3,283) of Pittsylvania-Danville white men of military age joined one of the regular army units, those front-line troops who fought in many of the major battles of the Civil War in the East.¹³ The percentage of military-age men mobilized from the area increases to over 83 percent (3,453) if those in the Virginia Reserves, Home Guard, and Otey's Artillery, a company made from the employees of Danville's Arsenal, are included.[14]

Given the enthusiastic send-offs many Civil War volunteers received and their naiveté about what the war would be like, it is not surprising that most soldiers from Pittsylvania and Danville shared a confidence and optimism early in the war. Years later, Robert Withers, a colonel of the 18th Virginia Infantry, claimed that at the start of the war he had "not share[d] the confident anticipation of speedy and glorious victory which seemed to animate a large majority of those around [him]." If this claim is true, Withers was one of few area soldiers who did not have that optimistic view of the Confederate Army's chances. Isaac Carrington of the 38th Virginia Infantry wrote to a friend in November 1861, claiming, "If there is one thing utterly impossible, it is that this army can be whipt by any force the Yankees can bring against us."[15]

Soldiers' Experiences during the War

As with other Confederates, the early confidence and optimism of the area's soldiers (and most civilians) was challenged by the experiences of those in service in the field and of their families back in Cascade, Callands, and Danville. Life as a soldier or as a member of a soldier's family was far from easy during the Civil War. Soldiers had to endure weather extremes out in the open, supply and food shortages, disease, separation from their families, battles, wounds, death, and, for some, time in Northern prisoner-of-war (POW) camps. Their families not only suffered from the separation from their men and from shortages but also had to survive without the labor and skills of their soldiers and manage despite crippling inflation on the home front. These experiences defined the Civil War for soldiers and their families, and they often shaped their postwar lives as well.

Exposure to bad weather was simply a part of life for Civil War soldiers. They often had to march and live in cold, wet, muddy conditions. Heading toward Richmond in early April 1862, the 18th Virginia Infantry had to deal with poor weather, "Hail and snow, mud and slush combined." One soldier in the 21st Virginia Infantry wryly described how poor conditions and marching had changed his view of mountains, which "are very pretty things when you wind along between them on a rail road, or even when riding slowly over them on horseback, but to have to walk over 3 of them in one day, through mud & water, detracts very much from their beauty."[16]

Extended exposure to the elements proved wearying, if not debilitating, for many soldiers. On the way to one battle, William Dame and his artillery battery had an exhausting trip. "It was an all-night march, and a most uncomfortable one. The rain had been pouring, and long sections of the road were under water. I think we waded for miles, that dark night, through water from an inch to a foot deep. And the mud holes! ... I suppose we did not go more than five or six miles, in that all-night march, and by the time day dawned we were as wet, and muddy, as the roads, and felt as flat, and were tired to death. We halted for an hour or two to rest; then pushed on, all day." Although soldiers' complaints often detailed the problems of rain, snow, and cold weather, heat could be just as debilitating. A physician in the 57th Virginia Infantry recorded in his diary during a scorching June march, "Excessively hot day[;] a great many men overcome by heat, one in my Regt. had coup de soleil [sunstroke] & had to be left on the road."[17]

Living conditions were so bad for Pittsylvania's soldiers, and for the rest of the Confederate Army, largely because of the inability of the government throughout the war to provide its men with adequate supplies, especially blankets, tents, and clothes. One soldier complained to his wife in late October, "Sue, I have been seeing a pretty ruf [rough] time for the last three or four days. ... We have had a very cold rain and we have had to take it all[;] we have no tents. I recon we will get some before long, if we dont we will see a hard time of it." As November began and the weather got even colder, his unit still had no tents and he had but "one blanket."[18]

The lack of clothes became a serious problem for some units from Pittsylvania. The 38th Virginia Infantry had problems at the beginning of the war because they had not been given enough shirts and pants. In one plaintive letter in the late summer of 1861, an officer wrote to people in Danville for help, noting, "my men are nearly necked." Even those who received clothes early in the war needed to have them replaced after two or three years of hard use wore them out. As one soldier noted in a letter to his family, "I observe that my shirts are beginning to exhibit signs of decay & fear they should give out suddenly & leave me shirtless."[19]

Given all the marching that the Confederate Army did during the war, the dearth of footwear brought suffering, even long-term damage, for the men (and lost manpower for the units). "I am almost without socks," one soldier wrote home, "the toes and heels being wornd away & I know of no place where I can get any." Rawley Martin and his men in the 53rd Virginia Infantry "had to make [the] long march[es] almost bare-footed," and their "bloody footprints ... marked the rocky" ground.[20]

For all the suffering that soldiers endured because of the weather and a lack of adequate supplies, most of their complaining seemed to focus on the very real problem of food shortages. "This hunger was much the hardest trial we had to bear," one Danvillian soldier remembered years later. "We didn't mind much getting wet and cold; working hard, standing guard at night; and fighting when required—we were seasoned to all that—but you don't season to hunger." It was a constant pain, always with the men: "Going all day with a gnawing at your insides, of which you were always conscious, was not pleasant. We had more appetite than anything else, and never got enough to satisfy it—even for a time." Another soldier wrote home, "we have to fast two days out of the five." Even when they were given food every day, the portions were too small to satisfy the men who made "awful complaint of short rations." Unfortunately, "that small ration dwindled until, at times, eating was likely to become a 'lost art.'"[21]

The constant life outdoors, often without proper food, clothes, or supplies, was too much for some soldiers. One protested in 1862, "I have been in the service about eight months.... My health is such, that I can not stand the exposure & hardship of camp life." Soldiers were weakened by the "hardship of camp life" in ways that had both short- and long-term effects on their lives. Not only did soldiers suffer during the war, but years later many veterans claimed that their wartime exposure had debilitated them.[22]

Illness was another significant part of the wartime experiences of the soldiers of Pittsylvania and Danville. Jed Carter wrote home to his wife from his camp in Charlotte County, on the James River, "This a sickly country down hear[;] some of the boys have chils every day[.] I am very fraid they will get holt of me." Jed's fears were justified. The lack of previous contact by the largely rural population with many illnesses, combined with inadequate sanitation, exposure to the elements, and insufficient or spoiled food, meant that infectious diseases were a serious, life-threatening problem for many individuals and potentially debilitating for an army.[23]

Although statistics on illness in the Confederacy as a whole are far from precise, most estimates indicate that at least half (if not two-thirds) of the deaths of soldiers in the South were caused by disease and that many more were seriously affected by sickness during the war. Pittsylvania's soldiers were not outside that trend, with disease causing about 55 percent of the deaths for which a cause is known (see table 1.2). Overall, nearly 12 percent of the soldiers from the county died from disease over the course of the war. Even if they did not die, almost half of the county's soldiers were sick enough to enter a hospital at some point during the war.[24]

Some infectious diseases spread during the war because soldiers from predominantly rural communities had not been exposed to them before and there-

TABLE 1.2
WARTIME DISEASE DEATHS OF COUNTY SOLDIERS

Disease deaths	383
As percentage of total deaths (831)	46.09
As percentage of deaths with known cause (696)	55.03
As percentage of total served (on front lines, 3,283)	11.67

Source: Soldiers Database.

fore had not developed any biological resistance. Measles and smallpox infected only a small number of Pittsylvania and Danville men (about 3 percent), but in most cases with deadly results. The most serious infectious diseases of the Civil War, however, were largely a result of poor sanitation. Typhoid fever, dysentery/diarrhea, pneumonia, and malaria—called by one prominent historian the "principal killer diseases of the war"—spread quickly, viciously, and continuously through Pittsylvania's troops and the rest of the armies because of cramped and dirty living conditions, contaminated water supplies, and what amounted to ideal breeding conditions for disease-bearing insects. Among Pittsylvanians, these four "killer diseases" caused over half the deaths from illness and nearly one-third of the deaths of county soldiers (see table 1.3). Overall, 15 percent of local troops caught one of these illnesses.[25]

One example is illustrative of the potentially catastrophic and debilitating impact of these infectious diseases on men and military units. Almost a month after the first battle of Manassas, an officer of the "Pittsylvania Regiment" (38th Virginia Infantry) expressed his concerns about the widespread illness in the regiment's northern Virginia camp in a letter to a friend in Danville: "A large number of our men are sick. Some fifteen have died in the Regiment: others will probably die as we have a number of cases of Typhoid fever." He then added that they had "lost a young man by the name of Hutson this morning." Matters only got worse for the 38th. A month later, the original letter writer was himself sick, and his subordinate wrote to his brother of the continued impact of the illnesses: "Our Regiment is now suffering more from sickness than it has at any time since we have been out. We have over 300 cases *Typhoid fever* so our Surgeon says." That number meant that out of roughly one thousand men, about 30 percent of them were ill with typhoid fever alone. In fact, only ten days later, the 38th moved from Manassas Junction to Manassas and left most of its men behind, taken out of commission by illness. Joseph Cabell and George Sutherlin's company, nearly one hundred men at the start, marched with only

TABLE 1.3
WARTIME INFECTIOUS DISEASES AMONG COUNTY SOLDIERS

	Cases	Deaths	Percentage of cases who died	Percentage who got disease of all 3,283 soldiers
Measles/smallpox (rubeola)	91	47	51.65	2.77
The four "killer diseases":				
Typhoid fever	169	100	59.17	5.15
Dysentery/diarrhea	254	62	24.41	7.74
Pneumonia	95	50	52.63	2.89
Malaria (intermittent/remittent fever)	29	10	34.48	0.88
Total of four "killer diseases"	504	222	44.05	15.35
Other infectious diseases:				
Catarrh/bronchitis (respiratory infection)	60	10	16.67	1.83
Syphilis/gonorrhea	23	2	8.70	0.70
Tuberculosis, consumption, phthisis	28	6	21.43	0.85
Yellow fever, scarlet fever	10	2	20.00	0.30
Erysipelas	14	3	21.43	0.43
Mumps	4	0	0.00	0.12
Non-infectious illnesses:				
Rheumatism	141	4	2.84	4.29
Scurvy	5	4	80.00	0.15

Source: Soldiers Database; Steiner, *Disease in the Civil War*, 9–12.

forty-five, and it was "the largest company in the Regiment as several does not number over 20 men."²⁶

Although less widespread, non-infectious illnesses also caused problems for Civil War soldiers during and after the war. The most common was rheumatism, which could debilitate its victims. At least one of every twenty-five Pittsylvania soldiers suffered from rheumatism during the war. George Jones's experience illustrates the potentially significant impact of the disease. In late 1863, George had an attack of rheumatism "for . . . six weeks," which meant he "was perfectly helpless[,] could not do anything for [himself]." George slowly recovered to the point where he was "able to go about again." Three months later, another attack—"for upward of six weeks"—left him too weak to "use [his] hand to write." Chilly weather only exacerbated the effects of the condition. That fall he wrote home, "I can feel the effects of my Rheumatism right smartly[;] am fearfull as the weather turns colder I shall be knocked up with it again." As a result, George and other sufferers came to "dread [their] Rheumatism" before every winter because of its crippling effect on their bodies. Many veterans continued to deal with these symptoms for the rest of their lives.²⁷

In late 1863, Jedediah Carter's frustration with his life as a soldier boiled up and over in a letter he wrote to his wife: "Sue, I wish this wicked war would come [to an] end. I am getting tyre of it. I don't get more than half enough to eat, all [the] handsful of lice and the sick, it is enough to make a preacher swain. Sue, I am nearly derange one half of my time, it looks like I dont care whatever of me[;] I want to go home. I wish every soldier that is in the confederate army would leave and go home to day. I would willingly go with them." Jed was tired and hungry and surrounded by disease. Like hundreds of thousands of other soldiers during the Civil War, he wanted to go home to his family, whom he missed a great deal. Homesickness, concern about one's family, anxiety about their safety and well-being, angst at separation from them, especially at times of great need, all these emotional burdens played key roles in the wartime experiences of the soldiers from Pittsylvania County and Danville.²⁸

Soldiers missed their families and hated being separated from them. Thomas Elliott told his wife he thought of his family while awake and asleep: "I lay here at nights and think of you while there is some sound asleep." About two months later he wrote her, "I dream of you & the children often." The feelings of separation could shape a soldier's attitude in general. Richard Waldrop wrote in his diary in the middle of the war, "I am suffering today from a severe attack of homesickness & therefore feel dissatisfied with everything."²⁹

Soldiers also worried about their families, especially during times of crisis at home. George Sutherlin explained to his brother, "since I heard from Mary [his wife] and as she was sick I am very uneasy about her." Jed Carter had good reason to be "very uneasy about" his family in October 1863 because his wife, Susan, was eight months pregnant. It was a time of excitement and concern for the family, and Jed's military service did not make the process any easier for them. He wrote her often, expressing his joy and worry: "I dream[t in] the night that I have a sweet little daughter[;] I hope it is true and I sincerely hope that you have an easy time of it and am most well again." When he finally heard that their child was born and that both Susan and their new daughter were all right, he was extremely relieved: "I was so glad to hear that you had such good luck and to hear that it was over." But he also agonized over his inability to get back to his family. "I would willingly give my horse to go home to see you and my little girl."[30]

The impact of soldiers' separation from their families was partly mitigated by the letters that went back and forth carrying sentiment and news, but those missives never seemed to come as often as the men from Pittsylvania desired. Soldiers wanted mail desperately, and when they failed to get it, they became unhappy, often criticizing their loved ones. When Jed Carter failed to receive a letter from Susan, he wrote to her with an injured tone, "I write to you every week as regular as it comes I haven't had any new [letters] since I wrote to you last [about one week before]."[31]

To be fair to Susan Carter and the others at home, at times letters were delayed or even failed to reach their destination because of the host of problems that arose with keeping the mail running during a war. Although letters sent from camps in northern and eastern Virginia to Danville and back took only a day or two at the start of the war, by 1862 correspondence began to take longer or not to arrive at all. The Martin family tried to explain why, although they had sent several letters to Rawley in camp, he had only received one of them: "Their must be some thing wrong in the mail some where." Such problems with the Confederate mail service, which worsened as war took its toll on the Southern infrastructure, exacerbated the tensions, unease, and distance that soldiers' family members felt during the war.[32]

Although most of the armies' time was spent marching or encamped, combat was a fundamental part of soldiers' experiences, as were wounds, deaths in battle, sharpshooters, and life spent near a hostile enemy. Soldiers' accounts of battles reveal the excitement and intimidating deadliness of Civil War combat. Two passages from William Dame's memoir of the battle of Spotsylvania Court House briefly illuminate both aspects. Dame's remembered excitement shone through when he described his unit's arrival at the battle: "As we passed out from behind [the] woods, we saw 'the elephant!' There, about six hundred yards from us were the Federals, seeming to cover the fields." The deadly nature of the battle tempered that excitement somewhat: "Then, after one volley, swiftly came the dreadful, venomous roll of musketry.... That withering fire tore the ranks of that Division to pieces."[33]

Artillery fire was a part of Civil War combat and occurred almost any time the two sides came near each other in sizable numbers. Its ability to wipe out large numbers of men, or to strike from a distance, apparently arbitrarily and almost anonymously killing or maiming, made it particularly frightening and awe-inspiring to soldiers. Dame, under fire from Union batteries in the battle at Spotsylvania Court House, wrote later of what he heard: "a sharp, venomous screech, clap of thunder, right over our heads, followed by a ripping, tearing, splitting crash, that filled the air; a regular blood freezer. We knew *that sound!* It was a bursting Parrott shell from a Federal gun! ... Another shell, and another, and another, came screaming over us. Then they began to *swarm*; the air seemed full of them,—bursting shells, jagged fragments, balls out of case-shot,—it sounded like a thousand devils, shrieking in the air all about us. [Later in that battle,] the artillery began to pour in their shells on us more furiously than ever! The air around us was kept in a blaze, and a roar of bursting shells, and the ground, all about, was furrowed and torn." Some soldiers, understandably, found such conditions difficult to take. Many years later, Robert Withers still vividly remembered his first serious shelling by heavy artillery: "The shriek of these large shells as they passed over us was decidedly discomposing.... Many officers and men would involuntarily stoop at the uncanny sound."[34]

One charge in one battle stands out as particularly definitive of the human impact of combat (and more generally of the war) for the soldiers of Pittsylvania and Danville. The battle of Gettysburg in July 1863 is the most famous conflict of the Civil War for many reasons, but in large part because of the massive casualties taken by both sides, some 23,000 for the North and 24,000 for the South. A sizable portion of the Confederate casualties were taken in the infamous "Pickett's Charge" on July 3 in which somewhere between 10,500 and 13,000 men attempted "to advance three-quarters of a mile across open fields" and break through the well-defended center of the Union lines.[35]

Sixteen companies of men from Pittsylvania and Danville made up over 10 percent of Gen. George Pickett's division, the most men from any single area in Virginia that took part in the unsuccessful charge. They suffered for their participation. A surgeon from the 57th Virginia Infantry (part of Pickett's Division) recorded the event and its aftermath: "The enemy could be distinctly seen a mile or so distant, but nothing but exchange of shots with the artillery occurred till about 2 O'clk when the signal, 2 guns, was heard & the battle commenced in real earnest. The cannonading was terrific, under wh[ich] our Division gallantly advanced but only to its destruction. The enemy were posted behind a stone wall with batteries enfilading our troops as they advanced wh[ich] mowed them down like grass. Every field officer in our Brigade was either killed or wounded. ... Our Division Hospital ... was soon filled to overflowing."[36]

The surgeon finished the entry with his summary of the action: "The Division covered itself with glory, but alas at such a cost." The sentiment of loss was echoed in a letter written home a week after the battle: "The fight was a very hard one and our company lost awfully. We carried in forty men and brought out fifteen untouched." A member of the 5th Virginia Cavalry watched Lee's army straggling back across the Potomac to Virginia and wrote to his sweetheart back home, "there was know end to the wounded[.] I think we got the worst end of the bargain this time."[37]

Although the soldier meant that the Confederates in general had "got the worst end" of the fighting at Gettysburg, the comment also applied specifically to the Pittsylvanian companies involved in the charge. They suffered 362 casualties in "Pickett's Charge," over 45 percent of those Pittsylvanians engaged, and 100 area men (about 13 percent of those engaged) were killed or mortally wounded (KIA/MWIA). These casualty and death rates were slightly higher than those for Pickett's Division as a whole (which suffered more than 42 percent casualties and about 12 percent killed or mortally wounded).[38]

Over the course of the entire Civil War, the soldiers of Pittsylvania and Danville took numerous casualties in battles and skirmishes with Union troops. These wounds received and deaths suffered often had lasting consequences for both soldiers and their families. Over 28 percent of the county's soldiers were wounded at least once during the war (see table 1.4). Some wounds were relatively minor, a scratch from a bayonet or a grazing blow from a bullet. Others were more serious, mangling arms or legs beyond repair or piercing vital organs. It was not unusual to be wounded multiple times in the same battle or multiple times over the course of the war. Some wounded soldiers lay on the battlefield for hours or days before they could be recovered and treated. Some wounds were deadly, killing instantly or within minutes, days, or weeks. Although records are not exact, over three hundred men from Pittsylvania and Danville were killed or mortally wounded in action (one of every eleven soldiers). Men were shot in the head or chest; soldiers were blown up by artillery shells; others bled to death from multiple wounds; a few were even killed by swords.[39]

Those Pittsylvania County soldiers wounded in battle or sick from disease were taken to one of the many Confederate hospitals, either a temporary field hospital or one of the more permanent facilities set up in Richmond, Farm-

TABLE 1.4
BATTLE CASUALTIES FOR COUNTY SOLDIERS

	Number	As a percentage of all front-line troops from county
WIA (not including KIA/MWIA)	761	23.18
WIA (includes KIA/MWIA)	933	28.42
KIA/MWIA	305	9.29

Source: Soldiers Database.

ville, Lynchburg, or Danville. Ideally—from the Army's perspective, if not the soldiers'—the men would recover and be sent back to their regiments to fight again. If not, they might receive a medical discharge. Of course, many men died in the hospitals, unable to survive their wounds, illnesses, or both. For the soldiers and their families, the diseases and wounds, the debilitation and death brought by military service affected many of them for the rest of their lives.

These hospitals, unfortunately, were often not the safest place to recover because of the limited understanding of the basic causes of disease and infection. Nosocomial infections were not uncommon. A soldier admitted for a small wound might catch from another patient in the next bed some disease that would kill him. Surgeons would move from patient to patient using the same bloody knife and covered in gore and dirt, spreading infection to the men they were trying to help. Brave men and women who worked in the hospitals as nurses often caught diseases themselves or served as carriers to further spread the illnesses among their patients.[40]

Recovery was also constrained by the limitations of medical ability. Large and slow-velocity minnie balls used by both sides did massive amounts of damage, often stayed in the body, and brought infection with them. Amputation of a wounded limb seemed the only way to stop gangrene once it had started, or even to deal with some particularly bad bone breaks. Torso wounds were often deadly because of the inability to treat sepsis and peritonitis. Diseases were often treated with calomel (mercurous chloride), opium derivatives, or other potions whose horrific side effects (ranging from mercury poisoning to drug addiction) may have obscured the ineffectiveness of almost all of them.[41]

If it became clear that a soldier's illness was chronic and debilitating, or if his wounds were too severe to allow him to return to any kind of duty, a surgeon would issue the soldier a medical discharge. Booker Adkins's rheumatism was so debilitating that he was discharged from the army in November 1861. Severe war wounds brought about the discharge of numerous Pittsylvanian soldiers such as Robert Withers, colonel of the 18th Virginia who was wounded three times at Gaines' Mill. About 7 percent of the soldiers of Pittsylvania and Danville were discharged for either illness or wounds received in the war (see table 1.5).[42]

For some ill or wounded soldiers, however, their bodies could not recover, and they died. Of those for which a cause of death is known, nearly 44 percent died from wounds received in battle. Another 55 percent died from disease. Overall, one-quarter of Pittsylvania's soldiers died during the war (see table 1.6).[43]

One crude measure of how much war affected Pittsylvania's soldiers (and their families) is the number of soldiers who seem not to have been physically affected by their time in the army. Only 37 percent of area soldiers had no evidence in their records of any illness, injuries, or death during the war. This percentage is almost certainly even lower in reality because problems with the records of the Confederate Army often mean that some soldiers, though identified as serving in a unit, have no other notations in their official service records.[44]

Additionally, hundreds of thousands of Confederates were captured by Union forces as prisoners of war (POWs). About one-fifth of Pittsylvania's soldiers spent some time in a Union prison. Although not pleasant, prison life was initially not horrible, but it got much worse in 1863 as politics suspended what had been a liberal prisoner-exchange policy.[45] For Confederates in Northern prisons, conditions worsened significantly because of overcrowding and because

TABLE 1.5
MEDICAL DISCHARGES FOR COUNTY SOLDIERS

	Total number	As percentage of soldiers with non-fatal wounds	As percentage of all Pittsylvania soldiers
Medical discharge—all	248	13.08	7.55
Medical discharge— amputee (who lived)	51	2.69	1.55

Source: Soldiers Database.

TABLE 1.6
WARTIME DEATHS FOR COUNTY SOLDIERS

	Died of disease	KIA/MWIA	Other miscellaneous death	Unknown cause	Total deaths
Deaths	383	305	8	135	831
As percentage of total deaths	46.09	36.70	0.96	16.25	100
As percentage of deaths with known cause	55.03	43.82	1.15		
As percentage of total served (in front line, 3,283)	11.67	9.29	0.24	4.11	25.31

Source: Soldiers Database.
Note: Miscellaneous deaths include soldiers executed for desertion and accidental deaths.

of a lack of food. Increased numbers meant problems with shelter. One Confederate POW recounted his experiences at Pt. Lookout, a prison in southern Maryland where there were "sixteen men to each tent, and one blanket to the man, and you were not allowed to have any more, even if your comrade should die and will his to you. The bare ground was our bed." Although the North had plenty of food to give to its prisoners, in 1864 it reduced the rations given to POWs in retaliation for the reduced rations that Union POWs were getting in Southern prisons. One account of prison life at Johnson's Island in Ohio noted that once rations dropped, the inmates there "began to show the effects of meagre fare, and the patients in [the] hospital rapidly increased—smallpox, erysipelas and pneumonia being the principal and most fatal diseases."[46]

Life in these overcrowded, reduced-ration Northern prisons took its toll on Confederate POWs. Many captives suffered a long-term degradation of their health because of their time in prison. Some died, largely because of diseases that spread through the confined, crowded, and unsanitary facilities, diseases to which they were more susceptible because of reduced food and inadequate shelter. Of the nearly seven hundred Pittsylvania soldiers who spent time in Northern prisons, about 16 percent died, compared to 12 percent overall for Confederate prisoners.[47]

Soldiers' experiences in camp and while marching obviously differed greatly from those in battle, but at times the two worlds seemed to overlap, with potential consequences for soldiers' mental well-being. It was common for two opposing Civil War armies to be located fairly near each other, divided by a river, by trenches, or even just by open space. The air between the two armies was often filled with bullets or artillery shells, making life for soldiers both exciting and dangerous. Being near enemy lines had an impact on the physical and mental environment in which soldiers lived, straining nerves and heightening tension because of the looming danger of snipers and the constant presence of artillery batteries lobbing shells. One Danvillian described daily life when "in close proximity to the enemy" as rarely lacking the sounds of war. "There is more or less cannonading every day from both sides, and occasionally some musket firing." Some soldiers could not adjust. Prolonged exposure to artillery fire has been linked to cases of "combat stress" or mental breakdown in soldiers in a number of wars in the nineteenth and twentieth centuries.[48]

The soldiers of Pittsylvania and Danville suffered a great deal during the war. They weathered the elements with shortages of tents and blankets; they dealt with inadequate or nearly inedible food; they endured separation from their families; they suffered the effects of a variety of illnesses; they fought in battles and were wounded, captured, and killed. The legacies of these experiences in the Confederate Army affected the rest of their lives and those of their families.

The Families at Home during the War

Stephen Ash has argued that the wartime experience of a Southern region was determined by its relative proximity to Union troops, more than by any other single factor. Unlike much of Virginia, the Pittsylvania County and Danville area was never the site of any battles, and the city was not occupied until after Lee's army surrendered at Appomattox. The area's distance from the conflict of the war placed it in a region that Ash calls the "Confederate Interior," the most protected and most stable of the four regions he describes in the wartime South.[49] Ash's focus on the importance of the location of the Union Army is certainly useful, but over-reliance on that dynamic risks overlooking the struggle for survival that soldiers' families experienced even in the most stable of Southern locations. These families, mostly women and children, faced numerous problems, ranging from a growing town to wartime inflation, food shortages, and worries about the men at war. Ultimately, the most significant factor shaping these families was the absence of so many of their husbands, fathers, sons, and brothers and the attempts to survive economically without them. In the end, these women and children coped by turning to sources of aid within and outside their families.

One key factor shaping the wartime experiences of women and children was the development of Danville as an important Confederate center. Its wartime prominence grew out of two factors: its location away from the fighting and the recently completed railroad, which linked the city to the Confederate capital of Richmond. This importance to the Confederacy brought to the city another, new railroad connection to Danville from Greensboro, North Carolina, as well as several wartime departments.[50] By 1863, in the words of one of the city's military leaders, "Danville had been made a Prison Post, as the several large tobacco factories located in that town were easily converted into comfortable prisons, which were pretty rapidly filled, as exchanges had then almost entirely ceased. Large hospitals had also been organized there. . . . The Government had also established an Arsenal there for the manufacture and repair of arms, and storing of ordnance supplies. When in addition, it is known that the town was crowded with refugees from the northern and eastern portions of the State, who filled almost every house to the limit of its capacity, you may judge that it was a pretty busy little place."[51]

In some ways, the residents of the area benefited a great deal from Danville's being such an important Confederate center. The arsenal and other wartime industries provided jobs for those men still at home. Merchants and manufacturers from Virginia's major cities, especially tobacconists, moved their warehouses to Danville, often to great profit for the city's businessmen and warehouse owners. Still, these changes rarely provided jobs or income for veteran families.[52]

Danville's being a Confederate center also had its downside for residents. Large numbers of Confederate soldiers came through the town, and their presence could be disruptive. For example, a few soldiers recovering in a Danville hospital got into a fight with a resident and overturned his wagon. After the servicemen were put in jail by civilian authorities in the town, their comrades formed a mob at the jail, threatening to break them out. Although the crisis ended peacefully, the people of Danville could not have been pleased by the actions of these soldiers, and perhaps a few of them questioned the benefits they received from the sizable military presence in their city.[53]

Another problem with the town's being a Confederate center was the presence of prisons for Northern soldiers. Despite the claims of the military leader, these prisons were particularly noxious, with unpleasant smells and waste from the prisoners who were crowded and ill treated. More serious, however, were fears in Danville and Pittsylvania County that civilians would catch the diseases of the prisoners, especially when a smallpox epidemic among the prisoners in late 1863 and early 1864 proved hard to stop. To make matters worse, several groups of prisoners, some potentially contagious, attempted to escape. Not surprisingly, the prison superintendent later remarked that "the outbreak [and escapes] caused much trouble and apprehension" among the families of the area. The political and business leaders of the city sent three letters to the Confederate War Department requesting that the prisons be removed from the city, but their petitions were unsuccessful.[54]

Of course, most veteran families did not live or work in the city. In fact, given the near ubiquity of farming for Pittsylvania and Danville soldiers' families, any discussion of the wartime economic problems caused by the absence of men must start with agriculture. The basic dilemma was that most farms required the labor of the entire family (or hired or slave labor) to be successful. For small-slaveholding or non-slaveholding families, it almost certainly proved difficult for family members—young children, aged relatives, but especially women—to replace the work done by their absent soldiers before the war. Tobacco farming was extremely skill- and labor-intensive, and although the secondary crop of the county, corn, was not especially difficult to grow, it did take time and effort away from the work that women needed to do to keep the household going.

The dual effort of the physical work of farming and of household labor almost certainly wore out many women in non-slaveholding soldiers' families by the end of the war.[55]

Given the difficulty of tobacco farming, the shortage of labor, and the need for food for the families and Southern armies, it may seem logical that Pittsylvanian farming families would have switched over to food production; however, the war brought on a tobacco shortage that drove prices up. Soldiers' families in Pittsylvania continued to grow tobacco throughout the war, despite Confederate laws restricting its growth, partly because the soil in the county was not suited to much else and partly because it made a great deal of money. Tobacco was valuable, and with increasing inflation it became worth even more. In fact, in 1863, a soldier wrote home to his wife instructing her not to sell their tobacco crop yet because "I had rather had it than confederate bonds.... It may be several years before they [the bonds] will sell for the full amount," whereas the tobacco would soon be worth even more. Most soldiers' families, therefore, despite their labor problems, grew at least a small patch of tobacco.[56]

Slaveholding farming families faced different problems related to the absence of their men. Before the war, men supervised the farming done by slaves, but with their absence some Pittsylvanian women had to move into the role of overseer. Although some women did fine in their newly expanded roles, the uncertainty and lack of experience in farming or supervising slaves made their jobs hard. Many slaves took advantage of the inexperience of their new supervisors to gain new freedoms or slack off their work. One soldier explained that his wife had been having problems because she found that "it is a hard mater to get any one to do anything for her."[57]

The behavior of slaves was a serious concern for white Pittsylvanians, especially since the black population had been 46 percent of the county before over thirty-two hundred white men left for military service. This concern was exacerbated by the perception that, according to one memoir, slaves were responsible for wartime "thefts of everything to eat." White worry about the black population can be seen in the officers, such as James Shelton, who resigned from the army to supervise slaves at home, and in the exemption of some men from conscription for similar purposes; the Confederate law known as the "20 Negro" exemption proved unpopular with the vast majority of Southern families who did not have enough slaves to qualify. White Pittsylvania's concerns about slave behavior can also be seen in the increased focus on slave discipline in some county churches. Shockoe Baptist conducted numerous investigations of the "christian character" of its black members in 1862, 1863, and 1864 and organized a committee "to report a suitable plan" to deal with "Instruction & discipline" for "our coloured bretheren."[58]

While life was difficult for the farming families who had to manage without the labor of their absent soldiers, some men off at war were artisans, whose work many of their families could not do. The families of doctors, lawyers, and many craftsmen who joined the army faced a similar dilemma earning a living without the necessary skills of husbands and fathers. Still, a few of these families were able to continue the work of their absent men—James Norman's family ran his mill without him (until it burned in January 1865)—but that was not possible for all the families of artisans and professionals in the army.[59]

In an attempt to continue to support their families from a distance, many soldiers sent their pay home. After the 18th Virginia Infantry got paid, a captain from Pittsylvania remarked, "many of the soldiers are sending their wages home." Unfortunately, families could not afford to depend on the money from their soldiers to support them. In fact, some soldiers could not send their pay home because they had spent all of it on food to supplement their tiny rations. Jed Carter explained to Susan, "it takes all of our wages to b[u]y something to eat." Others could not send their money home because the army did not pay them on a timely basis. In 1862, a member of the 21st Virginia Infantry noted, "We are getting anxious to receive our pay & there is a good deal of complaint & dissatisfaction on this account—very justly too for we haven't been paid a cent for nearly eight months & some companies haven't been paid for ten months."[60]

The attempts of soldiers' families to weather the conflict were made significantly more difficult by the rapid inflation of prices throughout the Confederacy over the course of the war. "Somebody says that one used to go to market with their money in their pocket & a basket for the marketing. Now you must take your money in a basket & bring home your marketing in your pocket," a Richmond woman wrote in her diary in late 1863. The slight exaggeration applied equally well to the experiences of families in Pittsylvania and Danville.[61]

Although prices on all goods increased over the course of the war, it was the rising price of food that was most harmful to soldiers' families (see table 1.7). In the first twelve to eighteen months of the war, food prices rose, but not precipitously. Then, in the winter of 1862–63, prices skyrocketed. Flour and bacon nearly tripled from their prewar costs, and one man wrote his family that it was not unusual to see "a turkey sell for ten dollars" in Danville. By fall of 1863, food prices had worsened, with the cost of flour more than doubling and tripling again. By the first months of 1864, a barrel of flour sold for $250, over

TABLE 1.7
WARTIME PRICES FOR FOOD IN COUNTY

	Flour (barrel)	Bacon (pound)	Turkey (whole)	Corn meal (barrel)
1860	$7.50	$0.10–$0.15	$1.50–$2.50	$1.50–$3.00
Early 1862	$10.00	$0.35		
Early 1863	$30.00	$1.10	$10.00	
September 1863	$30.00–$40.00			
December 1863	$80.00–$100.00			
Early 1864	$250.00–$275.00			
May 1864		$6.00		$200.00

Source: Blair, *Virginia's Private War*, 69, 94; Thomas Elliott to Sarah Elliott, March 31, 1863, Thomas J. Elliott Papers, DU; Allen Womack to Charles Womack, May 8, 1864, Womack Family Papers, DU; Martin, *The Standard of Living in 1860*, 57–66, 418–21.

thirty times its antebellum cost. By the middle of that year, Allen Womack told his son in the Pittsylvania Dragoons that bacon was selling for $6 per pound, an increase of some forty to sixty times over prewar prices, and that "corn is worth any price you would ask." For corn meal, that price turned out to be "$200.00 per Barrel," an increase of 67 to 133 times!⁶²

Such incredible inflation made soldiers' salaries, when they got them, virtually useless to their families. The $11 that each private was supposed to be paid each month would not have come close to feeding his family. In June 1864, the Confederate Congress increased soldiers' salaries by $7 a month, but it was nowhere near enough. By this time, $18 would only buy a family three pounds of bacon per month, less salt pork than one study indicates an adult slave received each week before the war began. Even the families of Confederate officers, with their significantly higher pay, were hard-pressed by the middle of the war to survive on just the salaries their husbands and fathers earned. In 1863, Col. Robert Withers was concerned because "owing to the rapid depreciation of Confederate money, my army pay now furnished but a meagre support for a family."[63]

Given the inflated prices and the absence of their men's labor, some soldiers' families in Pittsylvania County did not have enough food. William Perkins of the 38th Virginia Infantry explained to an acquaintance that his wife had informed him soon after his departure in 1861 that "she does not get enough of provision to support her and [the] children." The number of families in real need of food increased throughout the war and by the winter of 1864–65, the county's residents were in fairly desperate straits, in part because of the difficulty of feeding both the Confederate Army and the civilian population. According to the man in charge of the Confederate post in Danville at that time, "As winter approached, food became more and more scarce in the country and the people were called upon more earnestly to contribute of their supplies to the sustenance of the forces in the field." There were "Inspection[s] of corn cribs and smokehouses all through the country by officers of the Quartermaster and Commissary Departments . . . and all surplus food carried off [to feed the army]." In this man's understated phrasing, "They generally estimated the surplus at a very liberal figure[, so that] there was little meat consumed by the country householder."[64]

Although the Confederate quartermasters were generally able to keep the army supplied with some kind of limited nourishment, civilians all over Virginia suffered from shortages of food, whether in Confederate-controlled areas such as Pittsylvania County or not. "The countryside . . . was exhausted," and some soldiers' families were starving. Danville, along with Richmond and Lynchburg, still had rations stockpiled at the end of the war, but they were for the Confederate Army and not generally available to Danville's civilians, even soldiers' families.[65]

Ultimately, for the families of Pittsylvania-Danville's soldiers, the absence of their men proved not just an economic crisis but also an emotional burden to bear. Of all the war-induced difficulties that the families of soldiers faced, worry about their men in military service was perhaps paramount. Wives had "multitudes of fears" about what would happen to their husbands. Mothers' "dear boy[s] occupie[d] the most of [their] thoughts." Sisters were anxious about their brothers. Family members at home worried about their soldiers and voraciously devoured any information about them.[66]

Whether soldiers were ill, in prison, or perfectly healthy in camp, their families wanted and needed information about them. Typically that news came from newspapers or from letters they received from the soldiers. As a result, like their soldiers, they were also upset by the decline in the Confederate postal system over the course of the war. Rawley Martin's mother wrote to her son and expressed her frustrations with the mail: "I do hope the Post Masters will attend to it in the future, for it makes us very uneasy when we do not get our letter regularly and so it does you when you do not get ours." Families also avidly followed the newspapers for information about their husbands, fathers, and brothers; however, the newspapers were not always accurate. Three days after the battle of Fredericksburg, Rawley Martin's family still did not know his status, and the waiting made them uneasy. One sister wrote him and expressed a common problem with the lack of knowledge and the transmission of information during the war: "I wish we could [hear] something definite from the fighting at Fredericksburg. We hear so many different reports that we do not know what to believe, and the paper this morning give us not much satisfaction." Throughout the war, families' lack of knowledge about the health and status of their soldiers remained a source of significant anxiety.[67]

The economic and emotional impact of war for families meant trying to find ways to cope without their husbands, fathers, and brothers. Families had to endure separations that might be temporary or might be permanent and periods of little or no food. For many women, it may have meant being forced into new economic roles. In order for soldiers' families to survive the Civil War, they turned to their friends and relatives.

Familial Strategies during the War

After Bettie Penick found out that her brother, Rawley Martin, was in fact alive, although wounded, after the battle of Gettysburg in 1863, she wrote and reminded him of the support system he had waiting for him back in Pittsylvania County. "Our dear Parents are so anxious about you—indeed all of us are. Many fervent prayers my dear Brother are offered in your behalf. Pa, Ma, Sister & Mr. Penick have written to you. Beckie will write soon. Mattie & little Chessie send a kiss to you. All join me in warmest love. I have not space to write the kind messages your numerous friends send." Bettie's letter reveals the network of friends and family that offered Rawley Martin support during the war.[68]

Wartime strategies for the survival of a soldier's family typically involved marshaling the resources of the familial household, as well as turning to "extra-household" relatives and to close friends for additional economic and emotional support. The family within the house was the first place members looked for help, and not just during the war. It was natural for family members in a household to work to support one another since they were already an economic and emotional unit. The sprawling network of family and friends described in Bettie Penick's letter did not just support Rawley Martin during the war but also helped him when he returned home.

While separated by military service, veteran families worked hard to provide the emotional support each member needed, typically in the form of letters. The letters served not just to convey important information between family members but also as a means for people to continue relationships strained by distance and the exigencies of the war. Some husbands wrote their wives that "there is no news of interest," yet they still wrote several pages. Letters from family members cheered up soldiers and civilians alike. An enlisted husband excitedly responded to his wife, "I received your kind and most welcome letter ... and will assure you it gave me a great pleasure and satisfaction to hear [from] one whome I as dearly love as you." A sister replied to her sibling, "Your kind letter cheered me *very* much my dear Bro."[69]

Soldiers often wrote home to reassure their spouses. Pittsylvanian George Jones wrote to his wife, Sarah, throughout the war, telling her in most letters not to worry about him or her work at home. Early in the war, he tried to assuage her fears: "Do not be uneasy. I am inhopes all will be well and that in a short time we will be able to meet each other again." Unfortunately, in July 1863 George was wounded and captured at Gettysburg and sent to Johnson's Island prison in Ohio. Sarah's anxiety for his situation hardly lessened after that, so several of his letters from prison tried again to reassure her: "Do not be uneasy about me." George also tried in his letters to ease Sarah's concerns about running the couple's farm, usually with the phrase, "You must do the best that you can." First written in 1862 before his capture, the phrase was modified after his capture to note, "for it may be sometime before I get home yet." His letters encouraged her but also acknowledged the difficulties she faced. "You must do the best you can under the circumstances."[70]

Equally important, letters from family provided long-distance emotional support for soldiers. George Jones's emotional well-being improved significantly after he got mail from his wife telling him everything was fine. "I received your affectionate letter ... yesterday and was more than glad to learn that you were all well[;] this leaves me in very good health and spirits." On the other hand, when George did not receive a letter from his wife for a while, he became anxious and complained, "if I knew that you were all well and doing well I should feel a great deal better." He explained more fully in another letter: "To know that you and Jennie were happy would render me more happy and contented than I now am and make me more contented with my lott.... You must write to me as often as you can."[71]

In addition to letters, furloughs and even stays at Danville's military hospitals proved important for reinforcing the connections between soldiers and families, and their reactions to these contacts indicate just how significant that family support was for these men. William Dame later remembered how, when home for his sister's wedding, he had "spent a few happy days with the dear home folks in the dear old home.... It was a home to love; a home to defend; a home to die for—the dearest spot on earth to me.... I enjoyed it with all my heart for those *few short days*." In addition to furloughs, a number of wounded or ill soldiers from the area were sent to one of Danville's military hospitals, where they were visited and nurtured by family and friends. In some cases, area soldiers such as John Crowder and James Ragsdale were even allowed to stay at home while recuperating. Others, such as James Gauldin, took advantage of their proximity to their families to duck out of the hospital without leave for short visits, a practice apparently tolerated as long as the absences were indeed brief.[72]

Still, surviving the war while separated required more than just providing emotional support. Veteran families also had to figure out how to survive financially without at least one of the male members of the familial household performing his antebellum occupation. Many soldiers' families attempted to deal with the economic situation created by the physical separation of male earners by using the mail. A few soldiers left the military, temporarily or permanently, to address their families' financial situations.

Soldiers and their families used the Confederate postal service to relay money and supplies and to discuss economic strategies. Soldiers who sent their paychecks home attempted to continue to support their families economically, although the high rate of wartime price inflation, low pay, and infrequent payment undermined the ability of men to provide their family with enough from afar. In fact, families often sent money or supplies to soldiers. While in prison, Rawley Martin asked his father to send him $100 in "green backs (Yankee money)." His mother sent him pants made from "thick home made flannel that will be very warm." Susan Carter and Sarah Jones both sent their husbands several boxes of food and clothes.[73]

Although husbands in the military could not always send money home, they often attempted to run the family farm or business through their wives. In the spring of 1862, George Jones directed Sarah on how much corn and tobacco to plant and told her to focus on the corn, since "the best corn country in Virginia is now in the hands of the Yankees." A couple months later, George spent several pages of a letter to Sarah discussing tobacco and corn prices, plans for a factory, and the disposition of slaves and harvests. Even after he was captured and sent to a Northern prison, he continued to try to run their farm; he wrote Sarah, "tell me all about the crop in the [tobacco] Factory and how the Pork turned out."[74]

The sheer distance that the war placed between soldiers and their families, however, meant that some husbands eventually gave some control over household finances to their wives, or at least acknowledged the limitations on their authority caused by the physical separation. George Jones, despite his attempts to remain very involved in the running of his family's finances, indicated in October 1864 that he trusted Sarah to handle the business of managing property and overseers, including finding a renter or overseer for his dead brother's land. "I want you to settle James['s] place if you can. You can form an idea of what is best better than I can tell you." If George had been around, this redistribution of responsibility would never have occurred. Because of the situation, however, Sarah gained the power to run the couple's financial affairs. This responsibility was not necessarily something she would have wanted, especially since few women were trained for this role, but she may have enjoyed the increased control of their finances. George was not willing to relinquish control completely, however. In the same letter indicating that she could handle the family's financial affairs, he also indicated that she should turn to the men in his family for advice: "Tell John to assist you, also Father. I have written to both of them." Still, either George increasingly accepted his inability to do anything from afar or he gradually acknowledged Sarah's abilities, because he increasingly turned business decisions over to her: "You must do the best you can for I cannot advise you here. . . . I shall be satisfied with any thing that you may do."[75]

For some families, however, a soldier's writing home to direct family businesses or farms was not sufficient for their economic survival. For the soldiers of these families, desertion, whether permanent or temporary, may have seemed the best way to support their spouses and children. That is not to claim that all deserters had the noble intention of saving their family from economic ruin. Certainly many deserters ran away out of self-preservation or fear, but not all. Soldiers themselves were careful to make a distinction between good and bad deserters. One man wrote home to his wife about the two kinds of deserters in August 1863: "Many of them I am truly sorry for, men who have large families dependent [on] their labor for supports. . . . Many have . . . applyed for furloughs which having been denied them, have been tempted to visit home regardless of the consequences." The writer believed these men to be justified, but "The great bulk of deserters, are worthless characters, whose consciences are no checks to their desires to do meanly." As William Blair has noted in his study of wartime Virginia, when there was little or no punishment early in the war, soldiers often went home for extended periods of time without permission but then returned, often after planting or harvest season ended. Even after Lee increased the penalties for desertion, men who left to be with their families were rarely executed. Although it is extremely difficult to determine the desertion rates of Confederate soldiers, roughly 14 percent of Pittsylvania soldiers left their units

TABLE 1.8

DESERTION RATES FOR COUNTY SOLDIERS

	Number	Percentage of deserters	Percentage of all front-line area soldiers
Pittsylvania-Danville deserters	460	100	14.01
Permanently (subset of deserters)	169	36.74	5.15
To enemy (subset of permanently)	53	11.52	1.61

Source: Soldiers Database.

without permission during the war, as compared to about 11.5 percent for the Confederacy as a whole. One in twenty Pittsylvania soldiers left permanently, never returning (voluntarily or not) to their units (see table 1.8).[76]

Desertion may have been the only option for some enlisted men looking to support their families, but Confederate officers had another option. They could resign their commissions and return to their families and businesses. One-fourth of all Pittsylvania officers did just that. Timothy Stamps, captain of the Ringgold Battery resigned in June 1863 for the "health of wife & aged father of whom I am the only child." John Roy Cabell resigned to care for "five small motherless children." An adjutant in the 18th Virginia Infantry effectively resigned when he declined re-election, citing family and business commitments. If officers, typically wealthier people, needed to come home to care for their families, then clearly poorer people needed to do so, even if they were not allowed by the Confederate government.[77]

Of course, most veteran families also had other people to whom they could turn for assistance. Although the familial household was the basic unit of organization and the fundamental unit of economic and emotional support, during and after the Civil War, soldiers' families often had to look just outside the household for a little extra help. Extra-household family, friends, and neighbors meshed together in this local world as kin and fictive kin, at times operating as close relatives did, providing additional economic and emotional sustenance to members.[78]

Wartime letters between soldiers and their friends and family served to link those in the army to this familial and friend-based support network that had existed before the war and that continued to exist after it as well. Evidence of the breadth of these attachments can be seen in closings of letters from soldiers, such as "give my love to your Ma & Pa and all of the neighbours" and "give my love to enquiring friends." Soldiers wrote home and related their lives and the lives of those in their locally formed companies and regiments, while the people at home wrote to soldiers and gave them "all the news in the neighborhood."[79]

Soldiers also wrote home to pass on the news, through their family, that other soldiers were safe and healthy. George Jones told his wife Sarah, "You can say to Mrs. Fitzgerald that Budge and Sam are both well and Mrs. Oliver that the Captain is well also. Also Isaac Dodson, Wm Davis, Henry Atkinson and the entire Company that is with us." Perhaps some of the soldiers whom George discussed were illiterate and unable themselves to send their families word that they were safe; but even if such was not the case, his friends and neighbors certainly would have appreciated the news.[80]

In some cases, extra-household emotional assistance involved soldiers' requests of friends and relatives to watch over, comfort, and keep up the spirits of people in the neighborhood. Such acts of kindness provided encouragement to both soldiers and their families at home. George Sutherlin asked his brother to watch over his family when he found out his wife was sick: "I am very uneasy about her and I want you to go and see her." Sutherlin was relieved to receive a letter before long from his brother, who had checked on his wife and children, who were all fine. His relief shone through in his response: "Was glad that my family was better, had been uneasy about my wife." Along these same lines, some women at home were tasked with keeping up the spirits of extended family members. George Jones asked his wife to watch over his aunt and father: "do all you can to render her happy and my poor old Father . . . cheer him up as much as you can."[81]

Another facet of the extra-household emotional support system for the soldiers themselves came from the method by which the Confederate Army formed companies and regiments. Most Confederate soldiers enlisted in units along with their neighbors and relatives, and as a result they brought some of their emotional support system with them, albeit only the male part of that system. Friends and relatives in the military could be there for one another. Bettie Penick advised her husband that since he and her brother were in the same unit, they should "console each other."[82]

When a member of this extended network died, there was an outpouring of sympathy and even help to the deceased's family back home, from both soldiers and civilians. Dealing with a death was obviously difficult for a family, but friends and relatives tried to help cushion the blow. When a close neighbor and member of George Jones's company died of disease within weeks after getting out of federal prison, he quickly thought of the man's widow: "I am truly sorry to hear of the death of [Isaac] Dodson. . . . how I feel for Mrs. Dodson in her sad loss." Several weeks later, he expressed more concern: "How does Mrs. Dodson bear her sad loss[?] . . . I sympathize deeply with her."[83]

Although this emotional support was helpful, many soldiers' families also needed economic help of some kind from their extra-household relatives and friends during the war. Relatives and friends played a key role in helping veteran families whose husbands were absent, demonstrated well by the interactions between George and Sarah Jones detailed earlier. Even after George came to trust Sarah's abilities to run their plantation, he gave her this advice: "consult our friends in regard to what you think is best and get Father and John [his brother] to assist you." Relatives and friends could also provide much-needed money or supplies to soldiers' families. In late 1863, Jed Carter told his wife to appeal to their friends for financial help, especially since he was unable to send her anything: "if you need any money you must go to Len for it."[84]

For many of those soldiers' families who had lost a husband, father, or son, economic support from relatives and friends could be extremely helpful, if not necessary, for their continued existence. George Jones did not just offer emotional support to Isaac Dodson's widow, Jane, through his wife, Sarah. He also expressed concern about "Mrs. Dodson's" financial status: "I am fearfull that she will not have much left after Dodson's debts are paid off." And he was willing to be generous with the debts that she (and her husband's estate) owed him: "I do not intend to disturb her."[85]

Robert Withers later recalled that after he was severely wounded and forced to leave active duty, his friends enabled his family to survive. "Indeed, I scarcely know how we could have gotten along without suffering, had it not been for the kindness of friends in the country who generously ministered to our necessities." Withers's family got food and money from his friends in Pittsylvania County. "You may be sure their kindness and liberality were highly appreciated."[86]

Finally, during the Civil War, combining households or moving to the house of a parent, other relative, or friend was another option for soldiers' families looking to adjust to the economic and emotional strains of separation. After Susan Carter's husband was captured and placed in a Northern prison, she received a letter from her mother-in-law, H. S. Carter, offering her house as a place of refuge: "you must come and stay some with me the first chance you have."[87]

The War Ends

The end of the war came remarkably fast when it happened. Union forces broke through the Confederate lines around Petersburg and Richmond on

April 2, 1865, and both Robert E. Lee's army and the Confederate government had to flee. Jefferson Davis and his cabinet left the Confederate capital on the Richmond and Danville Railroad. Davis arrived in Danville that same evening, hoping to link up with Lee's troops and establish a new Confederate capital in this well-stocked supply depot. On April 10, however, Davis's hopes were dashed with the arrival of word of Lee's surrender at Appomattox. What remained of the Confederate government left the "last capital of the Confederacy" by train that same night.[88]

The departing forces left Danville's military warehouses full of food and supplies intended for Lee's troops. The chance at access to the Confederate resources brought hundreds, perhaps thousands, of women, children, and recently deserted or paroled soldiers to the city. Although "at first," one soldier remembered, "there was some order, and rations were distributed ... it was not long till the impatient ones tired of waiting, [and] began to crowd up too close." According to another recollection, a woman started a riot of looting by yelling, "Our children and we'uns are starving! The Confederacy is gone up! Let us help ourselves!" In the chaos, the massive Confederate Arsenal, full of gunpowder and artillery shells, blew up, killing some fourteen people, apparently because of a careless spark. Although the explosion gave the mob pause, the looting of food and supplies continued.[89]

The town council asked Col. Robert Withers, ex-commander of the 18th Virginia Infantry and lately commander of the Danville prisons, to institute martial law and shut down the town, which he did. Martial law lasted until Union forces arrived on April 27. Given the conditions in the town and the presence in the county of a few small bands of Yankee and Rebel deserters, it is not surprising that Withers and the town leaders "felt greatly relieved by the presence of the troop," as their "situation was both peculiar and dangerous." There seem to have been few problems between the occupying troops and the citizens of Danville, especially once Gen. Joseph Johnston surrendered the last sizable body of Confederate troops in the field to Gen. William T. Sherman, officially ending the war.[90]

From April to July 1865, soldiers returned home to Pittsylvania County and Danville, as they were paroled or released from Union prisons. Among the first to be reunited with their families (of those who remained in the army until the end) were those who surrendered with Lee at Appomattox. After the formal surrender to Grant's troops and release, William Dame, like many other local soldiers, went to his "home in Danville, and had to walk 180 miles to get there." Back home with their families, soldiers and their parents, siblings, spouses, and children began rebuilding their lives.[91]

Sources of Aid for Rebuilding

In order to survive the Civil War, to weather its economic, emotional, and psychological effects, soldiers' families turned to several sources of help and assistance. First, these families looked to themselves, to spouses and parents and children, and to the network of extended family members and close friends. If this initial circle could not provide enough assistance, however, soldiers' families went outside that circle to local networks, primarily in the form of churches and elite members of the community. If the sources within that circle were unable to meet all the needs of soldiers' families, families would again go further outside the circle for more help, to take advantage of services offered by the state of Virginia. Some of these circles of support were well established before the war, and soldiers' families were used to looking to them for help. Others had come about largely in response to specific circumstances brought about by the war. All these sources of aid that were first seen during the war, however, also played important postwar roles in the attempts of veteran families to survive and reconstruct their lives.[92]

Beyond their own family households and the assistance provided by extended families and friends, soldiers and their families turned to local networks of assistance. During the war, Baptist churches saw a significant increase in their membership numbers, including soldiers' families. Because of the county's location away from Union troops and fighting, its churches survived the hardships of the war and were able to help their members, providing emotional and spiritual refuges for all and financial aid for a few needy families.[93] Another source of local assistance to which Pittsylvania's soldiers and their families turned for help during (and after) the Civil War was local elites. During the war, elite women from the county organized the Pittsylvania Ladies' Soldiers' Aid Society: "to supply the destitute and needy, of as many companies from our county as we may be able, with fatigue shirts, undershirts, drawers and socks. Also to aid in furnishing the hospitals with necessities and delicacies for the sick." Soldiers' families also turned to well-off and powerful members of their community for a variety of much-needed help, including food or money for their family, advice on business issues, and assistance getting out of the army or into particular military and non-military positions.[94]

Beyond familial and local assistance, soldiers and their families turned to the state, and even the Confederate government, for help. Soldiers' families made numerous pleas to the Confederate government for assistance and, in doing so, became part of the Confederate Congress's larger debate about centralized government. Although bills were proposed to the Confederate Congress in 1862,

1863, and 1864 offering financial support in several forms to soldiers' families, most did not pass because of anti-expansion congressmen. Of much more use to Pittsylvania's soldiers' families was the sweeping legislation passed by Virginia's General Assembly in 1862, 1863, and 1864 aimed at helping the most needy families whose men were in military service. These laws enabled protection of soldiers' property from debts incurred while in military service. They also ordered counties to provide disabled "Indigent Soldiers[,] Widows and Minor Children of Soldiers ... who have died[, and] the Indigent Families of those now in the Service" with money and food at prices well below inflationary level "in such proportion as [the counties] may think just and sufficient for [the families'] maintenance." In Pittsylvania, these laws meant that some needy soldiers' families received hundreds of dollars a month in "cash & provision" from county officials.[95]

In providing for soldiers and their families, the state of Virginia showed that it felt some responsibility toward its soldiers, foreshadowing the state's postwar attempts to help out its veterans and their families with artificial limbs, commutations, and pensions. Virginia's wartime assistance to soldiers' families also indicated that the government was willing to take on what one historian has described as "the role of male protectors through charitable campaigns," a position it also assumed after the war in its awarding of pensions for widows.[96]

Finally, some of Pittsylvania's families needed something other than money from the state; they needed some way of dealing with a family member (soldier or civilian) who suffered from psychological problems, in some cases directly attributable to the war or its effects. Although family or even close friends would normally care for the mentally ill, in cases of dangerous behavior, this was not a viable option. The state's asylums provided a place to send the mentally ill, hopefully to be "cured" but at least to be taken care of. For many patients, however, time in the asylum was unpleasant, at best, and horror filled, at worst.[97]

Pittsylvania's soldiers and their families had to deal with many emotional and economic problems during the war, and they turned to all these sources for help. They looked to their immediate families first and then to their extended families and fictive families, their friends. When those support networks failed them, they took their pleas further and further out from their homes, to local assistance and then to the state. Their pleas for help, which started during the war, did not stop with its end, and they looked to those same sources for assistance when it came time to rebuild their lives amid the political and economic wreckage of the war's aftermath.

2

Loss and Reconstruction

The Impact of the Civil War on Veteran Families and Their Postwar Rebuilding

> No estimates in dollars and cents can cover the entire cost of one of those sanguinary struggles in which the nations so often become involved. Such estimates fail to cover the value to commerce and to human happiness, of the productive labor, in agriculture, or in the various legitimate arts of peace, of those engaged in the war.... And what computation can measure the misery... what a sum total of pain and sorrow is endured on the part of the wounded, all of which defy computation by the unfeeling scale of mere dollars and cents. And when we add to this, the many tens of thousands of hale, athletic men who are killed in battle, or who die as a consequence of the war... then it is that we are made to feel that one war does more mischief than any extent of material destruction of which it is possible to conceive.
>
> —"The Cost of War," *Religious Herald*, July 24, 1862

IN MEMOIRS written in the early twentieth century, veterans William Dame and Robert Withers wrote about their experiences during and after the Civil War. Dame's account portrayed the immediate postwar years in a heroic light: "Just after the war, in the far harder trials and soul agony of the Reconstruction days, [veterans showed] wonderful patience, and courage which... rebuilt their shattered fortunes and pulled their country triumphantly up out of indescribable disaster." Withers was a bit more practical: "the question of food for my large family was now the dominant one." With the war's end, Pittsylvania's soldiers gladly returned home to their families. Not all those who left for war survived to come home, however, and most of those who did return came back as changed men. They returned home to women and children also changed by the war, and those who did not return left behind widows and devastated families. The Civil War left a demographic hole and a physical, emotional, and economic legacy that significantly affected veteran families in ways that made their attempts at postwar rebuilding difficult.[1]

In a landmark 1989 article on the social history of the Civil War, Maris Vinovskis made a number of estimates about the conflict's demographic impact. Vinovskis's statistics provide a rough frame of reference for the demographic impact of the war on Pittsylvania's soldiers and their families. A higher percentage of white men aged thirteen to forty-three ("military age") in the area served in front-line Confederate forces (79 percent) than did military-age white men in the South as a whole (61 percent). The region's soldiers seem to have suffered war deaths at similar rates to the South as a whole. Twenty percent of white men of military age from the county died in the war (versus 18 percent for the South), and over 25 percent of Pittsylvania's front-line soldiers died in service (the same as the Confederate military as a whole).[2]

Although Vinovskis did not demonstrate the percentages of Confederate soldiers wounded, captured, or struck with disease for the South as a whole, those percentages can be produced for the Pittsylvania-Danville area using the databases created for this study. In addition to the 831 soldiers from the area who died, another nearly 1,600 soldiers suffered from wounds, disease, or Union capture and imprisonment over the course of the war but survived. (Many of these men endured more than one of these wartime experiences.) Over 38 percent of the county's white men of military age and 48 percent of its soldiers suffered from at least one of these measurable, non-fatal, but potentially life-altering wartime experiences. Perhaps the fullest broad measure of the impact of the Civil War on the white men of Pittsylvania County and Danville combines these statistics: over 2,400 of the region's soldiers (nearly 59 percent of the white men of military age and a staggering 74 percent of the soldiers) experienced something during the war that either killed them, damaged them, or put them in a hospital or prison.[3]

The deaths, the wounds, the diseases, the time in federal prisons, and even military service itself represented a key aspect of the direct human cost of the Civil War for the Confederate veteran families of Pittsylvania and Danville. The rest of this project assesses the price paid in human and economic capital by veteran families and explores the strategies, solutions, and sources of aid that the soldiers' families of Pittsylvania and Danville used to reconstruct their lives. After assessing the impact of war and arguing for the significance of soldiers' particular wartime experiences for families' immediate postwar economic and emotional status, this chapter examines Confederate veteran families' initial attempts to rebuild, reorganize, and reconstruct within their own households and in the households of extended family members.

The Impact of War on Confederate Veteran Families

One way to look at the cost of the war for Confederate veteran families is to look at its short-term economic impact on household wealth. One such measurement can be achieved by comparing the amounts of property (real and personal) recorded for each veteran family household found in the 1860 and 1870 censuses. The value of real estate per veteran family household in Pittsylvania County dropped from $2,584 in 1860 to $947 in 1870, a decline of over 63 percent. The value of personal estate per veteran family household in Pittsylvania County dropped from $4,494 to $352, a decline of over 92 percent, reflecting the significant financial dimension of emancipation. Overall, then, the total value of real and personal property per veteran family household from 1860 to 1870 declined from $7,078 to $1,299, a drop of almost 82 percent.[4]

The war and its consequences affected the financial situation of the county's veteran families differently based on their antebellum investment in slavery (see table 2.1). Veteran families who had owned slaves in 1860 faced more severe declines in overall wealth by 1870 than veteran families who had not owned slaves in 1860. Despite that precipitous drop in wealth, the average former slaveholding veteran family was still better off financially in 1870 than the average veteran family who had not owned slaves before the war.

Another way of looking at the economic impact of the war on veteran families is to examine what percentage of those households lost their land between 1860 and 1870. In the 1860 census, 58 percent of households containing at least one future soldier owned land. By 1870, only 46 percent of veteran family households owned real estate.[5]

Comparing the percentage amount of the county's total wealth held by veteran families in 1860 and 1870 reveals the relatively greater negative economic impact of the Civil War on veteran families than on Pittsylvanians as a whole. According to the 1860 population census, family members of households who were to send soldiers to war owned almost 50 percent of the total property (real and personal) in the Pittsylvania-Danville region ($11,563,540 of $23,417,820). By the 1870 census, however, veteran family households held only 30 percent of the total wealth ($1,720,852 of $5,687,039). This relative decline in control of wealth in the county, combined with a decline in individual household wealth,

TABLE 2.1
ECONOMIC IMPACT OF WAR FOR VETERAN FAMILIES
BASED ON PREWAR SLAVEHOLDING

For 1,113 veteran families found in the 1860 and 1870 censuses	1860 total wealth per veteran family	1870 total wealth per veteran family	Percentage change in total wealth per family
Veteran slaveholding families in 1860	$18,343.95	$2,183.11	−88.10%
Veteran non-slaveholding families in 1860	$1,161.57	$727.84	−37.34%

Source: Soldiers Database; Pittsylvania County Population Census, 1860, 1870.

made it more difficult for veteran families to rebuild their lives in postwar Pittsylvania.[6]

Although losing one's slaves or having a family member serve in the Confederate military were factors in shaping a family's economic fortunes during and after the war, another significant influence on finances seems to have been a soldier's experiences during the war. Examining the change in total wealth as reported by the 1860 and 1870 censuses for those affected veteran families allows two observations. First, veteran families all suffered greatly in terms of wealth because of the war. Second, these statistics indicate that the war more negatively affected soldiers' families' wealth when the soldier's military service included wounds, diseases, amputations, imprisonments, or death.[7]

The most fortunate families seem to have been those whose men all returned home and did so without having been wounded, captured, or struck down by a major illness. Alive and apparently healthy, these soldiers came back home at the end of the war and, with their families, attempted to rebuild their lives. Although they typically began that attempt without the physical problems faced by damaged returning veterans, even these lucky soldiers had been away from their farms or businesses for years. James Redd articulated his concerns about the financial effects of his absence in a letter to a friend after over a year in the army: "my business ... is suffering very much for the want of attention." Health also did not guarantee a veteran financial success by any means in the chaotic postwar South. David Harris Watson, a healthy veteran, was unable to pay his debts and found himself in court a number of times in the years after

TABLE 2.2
ECONOMIC IMPACT OF VARIOUS WARTIME EXPERIENCES FOR COUNTY VETERAN FAMILIES

For 1,113 veteran families found in the 1860 and 1870 censuses	1860 total wealth per veteran family	1870 total wealth per veteran family	Percentage change in total wealth per family
Alive and healthy	$6,522.66	$1,673.26	−74.35%
Alive, not healthy	$6,907.05	$1,161.29	−83.19%
Dead (all families with at least one soldier who died)	$6,532.54	$1,033.01	−84.19%

Source: Soldiers Database; Pittsylvania County Population Census, 1860, 1870.

the war, with three separate judgments against him in 1867 alone for a total of $50.42, more than his total worth in 1860.[8]

Logically, the families most affected by the Civil War were those whose soldiers never came home at all, those families whose husbands, fathers, brothers, and sons died on the field of battle, in some hospital, or in prison. In an economic world in which men were expected to perform a great part of the labor that earned the family the money needed to survive, the loss of a male laborer could be financially devastating to a family. The loss of the male household head, husband, and father could be particularly difficult for veteran families. Soldiers' widows, such as Mary Simmons, were left to support multiple children after their husbands died in Confederate service, often without the resources or skills to do so. Simmons's husband, Henry, died of disease in 1862, leaving her with $25 in personal property and six children, the oldest only thirteen. In even worse shape, typically, were those children who had lost both parents, such as Anderson Crowder's seven children, who were left largely to fend for themselves when their father died as a member of the 18th Virginia Regiment in 1862. Aging parents' loss of adult sons and their labor to the war could also devastate a family's economic well-being. Families who had lost a soldier seem to have suffered the most significant decline in total wealth (see table 2.2).[9]

Those families with soldiers who all returned alive but whose experiences during the war had injured or weakened them physically often faced similar obstacles to financial success, or even survival, to those families whose men did not come home at all. Wounded men had to struggle with the economic implications of the physical limitations imposed on them by their injuries.

Many wounded veterans whose occupations required significant manual labor found themselves hard-pressed to find the money to support their families. W. N. Layne, wounded during the war, made clear in a later pension application his concern about providing for his family if he could not farm: "I cannot do farm labor, ... and farm labor is my only occupation." Walter Mills's wartime experience included a debilitating illness that made it difficult for him to work after the war. Layne's and Mills's families both lost all their wealth from 1860 to 1870. As table 2.2 shows, as a group, those families with soldiers who returned alive but who had been ill, wounded, or a prisoner of war were more severely affected economically from 1860 to 1870 than the healthy soldiers' families.[10]

For the families of veterans, the most significant implication of the data in table 2.2 may be that those families whose veterans were "alive not healthy" were nearly as affected economically from 1860 to 1870 as those who lost a family member in the Confederate military. Even though their male family members had not died, the financial impact of a weakened or invalid husband, father, or son was severe. Such veterans would have been drains on family finances, not contributors. The women in these families would have been expected to carry a larger burden of the financial support than those with healthy men, and soldiers' wives in these families would not have had the opportunity to improve their economic status through remarriage that soldiers' widows might have had.[11]

Of course, the impact of the Civil War on veteran families was not merely financial in nature. In fact, the emotional and psychological effects of the war were felt for years to come. Soldiers and their families were affected psychologically by their physical separation during the war, by physical weakening or disabilities, by the Confederate loss of the war, by the end of slavery, by the postwar economic chaos, and, perhaps most seriously, by the deaths of so many for whom they cared so deeply. At the same time, the common struggle to survive and the numerous letters between couples or among family members may have brought some veteran families closer together.

Military service meant extended separations of soldiers from their families. That physical distance had an especially strong impact on two particular sets of relationships within veteran families: recently married couples and fathers and young children. The war's separation heavily shaped these relationships that were newly formed or had not even begun, which allows for a close reading of the war's emotional impact.

A number of soldiers went off to war recently married, some of them just days or weeks before their companies left town, and they left behind, sometimes for four years, their new spouses. George and Sarah Jones married about a year before the war began and so had spent only a little time together before they were separated for most of the war, especially the nearly two years during which George was a POW in a Northern prison. George's wartime letters to Sarah indicate his great desire to be with her but also the relative newness of their marriage: "how I wish I could see you.... We yet shall see each other and [I] am inhopes that there is yet much happiness in store for us." Jedediah and Susan Carter were also a newly married couple separated by Jed's military service. Jed's eagerness to return to his new spouse is clear in most of his letters to her: "I hope that this wicked war will soon be over so that I can go home to live with my dear companion."[12]

Jed and George clearly wanted to get home to their wives, and despite no extant letters from Susan or Sarah, it is likely that they wanted their husbands to come home as well. Unfortunately for scholars, as is the case for so many other couples separated by war, the letters between Sarah and George and between Jed and Susan stop with the end of the war. Still, there are some conclusions that can be drawn. When the men did return home, couples who were married just before the war such as the Joneses and the Carters would have had to work out what it meant to be married. They had to do so after several years of potentially life-changing events and experiences and in the midst of a stressful postwar, post-slavery economic world. For at least some couples, such a process of getting (re)acquainted amid such circumstances certainly proved difficult. For others, the way may have strengthened their emotional bonds.[13]

Another relationship affected by wartime separation was that between soldier fathers and their young children. George Jones's two children were both under three years old when he wrote Sarah from a military prison: "How I wish I could see the children.... It is nearly two years since I saw them." He was particularly concerned about what the separation would do to his relationship with his daughter: "I reckon that I am an entire stranger to her now." Similarly, when Susan Carter gave birth to a daughter, Mollie, while Jed was in the field, he worried that his daughter would not love him or get to know him. In almost every letter after her birth, Jed told Susan to give Mollie his love and "kiss her for me."[14]

As with newly married couples, fathers returning home from war had to reacquaint themselves with, or even meet (as in Jed's case), their children. Conceivably, the children and fathers might not have gotten along, two to four years being a long time for children (and adults) to grow apart. Although there are no sources for Pittsylvania families indicating the direction these postwar father-child interactions took, James Marten, a historian of children in the Civil War, has argued that wartime physical separation actually strengthened these relationships, made them more intense and explicit, especially if letters connected families to soldiers in the field. If Marten's contention is true, then George and Jennie, and Jed and Mollie, probably (re)connected after the fathers came back home, if perhaps after an adjustment period.[15]

Of course, the war, its events, its experiences, and the postwar world it helped create had also taken a toll emotionally and mentally on the soldiers (and on their families). Men who returned home missing limbs or permanently disabled because of wounds or disease (or both) had to cope with that disability, and with its implications for their economic survival, but also for their position as men in a Southern white world that had typically defined manhood in both physical and economic terms. For other soldiers, their wounds were not physical but mental, as they suffered from what today might be called post-traumatic stress disorder because of what they had seen, heard, and done during the war.[16]

All soldiers, regardless of mental or physical health, returned to their homes, their families, and their friends as defenders of a defeated cause, with the emotional weight of having lost. A palpable sense of loss pervaded their returns to Danville, to Chatham, and to their homes all over Pittsylvania County. C. Vann Woodward has described the legacy of Confederate defeat as the "burden of Southern history"; that burden lay much heavier on these homecomings and the postwar lives of these veteran families. Returning soldiers have always had some difficulty readjusting to civilian life, but ex-Confederates had to cope with losing the war and all that that loss entailed (including emancipation and economic difficulties). Given these circumstances, many former soldiers turned to their families for comfort, support, and a place to begin the rebuilding of their postwar world.[17]

In Pittsylvania, over eight hundred soldiers never came home to their families. In 1862, Bettie Penick wrote to her brother, Rawley Martin, who was fighting with the 53rd Virginia Infantry: "You are so often wished for my dear Brother—by us all—There is only one vacant seat in the little family circle—and that is yours." Like many families, the Martins at home comforted themselves with the knowledge that "We ought to feel so grateful that a temporary absence, and not *death* has made the vacancy." The Martin family was lucky. Although injured, Rawley came home and filled that seat at the table. For the other families who had not been so lucky, the empty seat (or seats) sat there, daily reminding family members of what they had lost in the war.[18]

Despite being an integral part of war, the death of a family member or a friend was obviously a severe emotional strain. Since over one-quarter of the county's soldiers died, many of Pittsylvania's soldiers and their families felt the pain that came with the death of someone they cared about. A New Hampshire soldier who gave food in May 1865 to a "poor widow woman" in Danville whose two sons and husband had died noted the intensity of her understandable grief: "To talk to her with tearless eyes was more complimentary to the tongue than the heart of him who could do it, even if his eyes were closed to her sad tale; for she looked too much of the deep and crushing sorrow that she felt."[19]

Parents keenly felt the loss of their children during the war. Beckie Martin wrote to her brother of their neighbors, whose son had died, "they are much distressed, it is such a blow on them." George Jones wrote home to his wife expressing his concerns about the effect that the death of his brother, James, would have on his father: "Tell father to take care of himself, I know that he is distressed about the death of a favorite son whose loss to him is irreparable."[20]

The mourning was not just for family members. The death of a young member of Rawley Martin's regiment who had gotten shot trying to help Rawley during "Pickett's Charge" devastated Martin. He lamented in a letter to his sister, "Thomas Tredway, poor fellow, he saw me fall just as our men were repulsed and he rushed to me exclaiming, oh my dear col[onel], and just as he got to me, was shot and fell on me. We layed upon the field together and I was taken off first." Tredway died of his wounds.[21]

The soldiers and their families of Pittsylvania and Danville felt the economic and emotional impact of the Civil War in a variety of ways.[22] Yet they did not passively accept the changes. They employed strategies intended to protect their way of life as much as possible.

Strategies for Rebuilding Veteran Families (1865–1870)

Home was the place to which soldiers wanted to return and rebuild their lives, nurtured within the strong emotional and economic support of their network of familial households, extra-household relatives, and friends. Still, this reconstruction of veteran families took place in the new postbellum world, a world full of obstacles to that rebuilding process, a world in which veteran families worked with disadvantages due to their soldiers' time away from businesses or farms and their wounds, diseases, and deaths.

Once soldiers returned home to their families, it was again possible to work as an economic unit within the household (or at least to try to do so). It was also easier for veterans to request and arrange aid from other relatives and friends since they were no longer physically separated by the war. With the end to separation came an end to those wonderfully revealing letters that demonstrate the emotional support and economic interactions and strategies within and outside familial households. Wartime experiences, strategies used, and aid given, however, provide some indication of the ways in which the familial household, as well as other relatives and friends, also served as postwar resources for veteran families. At its most basic, the rebuilding of veteran families required, as one household head wrote three years after the war, "using every economy & working every way to get along."[23]

"Working every way to get along" meant choosing one or more of a variety of strategies intended to maximize economic and emotional benefits. These strategies included manipulating the family household structure (particularly important for soldiers' widows), endeavoring to hold their families together; attempting to succeed in farming or other work in the postwar, post-slavery world by using the labor of all family members; moving away from Pittsylvania County and Danville altogether; and turning to friends and relatives outside the home. As families tried to rebuild and reconstruct their lives, however, some of them also found themselves weakened by problems brought on by military service, wartime actions, and the postwar world in which they lived.

Restructuring the Family Household

The basic unit of economic and emotional support in the nineteenth century was the family household. According to statistics compiled from the 1870 county population census, most Pittsylvania veteran families lived in single-family households. Such homes consisted of a married couple with or without children or of single-parent families. To be classified as a single-family household, all children had to be under the age of twenty-one. For example, William and Linda Simmons lived with their four children, who were all age thirteen or younger. Almost half these veteran families, however, did not live in a single-family structure.[24]

Living in households larger than just the single family was one way for veteran families to increase their economic base, to help endure the loss or disability of important financial earners, and to extend their emotional support system. Extended-family households made up some two-fifths of all veteran households in 1870. These extended-family dwellings included adult children living with their parents, elderly parents living with their adult offspring, aunts, uncles, and cousins living together, and widows and orphans living with their relatives.[25]

This strategy of living with family members in times of economic or emotional crisis was not new, nor was it restricted to soldiers and their relatives, but it was of crucial importance for some veteran families. For example, when soldier William Dodson and his wife both died during the war, his five young children were taken in by their maternal grandfather, Turner Gosney. It was also common among Pittsylvania's veteran families for children to move back in with, or continue to live with, parents well after reaching adulthood, even when married and having children of their own. Many soldiers had been living with their parents in 1860, not unusual for a group whose median age was twenty-three. By 1870, however, the median age of Pittsylvania's veterans was thirty-four, well past the time when most men would have married and moved out of their parents' house. Certainly a number of these extended families were created by the needs of the immediate families of disabled and deceased men, but many of the veterans, such as James Fulton, who continued to live at home or moved in with their parents (or other relatives) showed no overt health problems. Their residence with extended family members may just have been about consolidating economic and emotional resources.[26]

Another way of shaping household structure in order to improve the economic status of veteran families was to hire workers to labor in fields or in the house or to find boarders to pay rent. Almost 20 percent of veteran family households in 1870 contained boarders, workers, or both. Because of emancipation, many white Pittsylvanians were looking to hire workers (both white and black), but some veteran families needed to replace more than slaves; they needed also to replace wounded, sick, or deceased family members. For example, Thomas Poindexter, wounded in service but with a family to support, hired Thomas Barber to help with his farming.[27]

A few veterans and veteran family members (about one in twenty-five veteran households), however, lived in households belonging to people to whom they were not related. Typically unable or unwilling to live on their own, they may not have had family members with whom to live. Veteran John Logan had lived and worked with his parents in 1860, but by 1870 they had died. Logan lived with, and worked for, William Linthicum as a farm laborer. A few veterans lived as boarders, paying rent to stay with families to whom they were not related or residing at a boarding house in Danville or Chatham. Although these veterans had money, they probably did not have family with whom to stay.[28]

Finally, there were those veterans who lived in their own homes but without family. Although relatives may have lived nearby, these men lived apart from them. Making up about 4 percent of the veteran households in 1870, these men may not have wanted, needed, or had a family with which to live, share, and support. Regardless of their reasoning or options, these men who remained single did not take advantage of a key economic strategy for many soldiers (and for many young men at the time).[29]

Many soldiers who were single in 1860 (although sometimes living with family) married after the war, many of them by 1870. Getting married made good economic sense for single men and women. Although they certainly did not get married exclusively as an economic strategy—marriage also gained single men and women another emotional support system to replace or supplement the one that existed before—the world of the nineteenth century was one in which the labor of both men and women was needed to survive financially. Unmarried veterans could take advantage of the significant shortage of white men in the county after the war and use marriage to move up in the world. Calvin Moore had been a poor livery keeper with only $100 in 1860. He fought in the war and was wounded twice, and his first wife died, but his second wife (Ann P.) had some money (and a couple of children) from her deceased husband. By 1870 Moore was a farmer with $2,200 of real estate and $300 of personal property.[30]

The flip side of the significant shortage of white men of marriageable age was that the single and widowed women had fewer opportunities for (re)marriage. Therefore, the choices made about household structure by widows of soldiers were particularly important in economically (and emotionally) surviving the death of their husbands and rebuilding their families within the postwar world. Widowed wives had four basic options, although admittedly their choices were heavily shaped by the war's demographic catastrophe, their age, their antebellum financial status, and the number and helpfulness of their children or other relatives.

Certainly, widows' first alternative was to get remarried. This option was what had been expected of antebellum widowed women, especially if they were young, and seems to have continued to be what many men and women expected of them. Southern society, with its emphasis on patriarchy, had little room for white women who were not directly dependent on male relatives, husbands, fathers, or even sons. Once they remarried, as Ann Moore did, the former widows no longer challenged the patriarchal order. By remarrying, these women not only yielded to societal pressure to return to the patriarchal fold and to conventional behavior, but they also reestablished themselves and their children (if any) as part of a male-headed economic unit, a good strategy in the world in which they lived.[31]

At least 7 percent of the soldiers' widows found in the 1870 census had remarried. For comparison, about 30 percent of Suzanne Lebsock's antebellum Petersburg widows and Jennifer Gross's war widows in Brunswick County, Virginia, remarried. Despite the problems with finding widows in the census (a difficult process unless they had particularly distinctive first names or had children from a previous marriage), it seems likely that Pittsylvania's actual warwidow remarriage rate was still lower than those found by Lebsock and Gross. Since the wartime loss of so many young white men had created a significant gender imbalance—among whites between the ages of thirty and forty-nine in the county in 1870, there were only eighty-two men per one hundred women—remarriage was not always a choice that widows were able to make.[32]

So not all widows could get remarried, and not all of them wanted to. Those most capable of living on their own financially were also the ones most likely to have men interested in marrying them. Unfortunately for widows who wanted to remarry and who did not have great wealth, as historian Jennifer Gross points out, many of the remaining single men decided "to marry younger women who did not bring with them the 'emotional baggage' of a previous marriage." Barsheba Adams's husband, George, died in service in 1862, and she never remarried; that is not surprising, since she was almost fifty years old when he died and the couple had no money in 1860, and given the postwar gender imbalance.[33]

The second, and most likely, possibility for a war widow was to remain unmarried and continue to live on her own, often with her children. As Kirsten Wood and Suzanne Lebsock have shown for the antebellum South, some widows wanted to continue living without a husband and running their own affairs, assuming they could financially do so. These widows may have relished the independence they gained. Some may have been able to rely on the efforts of their older children. Others may have had to deal with the fact that the difficulty of finding available marriage partners for widows, combined with an economy largely structured around rewarding male labor, created, as one historian has noted, "a circumstance that no doubt relegated larger numbers of women to old ages marked by poverty and loneliness."[34]

Whether or not continued status without a male household head was a matter of choice, it was the dominant family structure for Pittsylvania's veteran widows, with over 70 percent of them living as independent household heads. The experiences of these widows who lived on their own varied widely. Lucy A. Payne, whose husband and son died during the war, was still a widow in 1870, living on her own. Despite suffering a massive economic loss (her family was worth about $50,000 in 1860 and only $2,250 in 1870) in addition to her familial loss, Payne still remained better-off than most widows who continued to live on their own. Over a fourth (twenty-two of seventy-six) of the widow-headed households in 1870 had no property, real or personal, while close to half (thirty-five of seventy-six) had less than $500 in total combined property.[35]

By choice or not, some widows did not remarry, nor did they live on their own. A third strategy for reorganizing widows' households was to move in with relatives. Roughly one of every six Pittsylvania widows took this option. One of these widows, Susan Terry, along with her two young children, moved in with her parents after her husband died. This movement of unsupported women to live with other family members in a different household was an old survival pattern, but it was one made more necessary by the death of so many men during the war.[36]

The fourth option, although apparently not a first choice of most widows, was to move in with non-family-members. Some widows and their families lived with others to whom they were not related, sometimes gaining a place to stay and food to eat for themselves and their children in exchange for their domestic service. In what was certainly the least desirable situation and a sign of great desperation, a few widows and their children moved into the county's poorhouse. In doing so, they acknowledged that the system of depending on families for help and assistance had failed them.[37]

Making a Living in Postwar Pittsylvania

Of course, whether or not veteran families' soldiers survived, whether or not they shifted their households around, they had to find a way to earn livings in the postwar world. Although there were other ways to put food on the table, for many of these Pittsylvania families, farming was their main occupation. In 1870, at least 72 percent of white men and 76 percent of veterans worked in agriculture.[38]

In postwar Pittsylvania, farming generally meant growing tobacco, even more than it had before the war. Production of tobacco had continued even during the war, although at a reduced level. In those four years, however, a significant change took place in the way bright tobacco (a standard variant for the Pittsylvania area) was used. Because of a variety of war-induced conditions, soldiers led a change from chewing to smoking tobacco. Before, bright tobacco had largely been valued as the wrapping on manufactured "plugs" made of darker tobacco, but because of its milder taste and smell, it was seen as the preferred source for smoking tobacco. Tobacco demand and prices jumped in the immediate postwar period (1865–70) because of the new smoking habits and because of Northern demand. Danville itself became a major center of bright-leaf tobacco sales and manufacturing until displaced by several North Carolina towns in the early twentieth century.[39]

The profit made from this bright-leaf growth, however, was not evenly distributed among all those who participated in the process. Pittsylvania's tobacco manufacturers and dealers profited a great deal more than the county's farmers, especially the smaller ones. Local growers also suffered more than the processors from the extended agricultural depression that started in the 1870s and lasted (to some extent) through the end of the century, made worse by competition from farmers in Kentucky and Tennessee. Despite these hardships, as one historian of the county notes, "Pittsylvania stood and fell with tobacco." For many years after the war, agriculture, and especially tobacco, remained the main occupation of the county and most of its residents, including its veteran families.[40]

As before the war, veteran families' postwar agricultural experiences depended on their economic status. Almost every family, veteran or not, suffered economically because of the end of the war, and many suffered major losses in their "personal property" with emancipation. Still, there remained significant differences between the resources with which various white Pittsylvanians had to work and, as a result, different approaches to take regarding postwar agriculture.

Wealthy landowners were most concerned with how to run their farms without slave labor. The focus on labor-intensive tobacco meant that a solution was especially critical for Pittsylvania's large veteran landowners looking to support their families. David Dyer, a veteran and landowner, complained right after the war that despite "good land & nine good hands," he had problems getting all his farming done. The solution for large landowners in Pittsylvania County and most of the South was to shift, in historian Gavin Wright's terms, from running plantations as "laborlords" to renting or sharecropping their farms as "landlords." As early as 1866 or 1867, according to several estimates, sharecropping had already begun to develop in tobacco regions of Virginia and North Carolina as a standard way of organizing postbellum plantations.[41]

Of course, most veteran families in postwar Pittsylvania were not wealthy planters. Many of them continued to work their own land and to grow their own tobacco to process and sell and their own corn to eat. Studies of postwar experiences of Southern yeomen or plain folk point out the increase in white tenancy and sharecropping after the war. Pittsylvania County farming families had a difficult time dealing with the economic consequences of the war and the end of slavery, even if they did not own slaves. Although most antebellum planters in the county probably kept their land, landlessness, tenancy, and sharecropping among Pittsylvania's yeomen and small slaveholders increased, including a number of the veteran families. Many of those veterans who owned land, such as Grief Lampkin, "had to give a lein on my real estate to pay off my creditors." Some people were not able to pay those liens off in time to keep their land.[42]

One admittedly crude way to measure the increase in tenant or sharecropping veteran farming families is to look at the percentage of farming soldiers' households with no real estate in the 1860 and 1870 censuses. Of all veteran households with farming family members, 41 percent were landless in 1860. By 1870, the proportion of landless veteran farming households among all veteran farming households had risen to almost 58 percent, indicating an increase in veterans who were working on someone else's land.[43]

Some veterans and their families therefore ended up sharecropping or working as farm laborers. William Harraway, from a previously well-off antebellum farming family, requested "to go your halves" with a rich landowner in 1867, hoping the man would allow Harraway to work the man's land, provide farming supplies and labor, in exchange for half the crop. For some veterans, injuries added to an already difficult postwar economy and cost them their land and any real occupational independence. By 1870, Thomas Cook, wounded veteran and antebellum landowner, had lost his real estate and become a farm laborer, working someone else's land.[44]

Most of Pittsylvania's veteran men and women, along with most whites of the region, attempted to survive wartime debts, postwar chaos, droughts, and emancipation and take advantage of the boom in bright-leaf tobacco prices while it lasted. Still, although agriculture dominated, it was not the only means of earning a living in Pittsylvania County and Danville. Like veteran family members involved in farming, many in non-agricultural positions continued to work in the jobs they had before the war, though some veterans explored other occupations because of war-induced disabilities, higher callings, or just a need to earn more money for their families.[45]

Some non-farming veterans successfully weathered the financial problems of the war. Charles Sublett and Frank Swanson, veterans and merchants, managed to survive the war economically intact and actually improved their financial situations, despite their military service and the war's economic effects. Both these men, however, had been wealthy merchants before the war, each worth nearly $10,000, and both remained healthy and unwounded during the war. Few veterans had all these factors going for them.[46]

Wartime injuries caused a number of veterans to look for other employment. Many disabled soldiers could no longer support their families through manual labor of any kind. William Baugh served in the 18th Virginia Infantry during the war and lost his arm at Gettysburg. As a result, Baugh could no longer work as a mechanic as he did before the war. He tried to rent Danville's toll bridge for up to "five years" and earn money running it, because, as he explained to one of the owners of the toll bridge, "I am disabled and must go at something else besides hard labor."[47]

Disabled farmers and agricultural laborers were forced to find new (occupational) fields in which to work. David Marshall, a laborer in 1860, was also forced to find suitable employment when gunshot wounds to his right hand and left shoulder left him unable to "perform manual labor without great pain," according to a later application for state financial assistance. He finally found a place working in one of Danville's tobacco factories. Even there he had problems with the constant pain of his wartime injuries, but it was better than agricultural work. Marshall must have been fairly desperate to find employment, because laboring in the tobacco-manufacturing plants of Danville would certainly have been seen as a step down in status for a white man, since most tobacco-factory workers were black.[48]

Assuming that disabled veterans were literate and could find a position, they could also work as clerks. Ludolphus Gunn's father, James, wrote to one of the town's richest men toward the end of the war asking for a position as clerk for his son. The young Ludolphus had fought and "was badly wounded an fell on the field & Taken Prisoner he has just returned home an has to start back soon." Gunn's family needed him to work, and clerking was a job in which his injuries would hamper him less than they would working in the fields or some other form of manual labor.[49]

Finding another good job if veterans were disabled from wartime wounds or illness, or just wanted to change occupations, was much easier for elite, well-educated men. They simply had more options than a less-educated, less-well-connected worker or yeoman farmer. Robert Withers, a doctor before the war, had to find a new job because of his injuries suffered as an officer. He later remembered, "I was so crippled by wounds that I was physically disqualified from following my old profession." Working with an acquaintance, Withers became a newspaper editor soon after the war's end. William Dame, son of a prominent Danvillian minister, was able to get "a place in the railroad service" almost immediately upon his return home, despite no experience in the field. Later, Dame decided to go to seminary and became a minister himself.[50]

One key strategy for the economic survival of many veteran families was a willingness on the part of their members to earn money in a variety of occupations. The experience of David Harris Watson—as pieced together from letters, receipts, military records, and tax bills—reveals the lengths to which many non-elite veterans went to try to support their families. Although listed in the 1860 census as a bricklayer, before his death in 1894, Watson worked as a house builder and shoemaker. Even after he obtained a small piece of land of his own on which he grew tobacco and corn to sell, he continued to do side jobs in these other areas. Many veterans listed as farmers or laborers certainly did other work on the side, even if few collections of records exist that are as detailed as Watson's. For families who did not have large farms, powerful connections, or elite educations, working multiple jobs was simply a way to survive.[51]

And it was not just veterans like Watson who worked in multiple ways to support their families. In late 1865, at a statewide meeting of Virginia's Baptists, the Rev. J. B. Jeter spoke to the ladies in the audience "on their obligation to conform themselves to the exigencies of the times." The *Religious Herald*, the Virginia Baptist newspaper, later reported, "The speaker complimented the ladies of Virginia on their virtues and their accomplishments. They were the pride and joy of the land. But with the change in the times their habits must be changed. Avoiding idleness and extravagance, they must seek to make themselves useful. They must show that those who adorn the parlor are capable of performing all the duties of the domestic circle. Thus they will prove themselves to be worthy mothers, sisters and wives of the young men who are hastening to redeem, by their honest toil and patriotic plans, our beloved commonwealth from its depressed and desolate condition."[52]

At a minimum patronizing, the talk suggested that the antebellum and wartime work that many white women did for their families was not well recognized by men, or at least not by this man. The reverend's speech also indicated a recognition that women's work, whether by "ladies" or not, would be essential to the rebuilding of postwar families and Southern society. Family survival had always been at least partly dependent on the actions of women, but that became increasingly true and obvious to family members during and after the Civil War, when women in veteran families worked in a variety of positions to support their husbands and children, siblings, and parents.

As they had before the war, women in Pittsylvania's veteran farming families continued to play important roles in household agricultural efforts. Women's gardening provided at least a supplement to, if not a significant portion of, family food supplies before, during, and after the war. Susan Carter grew "good apples and potatoes" for her family throughout these years. The Martin family's letters reveal that the women grew strawberries and raspberries and made jams.[53]

Women in the poorest of antebellum white families had actually worked in the fields, although typically as a last resort, since white Southern society perceived such work as inappropriate for white women. The war had forced many white women of non-slaveholding soldier families to work to grow corn and tobacco while their men were off in the army. In the postwar need for labor, some of the poorer white women probably joined their men in the fields, although, again, typically as a last resort at peak times such as planting and harvest. Despite the negative perception, a few white women actually described their occupation in the 1870 census as "farm laborer."[54]

For widowed farming households, women's agricultural roles were much more prominent. Veteran widows had to run farms on their own, but most had already had to deal with farming during the war because of the absence of their husbands. Of the widows listed in the 1870 census with an occupation, 30 percent were landed farmers. As with male farmers, the postwar experiences of female-headed farming households differed significantly according to their amount of wealth, especially real estate. Widows with substantial amounts of farming land were most concerned with supervising or contracting with agricultural workers, tenants, or sharecroppers. Widows with small amounts of land might work their farms themselves or have male relatives work them for them.[55]

The 1870 census also provides a partial picture of what other jobs women of veteran families were doing to support themselves and their families. White women did not have many opportunities to earn money outside the home, and the work that was available was the most menial and among the lowest paid. Of those women in veteran families with an occupation listed in the census, almost three-fourths worked as domestic servants for other households (although most continued to live with their own families). The other non-agricultural positions held by women of veteran families included work in the clothing field (seamstresses, weavers, and spinners), teaching, and clerking. Few women had the opportunities or education to take these latter positions, which might have earned them and their families more money.[56]

The most common occupational classification for veteran women (and white women as a whole) was not even a formal job in the eyes of most census takers, yet it hid work essential to their families' survival. Of all women age fifteen and over from veteran families in Pittsylvania County, over 92 percent were listed as "keeping house" (if she was the woman in charge of taking care of the home) or "at home" or "without occupation" (if she was an additional female relative in the home). Women "kept house" by cooking, cleaning, sewing, rearing children, gardening, storing food, nursing the sick, and caring for boarders. The categorization obscured women's agricultural efforts, especially among poor and yeoman families. Other veteran women listed as "keeping house" whose husbands were merchants, such as Sallie Swanson, helped out in the store when needed. Also, in-house manufacturing of cloth, clothes, and even tobacco, albeit on a small scale, took place during the war, proving that women such as Susan Carter and the Martins had the skills to do such work in the postwar period as well.[57]

"Keeping house" also masked the increase in domestic labor on the part of white women who had previously depended on the labor of enslaved women. Poor and yeoman white women had been doing their own family's (and sometimes other families') cleaning and cooking for years, and they continued to do so. As historian LeeAnn Whites points out, however, as black women gained some power over their work after emancipation, wealthier white women ended up having to do some or all of their own washing, ironing, cooking, and cleaning.[58]

"Keeping house" also obscured the essential role that women in all families played in the management of household resources. Women worked to save money by repairing and reusing clothes, by saving food scraps, by reducing household costs as much as possible. This responsibility was an important part of running a financially successful household. Robert Withers later praised the ability of his wife to keep the family going while he was gone during the war: "My wife had shown great business capacity, I thought, in the management of her household affairs." Part of that manipulation of resources meant making food go further and ensuring that it went to the most needy of the family. When the Withers family was short of food later on, the parents took the little meat they had and "boiled [it] with black-eyed peas to give them a flavor." The youngest child got "all the meat that was cooked for dinner," while the rest of the family "ate peas and other vegetables." In less-fortunate households during and after the war, parents probably went without food some meals so that children could eat.[59]

Like David Harris Watson, women in veteran families worked at different jobs, even if female occupations tended to be classified as "keeping house" or "at home." One veteran woman who worked both inside and outside the home to support her family was Katherine Moses. She was listed as "keeping house" for her family in 1870 and 1880, doing all the work that went with that position, but she also taught school from 1871 to 1884 in Pittsylvania County and then also ran her farm after her husband died in 1878. In order to survive the postwar era, women in veteran families did an incredible amount and variety of work.[60]

Children in veteran families worked, too. Sarah Wallace's father received a mortal wound when she was seven years old; in 1870, she worked as a domestic servant to support herself and her family. Although it is hard to tell how many veteran children ended up working to support their families, there are indications that many families thought schooling was a luxury that they could not afford for their children to have. In 1874, the local Baptist association proclaimed, "We would enter our solemn protest against the idea that education is needful for professional men alone, or for women who are to become teachers, or for those whose aspiration is to shine in polite company, but it is not necessary to those of either sex whose ambition is to be useful members of society." Comparing the percentage of veteran children between the ages of five and eighteen in school in 1870 (15 percent) to the percentage of non-veteran white children of those ages in school in the county as a whole (18 percent) indicates that veteran families were slightly less likely to have their children in school than non-veteran white Pittsylvanians as a whole, suggesting that they needed their children more for work than the other families did.[61]

Starting Over in a New Place

One other survival strategy for veteran families was to leave Pittsylvania County and Danville, hoping for better opportunities in a new place. In 1870, 61 percent of the veteran families located in the 1860 census were again recorded by census takers in Pittsylvania County or Danville. Not all the remaining 39 percent of veteran families (some seven hundred families) moved away from the county. Some veterans died without any clear family to trace, or their widows remarried, and other people may have been missed by the census takers, factors that would reduce indications of persistence.[62]

Despite these caveats, clearly a fair number of veteran families chose to leave Pittsylvania County and Danville. Of the 123 veterans and veteran families for whom there is specific evidence of where they went, 80 of them just moved somewhere else in Virginia. Robert Withers and his family moved to Lynchburg to take up his new job as newspaper editor, and others moved to Richmond, Roanoke, Charlottesville, and elsewhere in the state. The other 43 veterans moved farther away, to such places as Texas, Kentucky, California, Georgia, and Tennessee, anywhere they thought they might find better opportunities for themselves and their families. In a letter written soon after the end of the war, J. M. Hines indicated that he was willing to move away from the Pittsylvania area: "Should you find any position in 'New' Orleans or any point 'South' that you think I could make any money . . ." Hines explained that he wanted to leave because "Danville is remarkably dull[,] money very close with no better prospects ahead for some time." Other veterans, such as William F. Bentley, moved to newer, less-settled states such as Texas, hoping to find better economic conditions. People who moved left behind their local support network of family and friends, but perhaps they moved because that network was not helping them anymore.[63]

Stressors Faced by Veteran Families

Another important issue for veteran families was that, for all the essential support that many families provided for members, they also all faced numerous stressors. One historian of antebellum families notes that with the physical, emotional, and financial pressures on white marriages, "it is amazing that most remained loyal to and pleased with the institution." How much worse must it have been for postbellum white families, especially married veteran couples, who had to live with the greater tension of the postwar period? While some couples and families may have strengthened emotional bonds because of the war, the family-based support system on which so many men and women relied failed for others from a variety of stressors. Not all veteran families could provide the economic and emotional support needed to build or rebuild a strong, self-sufficient home. Most of those stressors were old, some were new, but all were exacerbated by the problems brought on by war and emancipation.[64]

First, veteran families had to contend with tensions brought on by the postwar economic depression that hit them as the South attempted to recover from the damage and privations caused by the war. Despite the region's freedom from direct Union destruction and the brief postwar boom in bright-leaf tobacco, such economic problems affected Pittsylvania-Danville too. One resident complained in early 1866, "There is perfect stagnation in business, everything is gloomy." In addition, as LeeAnn Whites has demonstrated with Jefferson and Gertrude Thomas in postwar Augusta, Georgia, one financially incompetent spouse could seriously exacerbate a family's economic problems and push a marriage and family to a breaking point.[65]

Adding to the strain on veteran married couples and families, soldiers returned from years of fighting having experienced some horrific events, incidents that may have changed them from the men they were before the war. Those who stayed at home also may have been changed by their wartime experiences. They all faced the added tension of working out what it meant to be married in a chaotic postwar world. They had to try to survive economically without knowing for sure what their particular roles were in dealing with family finances.

Veteran family households with additional relatives faced further challenges to their situation. When needy relatives moved in, it could mean extra workers, but it also meant the added economic strain of having more mouths to feed. Extra people also meant extra domestic work for the women in the house. In addition, not everybody gets along with their relatives at the best of times and while living in separate homes; the conditions under which these people were moving in with family members were far from ideal. It is not hard to imagine doors slamming and harsh words being exchanged. Finally, for those adults living with their parents, adult children may have felt burdened by elderly parents, and adult men may have felt dependent if they had to live with fathers who could continue to control their children through their power over familial resources. The return for some veterans to homes where their fathers retained or reasserted patriarchal control almost certainly resulted in increased stress on their families.[66]

In general, many veterans experienced difficulty re-adjusting to life back in their homes, which potentially created problems within their families, especially if it affected their ability to support their dependents financially. Some veterans showed signs of an emotional listlessness or depression, expressed well during the war by Richard Waldrop: "I have very little heart for writing or doing anything else." In others, there seems to have been a restlessness, even a potential for violence. Veterans returned home after having been away from Pittsylvania or Danville for the first time in their lives, having seen a great deal of the world and a great deal of violence. They returned to Pittsylvania County and Danville to find a smaller, different, even boring home, leaving them restless and unsettled, which placed greater strain on their family lives. Like a feedback loop, such depression or irritability would be exacerbated by economic problems, which would make financial success more difficult, which in turn could increase depression or irritability.[67]

Another problem that weakened the support that some veteran families were capable of providing for their members came in the form of alcohol. Given the stress that veterans were under when they returned and the depression and restlessness they faced, the use and abuse of alcohol by some of them is not surprising. Certainly veterans Frank Gosney, J. Blanks, and Samuel Chaney had extended problems with "intemperance," as all three men were kicked out of their churches after multiple incidents over a number of years with "habitual drunkenness." Alcohol had the potential to interfere with men's ability to earn for their families and to give family members the support they needed. Beyond alcohol's impact on work habits and economic success, there are clear connections between its abuse and domestic violence.[68]

Domestic violence, indeed, was a part of some of these supposedly supportive veteran families. Veteran James Ashby was kicked out of his church "for unmercifully whipping his wife." That the incident had come to the attention of the church, and that the church publicly stepped into an area that in the nineteenth century was considered private, indicates that the incident in question was particularly egregious and probably not the first. Many other acts of violence within veteran homes probably went unnoticed, or at least unchallenged, by others.[69]

Veteran marriages and families faced other stresses on their bonds that undermined the support that those relationships potentially offered. Some spouses committed adultery; some of them were caught, such as Griffith Evans. Some men brought home with them venereal diseases that they passed on to their wives. James Wyatt's syphilis can only have created stress between him and his wife, Adeline, on multiple levels.[70]

Although problems of money, depression, intemperance, domestic violence, and unfaithfulness were all part of some white antebellum marriages and families, many of these domestic issues were related to, and exacerbated by, tensions over changes in gender roles brought about by the war and postwar conditions. Before the war, Southern white male identity was based in the power that white men held over their households, over all their dependents: white women and children and all black men and women. That legal, economic, and social control, combined with the ability to support those dependents, defined antebellum white men as independent. Women's activities during and after the war, emancipation, the Confederate defeat, the weakened economic status of many white families, and the physical impact of war on soldiers all contributed to challenge Southern white male dominance and control. These tensions in gender roles and the threat to Southern white male power represented a serious danger, at least from a white perspective, to the ability of white veteran families to survive and rebuild in the postwar South.

During and after the war, the authority of white male household heads as patriarchs was challenged. Wartime white male separation from wives and dependents and white women's increased economic responsibility changed the role of women in families and changed the character of relationships between spouses. In the absence of men, women had been forced to take on roles and responsibilities typically designated as male, even if both members of a couple had tried to maintain male control through mail advice, as Bettie and W. S. Penick had done, or through surrogate husbands in the form of male relatives or friends, as George and Sarah Jones tried at one point. Several historians, including George Rable, have pointed out that "sexual confusion reigned as the course of the fighting seemed to make hash of traditional definitions of female propriety." By the end of the war, Sarah Jones had made quite a few important decisions on her own.[71]

Most recent scholarship indicates that after the war most white women wanted to return to their antebellum roles, if possible. Some women had been overwhelmed by the doubled work and responsibility. Other women had proven themselves capable of running businesses or farms but did not necessarily want to be in control of their families' economic future. When husbands returned, they likely would have taken back these responsibilities, and many wives willingly relinquished that role to their spouses, if that were possible.[72]

The problem was that in the postwar period, white male superiority and white men's roles as protectors of white women continued to be challenged—by defeat, by emancipation, by financial woes, by physical problems—in ways that prevented some white men from recovering the ability to support their families and from regaining their belief in their own independence and manhood. Their loss in war had forced Confederate men to accept a submission to the federal government that seemed unmanly, symbolized most explicitly at the end of the war by the Union capture of Confederate president Jefferson Davis allegedly wearing women's clothes. Emancipation had eliminated the position of slaveholder that before the war had defined some Southern white men and defined what other white men wanted to be. The end of slavery also challenged white male separation from black men, although white men who still owned land could at least point to their separation from the largely propertyless freedpeople. However, the similarities between poor veterans and black men—neither had property and both were free—were, at a minimum, disconcerting and, at worst, emasculating to the former soldiers.[73]

If a white man's worth came in large part from his ability to make money and support his family, then any failure to do so could be seen as a failure in his manhood. Many veterans were further emasculated by their inability to earn a living and support their families. One veteran wrote with glee after coming out of bankruptcy that he was "now working like a man. All I make now . . . is mine." Even successful, healthy veterans had difficulty supporting their families in the lifestyle to which they had become accustomed, a fact that continued to challenge their status as men in the postwar world. Disabled veterans, especially amputees, faced challenges to their masculinity that went beyond their ability or inability to support their families since their bodies were no longer whole. So, despite the apparent postwar desire of many Southern white women to return to antebellum gender relations and roles, if husbands, fathers, and brothers were not fully ready to take over, because of being wounded or an amputee, ill, depressed, or in an economic situation that still required women's labor both in and out of the home, or if soldiers did not come back at all, wives, daughters, and sisters faced the continuation of those extra wartime burdens and responsibilities, placing a massive strain on the ability of families to serve as adequate emotional and economic supports for their members.[74]

In the end, although Southern white masculinity was threatened, it eventually recovered some of its antebellum strength. This reassertion of white masculinity and male power was seen as necessary for Southern white families to survive the postwar world. This recovery of white male power occurred in a couple of different ways, but mostly by reasserting white men's dominance over white women.

Elite white women played a key role in the rebirth of white male dominance. As LeeAnn Whites and Drew Gilpin Faust have shown, "The rehabilitation of southern white men became a central postwar responsibility for Confederate women." At first, the rehabilitation simply involved these women willingly submitting themselves to their husbands' control. Later on, groups such as the United Daughters of the Confederacy and various other Lost Cause and women's memorial associations valorized the South's defeat and remasculinized defeated soldiers. Although some elite women may have had reservations about relinquishing control to men who had failed to protect them before, the postwar racial uncertainty seems to have convinced them that their interests lay in a united front with white men.[75]

White masculinity and male dominance could be reasserted in other ways too. James Ashby's "unmercifully whipping his wife" made a crude and violent claim for his power over and control of his family. Through physical or emotional intimidation, or even through assault, husbands and fathers could reestablish their own masculinity within their households, even if they were unable to do so outside their homes.[76]

Another way to deal with the changes that war and emancipation brought to gender roles was to assert different definitions of masculinity and femininity. Laura Edwards has shown that whereas elite white families continued to see men's duty to support their families on their own as the basis for masculinity, although now with their own labor, working-class whites rejected that elite notion, accepting the public work of wives and other family members as a necessary part of their survival. As a result, working-class masculinity and superiority was restored, if it had ever been seriously threatened, despite men's inability to support their whole family.[77]

Institutions also helped to reestablish white male dominance in the postwar South in two ways. First, as later chapters reveal, in assisting veteran families, institutions such as churches and the state reinforced feminine submission to men both as individuals and as a whole. Second, as some scholars have demonstrated, white male dominance was also reestablished by the violence directed toward, and the political and legal restrictions placed on, black men and women throughout the latter part of the nineteenth century.[78]

Going Outside the Household for Help

Beyond the family, the next circle of help involved relatives and friends outside the household. Historians such as Robert Kenzer have shown that close kinship and neighborliness were an essential part of the world in which white Southerners lived, even after the war. It is clear that antebellum and wartime life in Pittsylvania and Danville often involved spending time with and doing business with relatives and friends. George Jones's letters to his wife spoke about parents, siblings, aunts, uncles, cousins, and friends, a network of relatives and acquaintances with whom he and Sarah were closely involved. Such relationships and mutual assistance continued after the war, even if the vast majority of the letters that could be used to prove that point definitively and to explore fully the exact nature of that help—beyond taking in needy relatives—ceased to be created in the conflict's aftermath.[79]

A few extant sources support the idea of continuing extra-household assistance from kin and friends. One veteran in economic trouble explained to an acquaintance, "Our relatives help us some." In a pension application, Charles H. Owen, having been seriously wounded, explained the role of his friends in his survival: "[I] can only partially labor & have to be frequently aided by my neighbors to get support and but for their help for a number of years could not have gotten my support." It is clear that some veterans and their families were able to turn to their friends and relatives for help.[80]

In 1870, the Johnsons, the Merricks, the Hutchinsons, and the Barkers, all veteran families, lived in Pittsylvania County's poorhouse.[81] These veteran families had been unsuccessful in finding a job and in employing successful strategies to survive in the immediate postwar world. The vast majority of veteran families, of course, did not end up in the poorhouse. For some, marshaling the resources of their households was enough to survive the war and its effects, even if they could not live at the same level as they did before the conflict began. Sometimes turning to friends and extra-household family met the needs of a veteran household. In the end, however, relatives and friends failed to provide enough support for every veteran family, and some veteran families had to turn to other sources of help. Barsheba Adams, widow of veteran George, never remarried and lived on her own, eventually turning to her church for support. Adams and the veteran families residing in the county poorhouse were not alone in needing more help than they could get from relatives and friends. Many veterans and their families looked to the next circle of assistance, churches and elite members of the community, and eventually even farther out, to the state, for the help that they needed to survive in the postwar world.[82]

3
Local Support from Baptist Churches

> We consider it the duty of the people of Virginia, either by voluntary contribution or by State appropriation, to supply our maimed soldiers with artificial limbs, and to provide for the maintenance of the indigent widows of deceased soldiers, and for the support and education of their children.
>
> —*Religious Herald*, October 1865

VETERAN FAMILIES in Pittsylvania County and Danville turned to long-established local support systems based on churches and elite community members when their familial resources and strategies failed to meet all their emotional or financial needs. This chapter examines the role that area Baptist churches played in veteran families' lives. The Civil War increased the need for the support of churches, and men and women of veteran families turned to those churches in the postwar period.[1]

Most broadly, Baptist churches provided many Confederate veteran families with emotional and spiritual support within their religious communities. For some of the desperately needy, however, churches offered limited financial assistance. At times, Baptist churches seemed to take on responsibilities (such as education) previously belonging to families, yet churches also served to reinforce the traditional family household structure and gender relations through their behavioral standards for all members and through the paternalistic nature of the financial aid provided to those families most damaged by the war. Though the financial support was important to those people (typically widows and orphans), it was not enough by itself to meet the wants of the neediest families. Still, the increases in church membership among men and women during and after the Civil War indicates that veteran families found something useful or fulfilling in those religious communities.

Churches and the War

Almost every church in Pittsylvania County before the Civil War had some kind of policy about helping people in trouble. In addition to the emotional and spiritual support that was an integral part of church life, most churches in the county, state, and nation had funds for "benevolent purposes" intended to help out the impoverished. When Christians discussed their obligations to assist the needy, they often cited 1 Peter 4:8: "And above all things, have fervent charity among yourselves, for charity shall cover the multitude of sins." Chatham Baptist's antebellum church covenant typified this sentiment: "we will cheerfully contribute of our property ... for the support of the poor." Churches' financial, emotional, and spiritual support continued from the antebellum period into, and after, the Civil War.[2]

During the war, the most basic form of financial support consisted of churches' raising money to help out poor members of the congregation. In early 1864, the minister of First Baptist Church of Danville "informed the church that some of its members were in very destitute and needy circumstances." The church decided to take a collection on the first Sunday of every month during the war for the relief of the poor. Many of the poor members of Pittsylvania-Danville churches were veteran families. "Sister" Rebecca Adams, widowed in 1862 when her husband died in service, soon turned for financial help to her church, Mt. Hermon Baptist, which raised $10 in early 1863 to buy her a barrel of corn.[3]

Pittsylvania's churches also helped needy families by providing employment for family members. Instead of the potential shame of direct charity, people could earn money to support their families. Shockoe Baptist Church helped out the women of one poor family in the church by offering an ongoing job as sexton keeping the church buildings clean and neat. Impoverished before the war and with a male family member in the Confederate army, the Owens family had trouble making ends meet. In June 1862, Martha Owen started as Shockoe's housekeeper for $10 a year. Because of the severe inflation in the Confederacy, the church members agreed to double that salary when it came time to pay her in May 1863; they also agreed to pay her $25 for her next year of cleaning. In May 1864, however, inflation prompted the church to pay her $100 instead. Her sister Nancy Owen agreed to take on the position of sexton and housekeeper for the following year (1864–65). The church records fail to indicate the amount the church paid Nancy, but she agreed to another year of service in May 1865 "with the understanding that the church at the close of her service would remunerate her as well as possible." Female members of the Owens family, including two teenagers, continued to work as sextons for Shockoe Church throughout the 1860s, providing much-needed cash to the impoverished family.[4]

Church-based financial aid during the war was reserved for the most needy, the most impoverished, the most afflicted by the human cost of the Civil War. The emotional and spiritual support that the churches offered during the war, however, was available to all their members, including soldiers and their families. Churches served as a place where people could go to take comfort, both in their spiritual beliefs and in the company of their friends, their "brothers" and "sisters," their surrogate families. Church support took many forms during the war. Churches provided a place to meet and share burdens with others, furnished justification for the fighting and the loss, created special days and rituals to bolster morale and community at home, comforted people separated from loved ones, and aided in the spiritual relief of soldiers in the field.

Because of the chaos of war and the presence of hostile armies, many churches in the South could not continue to hold religious services for at least part of the duration of the conflict. People in these areas—regions that historian Stephen Ash has called "No Man's Land"—did not have this emotional and spiritual support system as a resource. The churches in Pittsylvania County and Danville, however, were in what Ash calls the "Confederate Interior." Baptist churches of the area missed few meetings or services during the war. Like most areas not directly touched by Union forces, the Pittsylvania-Danville region retained its emotional and spiritual support system largely intact throughout the war.[5]

Justifying the war effort in religious rhetoric was one important way that Virginia's churches helped to encourage their members. In June 1862, the annual meeting of the Baptist General Association of Virginia issued a series of "resolutions" aimed at buoying the spirits of the state's Baptists. Despite "a year's experience of the evils of war, which has served to deepen our sense of their horrors . . . with many of our fertile fields crimsoned with the blood of our sons and of our brothers," those at the meeting reaffirmed the justness of their fight: "we solemnly reiterate our firm conviction of the rectitude of the cause of the C.S.A., and our unwavering confidence in its final success." Finally, they asked for all to pray to God for their victory: "we will continue to pray, and we earnestly request our brethren to continue to pray, that the Lord of hosts—the God of peace—may enable us to maintain our independence, secure our cherished liberties, and gain an early, honorable, and permanent peace." In asking all their "brethren" to pray for the same thing, the state organization (a loose authority in the heavily congregation-based Baptist Church) tried to further a sense of community among its members. In June 1864, the annual state meeting reiterated its "undiminished confidence in the rectitude of our course, and in its ultimate and triumphant success."[6]

Fasting and prayer days sought to unite Southerners and create an atmosphere of joint sacrifice and emotional support. These ritualized events, suggested by churches and governments, often were observed by Pittsylvanians in their churches and with many of their fellow congregation members as "a day of humiliation & Prayer & Thanksgiving to Almighty God for his Mercies." Not everyone spent the appointed days in fasting or prayer, but many of these special events were, in the words of the Straight Stone Baptist Church clerk, "tolerably well attended." Some churches in Pittsylvania designated monthly fasting days to be held at the church, as Kentuck Baptist did during 1864 and 1865. These regular meetings brought these congregations closer together and tied them to the men in service as well as to the larger Confederate cause.[7]

Another part of the wartime emotional role of these churches was their support of soldiers' spiritual welfare, a movement that grew out of concerns about war's effects on soldiers. In 1861, the Roanoke Baptist Association (a group of Baptist churches predominantly from Pittsylvania County) warned, "war brings about a looseness in morals, that can only be counteracted by the most careful training." An editorial in the July 1862 issue of the newspaper of the Virginia Baptist Association echoed these sentiments and explained that these concerns were not limited to the war alone: "The injury which the characters of these men sustain, from the idleness and corrupt example of camp-life, from the absence of domestic influence, from the want of mental and spiritual training, and from similar causes is an incalculable evil, not only to themselves, but to society at large; and, should they survive the war, this evil will be one of continual experience down to old age, and may perhaps be entailed on their families."[8]

In the Baptist churches of the South, the attempt to fight the corrupting influence of war and assure soldiers' spiritual welfare consisted of sending "Books and Tracts of a religious character" to those in service to the Confederacy or sending ministers to the armies to minister to the spiritual needs of the soldiers. The churches of Pittsylvania and Danville followed this larger trend, appropriating money and "all suitable religious books, sermons and tracts, for the special use of soldiers." In 1864, Kentuck Baptist Church authorized its minister, William Plunkett, to spend up to two months each year "preaching to the soldiers if he wishe[d] to do so and the church agree[d] to pay his necessary expenses in so doing." In sending ministers and religious tracts, churches not only fought the corrupting influences of war and provided much-needed

TABLE 3.1
ROANOKE BAPTIST ASSOCIATION MEMBERSHIP STATISTICS, 1861–1865

	Total white members	White male members	White men as percentage of all white members	White male membership growth rate (%)	White female members	White women as percentage of all white members	White female membership growth rate (%)
1861	1,474	477	32		997	68	
1863	1,565	464			1,101		
1864	1,813	514			1,299		
1865	1,991	583	29		1,408	71	
Total white membership growth, 1861–1865	517	106		22	411		41

Source: Roanoke Baptist Association, *Minutes of the Annual Meeting*, 1861, 1863–1865.

emotional and spiritual support to soldiers, but they also used the war as an opportunity to gain more converts. By one estimate, some 150,000 converts were made from nearly one million members of the Confederate army.[9]

The significance of churches' assistance for the families of soldiers and other members is difficult to assess. One rough indicator of the appeal of the emotional and spiritual support system of Pittsylvania County's religious institutions is their growing church membership. Statistics from the Roanoke Baptist Association indicate that significant growth in county church membership took place during the war years (an increase of 35 percent from 1861 to 1865). Twenty-six people joined Straight Stone Church in the last three months of 1863, and twenty-six more were admitted in the last three months of 1864, an increase in membership of 49 percent from the start of the war. People kept joining because they clearly found something they needed in these churches, some measure of support, companionship, and assistance. This increase in membership, however, came disproportionately from women. During the war, more women than men joined Pittsylvania's Baptist churches and at greater percentages, increasing women's numerical superiority in these congregations (see table 3.1). This female-dominated growth at home is not surprising, however, given the number of men who were off at war.[10]

This growth in church membership from prewar levels was not limited to the churches at home. The religious revivals that swept through the men in the Confederate Army during the war have been well documented and indicate the success of chaplains, ministers, and religious tracts sent by congregations in providing an emotional and spiritual support network for the soldiers. The fears of many of the men in military service aided Southern religious groups in making converts. In June 1863, the Virginia Baptist Association's annual meeting noted how much the war had changed soldiers' attitudes about Christianity and revealed how much the rising numbers of converts had changed Virginia Baptists' view of the war in just a year: "Modern history presents no example of armies so nearly converted into churches as the armies of Southern defence.... In many who have been called to share the privations and perils of military service, there has been a marked development of the Christian character. The repose of home, before the war, had seemingly lulled them to slumber. ... But thrown among the stirring incidents, and confronting the doubtful issue of a campaign, they have awakened out of sleep."[11]

Such interest in wartime ministries, both in the camps and on the home front, indicates that churches constituted an important source of support for Southern soldiers and their families. These institutions and their congregations provided comfort, justification, spiritual strengthening, and sometimes financial support. Churches represented another important resource that soldiers' families used to survive the war intact. After the war ended, those churches and the network of emotional and spiritual support they provided made up an important part of the rebuilding strategies of many of Pittsylvania-Danville's veteran families.

Although faith in God and the support of the church gave important assistance to these families, it came with some limitations. Faith provided strength and solace, but some families whose worlds had been rocked by the horrors and chaos of the war questioned their beliefs. Disputes among church members also weakened solidarities of faith and community. Baptist churches were made up of individuals who did not always get along. Churches expected members to follow a fairly strict set of behavioral rules, but not all did.

Although Baptist church members were expected to behave with civility toward their fellow congregants, even to treat one another as "brothers" or "sisters," sometimes people just did not get along. With the additional stress and concerns brought on by the war, the conflicts that broke out in some churches during the war are not surprising. Greenfield Baptist Church met in two special meetings in the fall of 1861 to deal with one such conflict that involved four female church members. The dispute involved accusations of "unchristian conduct," lies, slander, and "abusive language." Such an atmosphere of tension and conflict weakened a church's ability to offer emotional comfort and spiritual refuge. The church membership resolved the dispute and restored the congregation by kicking out three of the four women for their behavior toward one another, specifically their "refus[al] to fellowship" the others in the dispute.[12]

Such questioning, conflicts, and resolutions existed before the war, but the wartime and postwar need for the church communities and the support they offered soldiers and their families made the results of these congregational disputes more significant than they were before 1861. The three women expelled from Greenfield Baptist Church lost the spiritual and emotional network created by the church community, as well as the potential for financial aid from the congregation as a whole. These forms of assistance remained available to veterans and their families, and to all church members, only if they continued to meet the expectations set out by the churches.

Churches and the Postwar World

Virginia's churches knew that the war severely affected Confederate soldiers and their families. As early as 1864, Virginia's Baptist churches discussed this impact and raised the significant question of how these families would survive:

"Thousands of our brave men have fallen, or have been disabled, and their little ones are growing up in rags.... Some who before the war were in good circumstances, are now dependant upon charity for their daily bread. What the soldier had accumulated by years of toil, has been consumed by his family during his absence from them at the post of danger."[13] In dealing with the problems of these veteran families, the financial assistance and emotional support that Pittsylvania-Danville area churches provided during the Civil War set the pattern for the postwar period. Religious institutions continued to serve as a source for financial support for desperately needy veteran families as well as an emotional and spiritual support network for all church members.[14]

The lack of destruction to the physical and religious infrastructure of the county proved an important advantage for Pittsylvania's churches going into the postwar period. In other areas of Virginia and the South, churches were in horrible shape. In June 1865, the Virginia Baptist Association's annual meeting reported, "Our churches are enfeebled, and in many cases torn to pieces; many of what were our best houses of worship are in ashes." Many areas of the Confederacy had to reestablish their churches and other institutions after the war, whereas Pittsylvania's residents had their religious-based support networks still in place. So intact were the county's religious institutions at the end of the war that Kentuck Baptist Church felt comfortable sending off its pastor in 1866, "for preaching to the destitute portion of the [Virginia] Association." The churches of Pittsylvania and Danville were well prepared to help their members, and veterans and their families took advantage of these opportunities for financial, educational, and emotional assistance.[15]

Financial Assistance

Jane Smith's husband, James, died in 1862 of disease while serving in the 38th Virginia Infantry. Not well-off before the war, the widow and her two young daughters were now in dire financial straits. She turned for help to her church, Kentuck Baptist. From 1867 through at least 1890, Smith received several forms of economic aid from the church and its members. This financial assistance proved essential for this veteran family's survival and was part of an organized system set up after the Civil War at Kentuck Baptist of "satisfying temporal wants" of the congregation's needy members. As the region's most sophisticated church-based poor-relief system in the immediate postwar years, Kentuck's financial-aid program merits further examination.[16]

Even before the war, Kentuck Baptist, like many other churches, collected money to assist "benevolent objects" within its congregation. During the war, according to its own minutes, "The church contributed to the wants of . . . Sister Ann Cole," an elderly member in financial distress. The poor continued to be an important focus of Kentuck after the end of the war, and the church took up several collections over the following couple of years to help out "benevolents," both impoverished elderly such as Ann Cole and soldiers' widows such as Jane Smith.[17]

In June 1868, however, the members of Kentuck Baptist made a significant commitment to help the poor. The church created a "committee on Benevolence" made up of three prominent male church members whose job was to collect money from the congregation and to decide who would get that money. The next month, the rest of the church members showed their support for the idea by "agree[ing] that all will contribute to a fund for the support of the poor of the church to be place in the hands of a committee for that purpose." This "charity fund of the church" began to grow from congregational gifts. A separate committee handled each impoverished family's case. One of the members of each of these committees was appointed to work directly with the needy families or individuals. The appointed man (and it was always a male church member) gave money, food, or supplies to the recipient of the church's charity and was then reimbursed from the church's charity fund.[18]

Kentuck Baptist's new system of helping its poor mostly assisted women who were impoverished for a variety of reasons. Generally these women were without family who could help them. Although the church assisted some elderly women such as Ann Cole, and the occasional elderly couple, most of the people to whom the church provided financial aid in the decades after the war were widows of soldiers, many with children they could not support on their own. The first person whom Kentuck's committee on benevolence decided to help was Jane Smith. The church appointed John Wells "to see to the wants of Sister Jane Smith." For four years, Wells served as the distributor of Smith's charity from the church, dispensing about $2 per month in cash and "provisions." When Wells stepped down from his position, other men stepped in to continue distributing the church's monthly (or quarterly) payments. In 1871, Smith apparently informed her committee of some specific needs, and after the church heard from the committee, its members contributed "Leather, Corn, & money for her wants." A decade later, Smith still received some cash aid from the church, but she seems to have been in better shape financially since she accepted only $3.00 of the $10.50 the church had collected for her. Five years later, however, she "was reported in a needy condition" and received another small cash grant. Two years later, in 1890, the church pitched in money and labor to help repair her house, which was falling apart. After losing her husband in the war, Smith had been unable to support herself and her daughters without the help of Kentuck Baptist Church.[19]

Kentuck Baptist helped several other widows of Confederate veterans, many of whom had children. These widows also had male church members assigned "to supply [them] with such things as may be necessary for [their] comfort." Unlike Jane Smith, who received church aid for twenty-three years, these women were much more likely to follow the pattern of Sarah Hay, who received steady aid for three years or less, with the occasional extra collection at a particularly difficult time.[20]

Kentuck Baptist's system of assigning a particular male church member to a particular family meant that impoverished women and men worked with certain people over long periods of time in ways that imitated other networks of support. For example, Lucy Earp received funds from John Dodson for over five years. Such a relationship may have made it easier for these needy families to ask for or accept charity. Since only one individual dispensed the church's benevolence to a family, the system operated as if the head of the impoverished household only had to go to a better-off relative or neighbor, rather than to the whole church membership, to ask for help. This personal, face-to-face procedure thus minimized potential shame, while taking advantage of the collective financial resources of the whole congregation.[21]

Kentuck Baptist's program of poor relief was significantly more sophisticated than any other Pittsylvania-Danville church (and more developed than many Southern churches) in the immediate postwar period. Certainly the church was conscious and proud of the work it was doing to help its needy. In an 1888 "Historical Sketch" of the church's first century of existence, the minister at the time wrote of Rev. J. B. Lake, one of the architects of Kentuck Baptist's poor-assistance programs: "Under his ministry a System of benevolance was rapidly developed and the church gained considerable notoriety in the State on account of her liberal donations to benevolance."[22]

Toward the end of the century, the First Baptist Church of Danville set up its own fairly comprehensive system of poor relief. Starting in June 1889, the church divided its members into districts assigned to and taken care of by a particular deacon. These deacons were responsible for making themselves known to all the church members in their district. The deacons made sure that members went to church and that their children went to Sunday school; each deacon was also told to "give information to the relief committee or Treasurer of the Poor Fund any cases which may come to his knowledge, needing their services & shall inform the Pastor of any cases requiring his attention." The church probably had deacons doing such things before, but this system gave the needy a specific person to go to for help. The poor of First Baptist in Danville may not have even needed to go to their deacon, since he was responsible for knowing when people in his district needed help.[23]

Kentuck's and First Baptist's postwar financial-aid programs were more extensive than those of other Pittsylvania and Danville churches (and perhaps more extensive than other churches in the state). Nevertheless, most religious institutions shared the sentiments of Kentuck and First Baptist. The constitutions of Pittsylvania's churches often included a brief statement about the church's responsibility to "take care of the poor" or, as explained by Mount Hermon Baptist, "we will cheerfully contribute of our own property according as God has prospered us, for the maintenance of a faithful and evangelical ministry among us, for the support of the poor, and to spread the Gospel over the earth." Churches saw their financial assistance to the needy as part of their larger religious mission. Even if the other churches did not have a program as large as Kentuck Baptist's, their help did assist some needy church families and individuals.[24]

The financial assistance available to needy veteran families from other churches in Pittsylvania and Danville tended to come in the form of specific collections of cash taken occasionally from church members for a particular person or family, typically women without men and "in destitute condition." Like the women at Kentuck, these women were not married. Usually, they were either recently widowed or elderly. But unlike Kentuck, one individual or committee was not assigned to make sure that their needs were being met. In the mid- to late 1880s, Barsheba Adams, an elderly war widow, found herself "in needy circumstances" and turned to her church, Mt. Hermon, for help. She received a total of $12 collected from church members over three occasions in six years. There is little evidence of regular visits by a church aid committee or of monthly or quarterly payments to the many women like Adams who received cash or food from churches other than Kentuck Baptist. Although Pittsylvania's needy veteran families could ask for and receive aid in the form of money or supplies from churches over an extended period of time, that aid did not generally come on a regular basis unless they were part of the immediate postwar welfare system at Kentuck or part of the poor-relief program set up twenty-five years after the war ended at First Baptist, Danville. Still, the differences between the programs of poor assistance at Kentuck and First Baptist and the individual assistance at the other churches were largely differences of scale and regularity of payment and not of kind.[25]

All church charity given in the form of cash or "provisions" took place within a framework of gender relations that resembled the idealized relations in the family and represented an attempt by churches to replace male family members, who by their death or absence had left their families without clear patriarchs or protectors. This gendered nature of financial aid was most clear at Kentuck. The poor helped by the church in this way were almost always female or female-headed families, and the person appointed by the church to dispense that aid was always male, reflecting the fundamentally paternal nature of Kentuck Baptist's church-based aid. Male members managed money for women out of a belief that the women were not capable of handling such affairs themselves, either in assessing how much they needed or in how to spend money given them. When Lucy Earp asked the church for cash or food in 1876, the congregation appointed William Clark "to supply Sister Earp with such things as she actually needs & present his a/c [account] to the church for payment." In 1874, the church raised $18.70 for Harriet Henderson, a widow of a veteran, and the money was "given over to Brother N. M. Gardner to be by him distributed to her as occasion may deem necessary." As further proof of the gender-biased nature of Kentuck's aid, when a "collection was taken up for the benefit of Brother William Hankens resulting in the sum of seven dollars & ten cents," the entire amount "was paid over to him" directly, without any male church member doling out the money to the seventy-five-year old Hankens as the member saw fit.[26]

Cash aid for women without men took place within a paternal framework at other churches too. A widow "in distress circumstancy" at the start of the war asked her church, Straight Stone Baptist, for help. "The church acknowledge[d] its Christian duty to aid to the wants of widows in distress" and selected two male members to "contribute judiciously to her wants out of such contributions as may be put into their hands." By implication, the "Bretherens'" assignment indicated a lack of trust in the ability of the widow to help herself or handle money, and it gave her two fictive husbands or fathers who were responsible for her economic well-being. Similar gendered charity-distribution procedures existed at the other churches in Pittsylvania County.[27]

This emphasis on paternalistic aid probably also reflected fears of the men in the church about a perceived postwar assault on traditional patriarchy. Southern white women—daughters, wives, and widows—were working outside the home, while Southern white masculinity was weakened by Confederate defeat and a host of other issues. In this context, church aid offered one way to reinforce a previously understood gender order.[28]

Some women probably chafed under such aid restrictions, but many others probably accepted what they saw as the religiously ordained social order. After all, many of them were active members of a church (and a society) that supported the subordination of women to men. In Baptist churches, women were generally not allowed to vote on church matters. In such an atmosphere and given their financial needs, female recipients of church charity probably took the paternal distribution of the aid along with their money.[29]

Of course, not all church-based financial assistance available to postwar veteran families came in the form of direct cash or food grants from their congregations. Other forms of aid included being given jobs cleaning or repairing the church and receiving cash from one of two Virginia Baptist funds. Not as widespread as direct charity from individual churches, these forms of assistance still proved valuable to some of the county's veteran families.

Getting a job from the church had several advantages over direct charity for veteran families. Unlike most direct charity, church jobs were given to men too, allowing another option for male veterans having problems making ends meet after the war. Perhaps more important, however, working for the church avoided the stigma of being a charity case. It allowed a measure of dignity while earning a salary, and although the pay was often small, it was more money and a steadier income than an occasional charity collection.

Some churches used the position of sexton or housekeeper as a way of helping families during and after the war, as Shockoe Baptist did with the women of the Owens family. Such positions proved an important source of income for some veteran families after the war. Samuel Richardson of the 38th Virginia Infantry suffered from a "debility" during the war. After the war, he served as Kentuck Baptist's sexton from 1865 to 1873, making between $10 and $15 per year. A farmer before the war, his wartime illness prevented him from making enough money in agriculture in postwar Pittsylvania, and the position as sexton allowed him to make a little extra. Although not defined as charity by churches—the fact that it was not so baldly stated as such probably served as an inducement for proud people, especially men, to take the position—the position of sexton seems generally to have gone to people who needed the money.[30]

Another way for veteran church members to earn money from their churches was by doing repair work on the building. Robert H. Williams, a painter and veteran wounded during the war, painted Kentuck Baptist for $41 in 1873. Williams had five children and only $100 in personal estate before the war; the church painting job helped support his family. When Shockoe Baptist decided to build a new church building in 1883, it hired Enoch Johnson, veteran and member, and paid him $1,250. Admittedly, these jobs were not explicitly designated as charity for these men, but congregations clearly helped by sending some business the way of their veteran members, especially wounded ones such as Robert Williams.[31]

Ultimately, the reason that most Pittsylvania and Danville churches did not establish the system of poor relief in the 1860s, 1870s, and 1880s that Kentuck Baptist did is fairly simple: most churches could not afford to make regular payments to their poor members. Several of the Baptist churches in Pittsylvania and Danville provided little or no money to the poor in the immediate postwar period. Smaller churches were probably less able (if not unwilling) to help their impoverished members. Chatham Baptist, a smaller church of about sixty people, could not even pay its minister his full salary in 1866 and 1867. Such financially weakened churches were not able to help the most needy among their congregations (at least not monetarily) until their members recovered. In general, larger churches such as Kentuck and First Baptist, Danville, weathered the financial impact of the war and later economic downturns with less trouble. According to church records, Kentuck Baptist members averaged giving $1.26 each in direct aid to the needy of their church from 1861 to 1880, an amount per member that no other Baptist church in the county came close to matching.[32]

Poverty was not the only reason churches did not organize formal poor-relief programs. Some churches may have provided cash to needy members but simply decided not to record acts of charity in the church minutes, perhaps out of some sense of protecting the dignity of the petitioning family or individual. Wealthier church members may have helped needy individuals and families outside the church; the destitute often went directly to the elite of the church (and town) to get assistance. Some of these congregations, in interpreting the stated commitment in almost every church constitution to "take care of the poor," may have limited their care to emotional or spiritual assistance. From such a perspective, the three collections taken by County Line Baptist for poor members over a forty-year period (1861–1900) were exceptions and were done only in cases of extreme need. Other churches may have felt that they gave in other ways to support the poor, either through their local taxes, which supported the county poorhouse, or through general Baptist programs. By the 1870s, Chatham Baptist's members apparently had recovered from their financial crisis of the late 1860s, but they contributed significantly to two statewide Baptist programs, the Education and Ministers' Relief funds, rather than giving money or provisions directly to any individual church members.[33]

Like Chatham Baptist, most of Pittsylvania's Baptist churches gave money each year to these two statewide organizations, which at times provided some measure of assistance to the veteran families of the state, although it was not necessarily intended specifically for them. (The Education Fund is discussed later in this chapter.) The Ministers' Relief Fund was initiated in 1871 by the Baptist General Association of Virginia to assist old or disabled ministers and their widows or orphans. Soon, however, it took on the added responsibility of caring for the children of slain soldiers. The Roanoke Baptist Association called in its 1875 annual meeting for each church to appoint a male and female church member to raise money for this cause: "We have in our bounds orphans of men who fell on the field.... God has committed them to our care. *Shall we prove worthy of the trust?*" In a sermon given at the meeting, Rev. J. E. L. Holmes of Danville expanded on these concerns: "It is well to raise monuments to the dead, but I think it is far better to take care of the living; it is well, indeed very commendable, to care for the children of those who have fallen upon the field, but it would be so much better if those dying could be assured of the support of those whom they are leaving behind them."[34]

Unfortunately, there is little surviving evidence of the children of dead soldiers who were helped by this fund, and by the 1883 Roanoke Baptist Association meeting, there was a clear attempt to refocus the Ministers' Relief Fund back on the people it was originally intended to help: "The object of the Ministers' Relief Fund is to provide a fund for the relief of infirm and disabled Virginia Baptist ministers, their widows and orphans." Afterward, the fund provided some financial assistance to several widows and children of deceased ministers in Pittsylvania and Danville but not to soldiers' children.[35]

Regardless of the form, during and after the war the churches of Pittsylvania and Danville offered limited measures of financial relief to its poorer members. As would be expected, the helpfulness of this aid to veterans and their families varied, and it was restricted in the number and type of recipients to the most needy. Overall, however, the financial aid provided by this support network proved an important supplement to the postwar survival (and rebuilding) of some of the most damaged veteran family households, especially those who had lost a husband or father.

The cash from Kentuck Baptist's postwar system was the most helpful, because of its amount and regularity. At times of extended need, veterans' widows such as Jane Smith received between $20 and $30 a year in aid from the church, an amount as much or more than many state widows' pensions later provided. Still, the needy in Kentuck's aid system only received about one-tenth of what white public-school teachers in Alabama made in a year in 1880. Thirty dollars was not enough to support a family by itself, but all capable members of these female-headed veteran families were also working to add to their income. As a supplement, $20 to $30 could go a long way.[36]

Still, Kentuck's aid system for its poor, though extensive for those it helped, was not very large in numbers, relative to the needy in the county. It helped seventeen families for an extended period between the start of the war and 1880, which is not bad considering the church averaged about 230 white members (roughly forty-five to fifty families) during that time. Many of Kentuck's church members were not well-off. Their contributions to nearly a third of the congregation's families must have represented a significant sacrifice on their part. Kentuck's system, of course, could only help a few of the over three thousand veteran families in Pittsylvania and Danville.[37]

During and after the war, at the county's other churches, less-organized church collections also assisted needy veterans and their families. These occasional payments were helpful but less so than the poor system developed by Kentuck. The infrequent church collections of $5 to $10—averaging $8.20 per recipient per collection—came at critical times, and again, though the amount was not enough to live on for any extended period, it may have made the occasional difference between a family starving or not.[38]

Alternative work also proved an important source of economic and emotional support for veterans and their families. The job of sexton usually paid only between $5 and $18 per year, so it most likely served as a supplement, rather than an entire income, for a family. The impact of such a position or of being hired to do repair work on the church building went beyond the money paid; the chance to work and earn money with dignity rather than accept charity made these church jobs more than just financial support.

The impact of financial aid on Pittsylvania's veteran families from other Baptist programs like the statewide Ministers' Relief Fund or First Danville's own late-nineteenth-century program is hard to measure because of a lack of records. The aid from the Ministers' Relief Fund to war orphans seems to have been limited to a brief period between the early 1870s and 1883. In addition, there was not enough money in the fund to meet the demands. In 1875, the Roanoke Baptist Association noted, "We learn from the trustees of the Ministers' Relief Fund that they have more applications for assistance than they can meet." As for First Danville's program, though it provided essential assistance to the poor of Danville at the end of the century, it came along too late to help veteran families get back on their feet in the immediate postwar years. Still, First Danville's aid system may have eased the later years of the aging veterans and their wives or widows who lived in or near the city.[39]

Educational Assistance and the Soldiers' Children Fund

In addition to the more direct forms of financial assistance, some churches offered help in other ways. Historian Beth Barton Schweiger has argued that in the postwar world, education was the central avenue of benevolence for

Southern ministers and churches. In the mid- to late 1860s, some of Pittsylvania County's veteran families could turn to their Baptist churches for an education for their children. This Baptist-funded education was intended to provide basic schooling for children in the neediest veteran families during and after the Civil War. By 1871, the Virginia public-school system had been set up and took over the education of Virginia's children. The impact of this brief program on veteran families is hard to measure since little direct evidence exists from the families who participated in the program. For several years after the war, however, it did offer some limited alternative to illiteracy for the children of some veteran families.[40]

The program of education for needy veteran families grew out of an 1864 plan from the Baptist General Association of Virginia to provide "for the maintenance and education of the children of soldiers who have died or been disabled during the war." As the idea moved forward, practical exigencies forced the Baptists in Virginia to focus the program just on the education of the children of poor, disabled, or deceased soldiers. Unlike most antebellum Northern states, Virginia and other Southern states did not have requirements for public school systems, meaning that only parents who could afford to send their children to the private institutions were able to educate them. The Baptists were correct in believing that most children of war casualties would not be able to attend school. The Virginia Baptist state convention in 1864 pleaded, "All that we ask for the representatives of these slain heroes is that they be cared for during the season of childhood, and provided with such instruction as may prepare them to become useful members of the community."[41]

The Roanoke Baptist Association agreed with the state association's plan at its annual meeting in August 1864 and agreed to "go at the work immediately." In September 1864, Chatham Baptist and First Baptist of Danville each pledged to "educate 20 children [of dead or disabled soldiers] for the next 12 months." Six months later, Chatham Baptist began paying for eight indigent children to go to school, and the church was looking for more.[42]

The first postwar annual meeting of Virginia's Baptist Association in June 1865 claimed that the Soldiers' Children Fund had made a significant impact in its first year. "Hundreds of little children, who, but for such aid, would never have learned to read God's word, were collected in schools, while the discussion of the subject had led several benevolent and patriotic individuals to adopt and take into their own family circle some who would otherwise have endured all the suffering which orphanage and poverty could inflict." Pittsylvania's Baptists continued to support the program and stressed the importance of education.

The Roanoke Association announced at its annual meeting in 1867, "There never was a time in our history when to educate was so vastly important as now."[43]

Statewide, the program expanded in the second half of the decade. In 1867, the program paid for 551 children (and "several *men* who lost arms or legs in the service") to go to school. Only two fewer children went to school in 1868 with Baptist scholarships, but the fund was beginning to have money problems. In 1869, over eight hundred soldiers' children in Virginia received schooling from the Baptists, but "the contributions ha[d] been, for the most part, small," leaving the program $1,400 in debt. By 1870, over one thousand "soldiers' orphans ha[d] been placed in various schools throughout the State." Once again, the fund was not able to pay for all the students, leaving the fund in debt to teachers for over $2,000.[44]

By 1870, however, the need for the program began to come to an end. "The inauguration of the 'free school' system in Virginia will make it next to impossible to continue this work," according to the statewide director of the program that year. The public system and the Baptist system of paying for soldiers' children to go to private schools overlapped in early 1871, but the fund ceased sending children to private school later that year as the students entered the new public school system.[45]

The impact of these five years of schooling for the children of the soldiers of Pittsylvania County and Danville is hard to measure, but the program faced a number of limitations. The children whom the program aimed to help came from families with deceased or disabled soldiers, and that presented a problem. Veteran families who had lost the full earning power of an adult male could ill afford to lose the labor of the children while they were in school. Another factor that undermined the effectiveness of this program of schooling was its small size. At its peak, it helped about one thousand students across Virginia, but Pittsylvania and Danville alone had over five hundred families of dead soldiers; add to that the families with disabled veterans, and there were well over a thousand potential students for the program just in the county. For the children who did go to school, the time spent may have been helpful in advancing their education and providing a transition to the new public school system, but overall, few Pittsylvania and Danville veteran families benefited from this program. Still, it was an alternative to illiteracy that was available briefly to some of the county's veteran families.[46]

The Baptist program, in its attempt to educate the children of deceased or disabled soldiers, stands as another example of the church assuming a role that had largely been occupied by family members until that time. Fathers and older brothers were supposed to ensure that their children or younger siblings were able to go to school. The state took over ultimate responsibility for public education, however, and it began to do so in other areas of assistance as well, as the government began to play a paternal role itself in the families of Virginia.

Emotional and Spiritual Support

Ultimately, while churches made monetary and educational support available to a few members of veteran families, the emotional and spiritual support that the churches of Pittsylvania and Danville offered was a key part of the survival and rebuilding of many of the county's veteran families. As they had before and during the Civil War, after April 1865 churches served as places where people could go to take comfort in the community of others who shared their spiritual beliefs. In addition to the empowering strength of spiritual fellowship, the Baptist religious institutions of the county and state helped their members adjust to the postwar world by suggesting ways of coping with the Confederacy's defeat and by continuing wartime traditions of special days of fasting and prayer. The veterans of Pittsylvania and Danville and their families turned to the emotional support networks created by the churches as part of their postwar struggle to rebuild their lives.

A commitment to assist and tend to the other members of the congregation lay at the heart of these supportive church communities. Mt. Tabor's congregation made that commitment clear in their constitution when they pledged, "we will participate in each others' joys, and endeavor with tenderness and sympathy to bear each others burdens and sorrows." Mt. Pleasant's members made a similar vow: "We promise . . . to avoid tattling and backbiting[,] to watch over each other in brotherly love[,] to remember each other in prayer[, and] to aid each other in sickness and distress." Churches and church members saw themselves as creating helpful, nurturing, caring places where they could bring and share their "burdens and sorrows."[47]

One of these "burdens" with which Southerners had to cope in the postwar period was their defeat by the Union forces. Soon after the war ended, the Virginia Baptist Association stepped in to help its members deal with that loss. The attendees of the annual meeting in June 1865 recommended coping with defeat by embracing Union. They decided, "whatever may have been our past views, aims or efforts regarding the issues which have decided the Northern and Southern States, we deem it our duty as patriots and Christians to accept the order of Providence, yield unreserved and faithful obedience to the 'powers that be,' and to cultivate such a spirit and to preserve such a course of conduct as shall best promote the peace and prosperity of the country; and we earnestly recommend to our brethren throughout the State to prove themselves to be loyal citizens of the United States, and to enter with zeal and activity upon the discharge of the responsibilities devolved on them by their new social and civil relations."[48]

Virginia Baptist leaders also made it clear to their members, however, that there was no shame in these actions. In October 1865, the Baptist state paper, the *Religious Herald*, explained, "it is our duty to submit, and conciliate our late enemies." But this was not to be "an obsequious, but a dignified and manly submission to the United States Government, since it is irreversibly decreed that we must live under it. In this course, there is no dishonor." As for those families who had lost a father, husband, son, or brother in the war, the same page in the *Herald* included a promise to "ever regard it as a most sacred duty to guard the reputation and cherish the memory of those noble men who laid down their lives in the Confederate service." Although similar to what many white Southerners were saying as the war ended and Reconstruction began, for religious men and women, such words from their church leaders and fellow members lent authority to this way of dealing with the losses of the war and moving forward.[49]

As during the war, postbellum Baptist churches in Pittsylvania and Danville designated certain days for "fasting & Prayer." Individual churches or regional or state Baptist organizations called these days of fasting, prayer, and reflection to increase and reinforce a congregation's spiritual strength and "to return thanks to God." These special days, generally held by Pittsylvania's Baptist churches about once a year between 1865 and 1885, combined with regular church services, served to bring these church communities together both locally and regionally. Some churches also held regular prayer meetings. Starting in September 1865, the members of Kentuck Baptist agreed to hold weekly prayer meetings. Although they reduced this schedule to one or two prayer meetings each month starting in 1869, they continued to gather together. Mt. Tabor also held weekly prayer meetings for several years. A fair number of members attended Kentuck's prayer sessions, according to the church minutes.[50]

Prayer meetings, special fasting days, and regular church services sought to bring people closer to God and to one another. Churches attempted to create an environment in which community would flourish. In the postwar South, some people, including veterans and their families, turned to that community for emotional and spiritual support. In fact, the words of the constitutions of

TABLE 3.2
ROANOKE BAPTIST ASSOCIATION MEMBERSHIP STATISTICS, 1865–1880

	Total white members	White male members	White men as percentage of all white members	White male membership growth rate (%)	White female members	White women as percentage of all white members	White female membership growth rate (%)
1865	1,991	583	29		1,408	71	
1870	2,045	620			1,425		
1875	2,233	713			1,520		
1880	2,833	987	35		1,846	65	
Total white membership growth, 1865–1880	842	404		69	438		31

Source: Roanoke Baptist Association, *Minutes of the Annual Meeting,* 1865, 1870, 1875, 1880.

Mt. Tabor and Mt. Pleasant paint a picture of the church as an ideal place to recuperate from the chaos and problems of the postwar world, a true sanctuary and the perfect support network for the veteran families of the county.

Yet, although some veterans and their families found the churches of Pittsylvania and Danville to be supportive, a number of ex-soldiers, by their actions and words, indicated that the churches failed to provide the environment that they needed. Some veterans skipped a number of church meetings and services after returning home from the war, implying some kind of unhappiness with their church. Griffith Evans failed to attend church for several weeks in July and August 1865, leading a committee from his church to visit him to find out why. The same thing happened five years later for Jackson Evans (no relation). Other veterans were more direct. Kentuck's minutes noted with concern that William Slayton had written "a letter to the church expressing dissatisfaction." A few of these ex-soldiers simply renounced their church membership, attempting to cut their ties with the congregational community. Henry Hall asked to be removed from the church membership rolls because "he made his profession of religion very young and felt that he was deceived." James Collie told the church leaders that he was leaving the church "feeling that he was not fit to be there."[51]

These men's dissatisfaction with their churches stemmed from multiple sources. Some veterans may have felt uncomfortable at church after their experiences in the war; others may have been disillusioned with religion or depressed, or they just did not want emotional support from the semi-public church community; some may have felt economic pressure and decided that they needed to work more than they needed to go to church; others like Jackson Evans may simply have been poor and ashamed of it, deciding not to attend services because of their "want of suitable clothing"; still others may have come into conflict with other church members or even the minister, as Stephen Townes did. Whatever the reason, for these veterans, the church and its community was not their first priority, and as a result, they no longer had (or wanted) access to the church's emotional support network.[52]

Despite these cases in which a particular veteran did not find emotional or spiritual support in a church, a return to the rough system of counting church members indicates that in the postwar years, the Baptist churches of the county and town provided some kind of support to their members that kept them there and that induced some non-members to join (see table 3.2). Although the churches never regained the sizable total membership growth of the wartime years (35 percent, or an average of 7 percent per year), they continued to increase in size after the war (almost 3 percent per year from 1865 to 1880). That postwar growth consisted of roughly equal increases in the numbers of male and female members. The growth rates by gender, however, reveal that men were joining the church at much greater rates, if not in greater numbers, than were women. This relative remasculinization of the church meant that by 1880, men made up a higher percentage of the county's Baptist churches than they had at the start of the war (35 percent versus 32 percent in 1861), although they were still vastly outnumbered by their female co-religionists. Some men joined churches back home because of wartime conversions in the Confederate Army; others may have become members of churches to which their female relatives already belonged. Still, this significant postwar membership growth from men and women suggests that churches offered a community that appealed to both sexes.[53]

Conforming to Behavioral Expectations

The price to be paid for the financial and emotional support of one's church was conforming to that church's expectations for proper "Christian behavior." Precise definitions of appropriate conduct for a Christian varied among denominations and churches, but the records of the county's Baptist churches suggest that their major concern was maintaining and protecting the church community and its constituent families. Generally, Baptists were expected to attend church, get along with other members of the congregation, avoid intoxication or even abstain from all alcohol, not commit adultery or fornication, and not mistreat their families, including all their dependents. By becoming involved in domestic affairs—especially alcoholism, adultery, and domestic abuse—churches monitored the welfare of families, sometimes even when patriarchs were still around. If formal charges or informal rumors about the "Christian character" of a member came to the attention of church leaders, a committee was formed of two to four of the prominent men in the church, often deacons. The committee investigated and reported back to the church as a whole, which then voted whether to exclude the accused member on the basis of information gathered by the committee. Although there was a great deal of wartime concern about the impact of military service on the character of the soldiers, there is no indication that veterans in these churches were more closely watched for good behavior than other church members after the war. Still, for those who were excluded from the church, expulsion meant losing access to the financial and emotional support system of the church and perhaps social banishment from the other members in the world outside the church.[54]

Lack of attendance was a common and obvious reason for churches to exclude people since the absence of those members implied that they had other priorities. Riceville Baptist's congregation claimed that absences showed "contempt for the church." Chatham Baptist passed a rule before the war that stated, "any member absenting himself from church meeting 3 times in succession shall be visited by the Deacons and his reasons given for nonattendance." Veterans such as Jackson Evans had to justify their absences.[55]

Ensuring the maintenance of the religious community also necessitated that church members not fight with one another, especially outside the church. Most churches had a rule similar to that of Riceville Baptist: "No member shall go to Law with another member with out first bringing the matter before the church." Congregations tried to mediate disputes among its members and threatened expulsion if the combatants failed to resolve their problems. In 1873, veteran W. W. Walker got in a vicious fight with another member of New Prospect; after several months, Walker "was charged with going to law with Brethern." The congregation voted that they "had lost confidence in his christian character and [ordered] that he be excluded from the fellowship of the church."[56]

People were also investigated and sometimes excluded from Baptist congregations because of behaviors that threatened families within churches. Virginia's Baptists in the postwar South saw alcoholism as a particularly noxious problem and a great "evil." An editorial in the *Religious Herald* in early 1866 blamed an increase in intoxication—seen in the "multiplication of drinking houses, and the patronage which they receive"—on postwar problems, including unemployment and a failure to cope with the Confederacy's defeat. The editorial claimed that many people, "it is likely, for lack of remunerative employment, and discouraged by the overthrow of the Confederacy, and the general prostration of the country, have been driven to seek relief from that worst of all comforters, the bottle.... When to all other influences, we add the general demoralization consequent on the war, we need not be surprised at the growth of this dreadful evil."[57]

In 1867, the Roanoke Baptist Association advocated that because of the threat to the church community, the Baptist churches of Pittsylvania and Danville remove members who became intoxicated. "We recommend that the churches deal strictly with any member who shall be guilty of the sin of drunkenness, and thus wipe out the reproach brought upon the cause of Christ by retaining drunken members in their fellowship." All the cases of intoxication investigated by area Baptist churches involved men, several of whom were veterans. Some, such as David Herndon of Mt. Hermon Baptist, were expelled; others, such as Thomas Hodnett of Kentuck Baptist, admitted their drunkenness and were forgiven, sometimes multiple times. In the 1870s and 1880s, as problems with alcohol continued, churches in Pittsylvania County expanded their focus to include those who were "engaged in this pernicious business," the "traffic of intoxicating liquors." Thereafter, alcohol sellers were to be kicked out of the church, unless they stopped what was probably a lucrative business. A few of the county's Baptist churches expelled members (including some veterans such as Thomas Anderson) who continued to sell "alcaholic liquors," explaining that these members' "general deportment is not commendable as a church member."[58]

Although one work on the subject of alcohol in the United States in the nineteenth century actually shows a decline in per-capita alcohol consumption in the whole nation from 1860 to 1875, by 1880 alcohol use was again on the rise, as it continued to be through 1910. Even so, the decline during this period does not mean that Southerners in general, and veterans in particular, were not drinking as much or more alcohol than before. Some studies of postwar Confederate veterans' lives indicate that alcohol was consumed to excess by a number of former soldiers, and it was not just the Baptists who expressed concerns about perceived increases.[59]

For many Baptists, just as members who were drunkards and alcohol sellers made churches appear lax and threatened to disrupt the system of emotional and spiritual support that congregations offered, so too did those who engaged in adultery or fornication. (Pittsylvania's Baptist churches used both terms to mean sexual relations outside marriage.) As with drunkenness, Baptists saw such behavior as inappropriate for Christians and as threatening to the family. Unlike intoxication, however, most of the people investigated for sexual misconduct were women, in part because they often carried evidence with them for nine months. Most of these women were not married at the time, although several were widows of soldiers who had died in the war. Shockoe Baptist Church expelled Mary Simmons when the widow admitted having sex four years after her husband had died of disease while in Confederate service. Shockoe Baptist also expelled Eliza Walker for fornication six years after her husband was killed at Gettysburg. In one exceptional case, Straight Stone Baptist Church expelled Julia Templeton for "prostitution." Church records fail to implicate these women's partners in intimacy, and there is no indication of church punishment of those men. Churches did go after a few men for sexual affairs, but generally only if they were married and thereby threatened the sanctity of marriage. Married veteran Griffith Evans was kicked out of his church for adultery, and Hubbard Hall was "expelled from the fellowship of the church for leaving his wife and children and runing off with another woman."[60]

Another necessity for the maintenance of a church community was that men would not severely abuse their dependents. Although rare, in particularly egregious cases churches got involved in the way certain men treated the members of their household. Veteran James Ashby was "excluded from the membership of [Kentuck] church for unmercifully whipping his wife." Although most nineteenth-century churches accepted, even encouraged, the supremacy of male household heads over their households, these churches could step in if the congregation felt that such control was being abused.[61]

Pittsylvania's Baptist churches did not expel everyone who was guilty of violating their understanding of proper "Christian behavior." If guilty persons showed remorse, the church tended to be much more willing to accept their promises to "try and do better for the future" and to keep them as members. Veteran Henry Terry admitted to his intoxication and told the congregation at Mt. Tabor "that he believed it was wrong to get drunk & asked the church to excuse him." It did.[62]

Sometimes the accused church members were found innocent of the charges against them. Although most of these members continued in their membership, a few left the church after their acquittal. A member of First Baptist Church of Danville charged veteran Syd Payne with "conduct unbecoming in a christian on the street." After a couple months of investigation, the charges were dropped. Soon after, Payne and his wife left First Baptist and joined the Methodist Episcopal church in Danville. To some of these people, whatever emotional or spiritual support they had been getting from the church disappeared with the charges laid against them. Even though W. W. Walker's fight with another member had cost him the support of the church network, by the time he was excluded from the congregation he may not have cared, since the members had clearly ceased being a support system by that time. Walker, the Paynes, and others in similar positions no longer felt they were members of that church's community, although some of them soon joined other congregations.[63]

Whether leaving voluntarily or having been kicked out, a former member, if unable to find another church, lost access to the support network that churches provided. Losing one's church for whatever reason may have been most significant for widowed women since they lost access to the greatly needed social and financial network of the church. If they had been expelled for perceived sexual misconduct, then that separation was even more traumatic. The actions that got them expelled took place in secret, and they had not been alienated from the support network before their exclusion, as had been the case for others such as W. W. Walker. Already in a more precarious position as single women in a world dominated by men, if the men they had had sex with did not provide for them, separation from the church network could have really hurt them, especially if they had any children.

Veteran families turned to the spiritual, educational, and financial resources offered to them in churches as they worked to survive the Civil War. The Baptist churches of Pittsylvania County and Danville provided important assistance to veterans and their families during and after the Civil War as part of their self-defined roles as loving community and fatherly protector of the needy and because of their belief in a Christian charity for the less fortunate. The price of these resources, however, was conformity to Baptist standards of behavior and a traditional view of gender relations. Some veteran family members could not meet these standards and were expelled. Others chose to leave churches because of the high expectations that those congregations set for their members. For these people, the price of the church's support network was too high, and they had to look elsewhere for the assistance they needed to rebuild and survive. Ultimately, rising church memberships indicate that many veterans and their families seem to have accepted, even embraced, the church community on its terms.

4

Appeals for Local Elite Assistance

The Case of William T. Sutherlin

> I . . . cannot call to mind any one who would be more likely to have it in his power to lend me a helping hand such as I ask for.
> —Grief Lampkin to William T. Sutherlin, February 22, 1877

ON JULY 26, 1865, C. B. Ball, a veteran of the Danville Artillery, appealed for assistance to one of the richest residents of Pittsylvania County and Danville, William T. Sutherlin. In his letter, Ball asked, "Can't you let me have six or seven hundred dollars to start me in the world again?"[1] Ball's written plea for help serves as another entrance into the world of needy veterans looking for help from the people near them.

Pittsylvania-Danville's upper class made up another part of the local support network of the community. Part of a long-existing system of local aid, elite men and women took on renewed importance as potential sources of cash or job opportunities for the less fortunate members of their community during and after the Civil War. Although members of the upper class could, and did, refuse to give their assistance, many veteran families (and other impoverished Virginians) felt they had little to lose by asking the wealthy for help, especially when other sources of aid had failed them. Some of these petitions succeeded, and the ones that did suggest that a new category, that of the Confederate veteran family, had been added to the obligations felt by upper-class men and women toward the needy. Few historians have addressed the question of what happened to the antebellum system of elite assistance for needy Southern whites, and none have looked at the way veteran families attempted to tap into that older tradition. This chapter examines the wartime and postwar appeals to the upper class through a focus on William T. Sutherlin, a wealthy citizen of Pittsylvania County and Danville.

Sutherlin was a prominent and rich member of the elite of Pittsylvania

County and Danville. He manufactured and sold tobacco, owned several farms, and served as president of the Danville Bank. He was mayor of Danville from 1855 to 1861 and served as one of the county's delegates to the 1861 state secession convention, where he and the other Pittsylvania delegate opposed secession as moderate or conditional Unionists. During the Civil War, he thought he might have a chance at an appointment to a field generalship. When that appointment fell through, he accepted a position as major and quartermaster stationed at Danville. At the end of the war, when the Confederate government stopped at Danville in its flight from Richmond (making the town the "Last Capital of the Confederacy"), Jefferson Davis stayed at Sutherlin's house. Despite the financial impact of emancipation, William Sutherlin continued to play a prominent role in the postbellum business and political community, operating several farms in Pittsylvania and Halifax counties, buying and selling tobacco all over the Southeast, and working closely with the area railroads as director, commissioner, builder, and president. According to the 1870 Census, Sutherlin had become the richest man in the county and was valued at over $200,000 in personal property and real estate. He served in the House of Delegates from 1872 to 1874 and as president of the state agricultural society. Sutherlin chaired the infamous "Committee of Forty," which defended the overthrow of black political power in the 1883 Danville Riot by placing blame on an allegedly aggressive black mob. He was also among the early founders of the city's cotton mills.[2]

Sutherlin loomed large in the life of Danville, Pittsylvania County, and the surrounding region throughout the second half of the nineteenth century. He married Jane Patrick in 1849, and had two daughters, one of whom, Janie, survived to marry and have a child of her own. Sutherlin was an active member of the Methodist Church and was active in local and state politics. He participated in a number of fraternal orders, including as a leader of the Roman Eagle Masonic Lodge. He was known as a supporter of education and served as a trustee of Randolph Macon College and Danville Female College. A brief biography of him concluded at his death in 1893, "emphatically a good man and a public benefactor."[3]

Sutherlin, prominent and wealthy even after the Civil War, was the subject of many appeals for assistance from people who needed something from him. Although his home and office were in Danville, Sutherlin spent a lot of time away from the city, visiting his holdings, serving in state political offices, or vacationing and recuperating in the West Virginia resort of White Sulphur Springs. Generally, needy men and women made personal appeals to elites all over the war-torn South in the form of face-to-face requests or in letters laying out their petitions for assistance. Not surprisingly, the content of the vast majority of those face-to-face encounters is lost forever, but some of the petitions have survived. Because of Sutherlin's extended travels, some of the people who would have gone to visit him in person to request aid ended up writing him letters instead. The letters capture some of what would have been said in face-to-face encounters, thus making his case valuable for studying the appeals of the needy to the surviving members of the upper class, an important aspect of the local support network accessed by Confederate veteran families.[4]

This chapter describes one part of a network of wartime and postwar assistance that was based on deferent supplicants and helpful members of the elite and was lubricated by reciprocal obligations. This system was not a new concept. Rather, the paternalism used by wealthier members of society to gain and maintain the backing of laboring whites was a key part of antebellum Southern white society. It is important to point out, however, that while Sutherlin had survived the war with much of his fortune intact, many other members of the Southern elite class struggled to retain their land and status, and still others were ruined completely. Even Sutherlin could not help everyone who asked him for assistance. The long-standing system of elite aid to the needy was severely strained, if not broken, by the postwar crises.[5]

Petitioners and the Petitions for Assistance

The extant wartime and postwar petitions suggest that a person who applied to William T. Sutherlin for help was most likely a member of a veteran family and from Pittsylvania County or Danville. Of the seventy-two surviving wartime and postwar appeals for help to Sutherlin, almost 57 percent came from soldiers or their families. Of those same petitions, over 76 percent came from people from the Pittsylvania-Danville area. These people turned to Sutherlin for help as part of their local support network.[6]

Although the appeals largely came from Pittsylvanians, a sizable proportion of them came from other people. Sutherlin's prominence within Virginia caused him to be the focus of needy people from far outside Danville. Some of them were important people in the state who fell on hard times after the war. John McCue, a major in the Augusta Raid Guard and a lawyer and justice of the peace from Augusta County, asked Sutherlin for a large loan in 1868. Henry Wise, former governor of Virginia and former Confederate brigadier general, unable for several years to get his land back from federal occupation, appealed to Sutherlin for financial assistance in 1867 from Richmond. Other petitioners were complete strangers, such as William Robertson of Nottoway County; in Robertson's appeal for financial assistance, he asked Sutherlin, "please pardon me for the liberty I am taking in addressing you," since they had never met. The appeals from the Pittsylvania area, however, greatly outnumbered the appeals from outside the area.[7]

Of course, appeals to Sutherlin for various forms of assistance did not begin with the Civil War. People had been turning to Sutherlin (and other members of the elite) before the war started. Fourteen requests for aid can be found in Sutherlin's papers just from 1860 and the first three months of 1861. Needy Virginians continued to turn to this form of local support during and after the war. Of the seventy-two surviving wartime and postwar requests for aid from Sutherlin, fifty-one come from the postbellum period.[8]

In these letters, the request for aid was usually the main subject, but occasionally the appeal was a larger missive that discussed many other subjects such as politics and business. Most applicants made a request for money, for help getting a job, or for Sutherlin to use his influence for them. The petitioners explained why they needed the assistance and offered justification for Sutherlin providing that assistance, often by attempting to reinforce or create connections between themselves and the "Major," as he was called even after the war. They also expressed their shame at having to ask for help, and they apologized for bothering Sutherlin. Applicants flattered Sutherlin, expressed their indebtedness to the Major, and showed him deference and respect. Finally, they attempted to coax Sutherlin into giving them the help they asked for through guilt. These constituent parts appear in most of the appeals and reveal the process by which people in need attempted to get help from the members of the local upper class.[9]

Although generally petitioners asked for similar favors from Sutherlin— money, jobs, influence—certain types of requests predominated during the antebellum, wartime, and postwar periods. Prewar petitions made to Sutherlin included requests for loans and the use of his influence, as well as pleas for contributions to the Danville Female College library. But half the requests made of him in 1860 and early 1861 called for his help finding the applicant a "situation" or job.[10]

During the war, although people continued to ask for money and jobs, the most common request (from over half the applicants) was for Sutherlin to "use your influence" to help the petitioner in some way. As quartermaster of Danville and a railroad commissioner, Sutherlin had contact with powerful figures in the Confederate government, including the secretary of war and even the president, who stayed at Sutherlin's house when in the city.[11] Not surprisingly, a number of soldiers, such as James Redd, wanted Sutherlin's help to get out of the Confederate army. Others wanted the Major to use his influence or pull for various ends: to get Danville's city council to provide uniforms for the petitioner's company, to advise the Pittsylvania Bank and publicly support its currency, to find a safe place to which a Treasury Department official could move his family, and to help a sick soldier get out of prison. Most of the appeals Sutherlin received for jobs asked for positions in Danville, some from soldiers such as Abner Anderson who wanted to stay in the military but not in the field. A few letters came from women such as A. E. Wiseman who wanted wartime clerical work. Wartime requests for money came largely from soldiers and their wives, who often asked for loans to tide them over since they were "out of funds." People turned to Sutherlin for all kinds of assistance during the war, even to bring separated lovers together, as when a soldier on "a short furlough" asked to borrow a horse "to see my wife (I have been recently married)."[12]

Given the postwar economic needs of many people in Pittsylvania County and Danville, it makes sense that Sutherlin would have continued to be the focus of more requests for help after the war ended. Although people continued to ask Sutherlin for jobs and for him to use his influence on their behalf, there was a noticeable shift toward requests for monetary aid in the postwar period. (There may have been a greater immediate need for cash than before the war and less of a need for Sutherlin's influence than during the war.) In fact, two-thirds of all postwar requests and three-fourths of all postwar Confederate veteran family requests for assistance from Sutherlin asked for money. Of these requests for financial assistance, 80 percent asked for loans, and the others asked Sutherlin for outright cash gifts.[13]

For petitioners who asked for loans, the amounts ranged from J. M. McCue's request for "a few thousand dollars" to S. S. Saunders's "Please be so kind as to lend me $10, or even $5." Although a few large requests tipped the average amount requested to over $400, the typical loan amount requested was closer to what David Dyer wanted from Sutherlin; Dyer, a veteran and officer of the 57th Virginia Infantry, asked for a "hundred dollars more or less."[14]

Of course, some people may have asked for loans knowing that they could not pay them back. Henry Wise, exhibiting timing worthy of his name, waited until after he received Sutherlin's loan of $100 to tell him, "I . . . will try to pay, but whether I can or not ever is doubtful, I am obliged honestly to confess. If not, I will leave the debt an heirloom to my children."[15]

Although not as common as postbellum requests for money, one-fourth of all postwar appeals and one-third of all postwar veteran family appeals to Sutherlin asked for his help getting a job. People wrote to the Major for a remarkable array of job possibilities. Some wanted sharecropping or other agricultural positions on one of Sutherlin's farms. William Harraway asked "to take a portion of your Pollock farm." Some petitioned for Sutherlin's help getting "a good situation on the Rail Road or any other public business." One veteran wrote "to ask you to assist me in Renting or Leasing the Toll Bridge for the next one, Two or Five years." These requests involved positions with which Sutherlin was directly concerned, but job appeals sometimes involved fields with which he apparently had little to do. "I will venture to ask your assistance in getting a situation as 'teacher' or some other profitable business in, or near Danville," wrote a female petitioner.[16]

As during the war, some postwar petitioners wanted access to Sutherlin's influence in town or advice on business, although there were not as many of these appeals as during the war. One petitioner looking for a raise in his job at the Danville Railroad Depot asked Sutherlin to talk to the man making the decision. Another petitioner requested Sutherlin's help in getting a legacy, left nine years earlier by a friend of Sutherlin's, to her two sons. Several others wanted "to counsel & consult" with him on a variety of topics, including farming, tobacco sales, and business.[17]

Almost every letter requesting aid from Sutherlin included an attempt to explain why the petitioner needed help. Occupational requests came with an explanation for the petitioner's job seeking. Extensive justification accompanied requests for financial assistance, as petitioners sought to convince Sutherlin of their need.

Finding a job in postwar Pittsylvania and Danville turned out to be difficult for a number of men. One man wrote Sutherlin, pleadingly, "I *want, need & seek work, labor* and will gladly be employed at any reasonable rate of living." Others needed to switch jobs, sometimes as a direct result of the war. Veteran William Baugh clarified why he needed Sutherlin's help in getting a chance to run the toll bridge in Danville: "I am Disabled, and must go at something else besides hard Labor." Baugh had been wounded at the Battle of Seven Days and at Gettysburg and could no longer farm or work as a wheelwright as he had done before the war.[18]

Several claimants asking for financial help explained that postwar Pittsylvania and Danville was impoverished and so were they. One veteran claimed, "there is no money in this section," and another bemoaned the impact of a poor economy: "These hard times have fallen rather heavily on me." Others reminded Sutherlin of their financial status: "as you know we are very poor." One Pittsylvanian explicitly stated what he needed and why: "I am out of meet & corn & I cant get it with out money."[19]

Some postwar petitioners told Sutherlin that they needed his help to support their families. One Pittsylvania widow laid out how she would use his money: "if I can secure the above amt just now 'twill enable me to carry out a plan by which I can support my family." Another applicant told Sutherlin of his plan to help the extended family for whom he was now responsible: "If I only had six or seven hundred dollars, I could restock my farm & be in a condition to support my family, and my mother and sister also, who are ... now wholly dependent on me." A member of a veteran family made clear that without some kind of help from Sutherlin "my land is sold [and] my wife & little children will be turned out of Doors." For other applicants, such as S. S. Saunders, family sickness had exacerbated their economic problems: "We have a very ill child with pneumonia that prevented me from attending to business. I am very much in need of money to get some supplies."[20]

A number of Sutherlin's petitioners told him that they just needed a brief loan to help them through a particular rough spot. For some, that meant getting enough money to survive until their crops were sold. David Dyer had "good land & nine good hands" but no money to get their provisions. Dyer wryly claimed, "if I could get the use of some hundred dollars more or less until I could put something in market I think I would be set until the next war." Thomas Jones cheerfully insisted that a brief cash loan would tide him over until he sold his tobacco: "After the lapse of a month or six weeks, I feel confident of being perfectly easy." A few widows were forced to seek loans to survive until their husband's estate was cleared of legal problems. That was the reason that Adie Ferguson gave to Sutherlin when she asked for "twelve months time to pay [his money] back." Some petitioners, such as Robert Baugh, just wanted money to tide them over until they got their new job. Baugh needed $25, he told Sutherlin, but only "for a short time as I will return the same to you as soon as I get paid off [in my new] situation."[21]

After the petitioners had explained to Sutherlin why they needed money or a job, they attempted to show why they deserved his help, either by demonstrating their worthiness or by pointing out the claims they had on him. This justification process was part of a larger problem that people with financial needs had in the nineteenth century, namely, how to prove that they deserved assistance in a world that largely believed that the poor had simply not put forth enough effort or suffered some other character flaws that prevented their worldly success. As a result, these petitions often were balancing acts in which applicants had to demonstrate severe need to get financial assistance but also had to prove that their needs had nothing to do with their own character or any lack of effort on their part.[22]

This balancing act led many petitioners to make a similar argument, basically telling Sutherlin that although they were poor, they worked extremely hard. In taking this approach, they tried to demonstrate their worthiness and head off any question of laziness or bad character as the cause of their impoverishment. One applicant for Sutherlin's assistance described his whole family this way: "I am working like a hero. Just a little start would push me up. . . . I have a wife & 5 children[,] all work like Trojans." Applicants believed that by working to help themselves they had demonstrated their worthiness and that Sutherlin would be more likely to grant them their requests. As Edwin Redd observed, "Now Major I know you are able and very generous to those who are helping themselves."[23]

For some petitioners, the process of proving themselves worthy of assistance could be most easily accomplished by showing that their current poverty was not their fault. In the immediate postwar years, many petitioners claimed that their present need was a unique situation; they swore that they had never sought assistance before. Veteran Robert Baugh told Sutherlin, "this is the first time I ever asked this favor of anyone in my life. . . . If I was not in the situation I am in I would not ask it of you." In a similar vein, another petitioner claimed, "It is the first time I ever begged any one." These applicants also assured Sutherlin, albeit tentatively, that since their situation was unique, they needed assistance just this one time. "I hope & presume that the time will never arise again," wrote one veteran. Another petitioner claimed that the loan he wanted from Sutherlin "would place me in comfortable circumstances & then I think I can weed my own row."[24]

Another way for petitioners to deny responsibility for their impoverishment was by blaming something else. An obvious scapegoat would have been the war itself, yet few of the applicants blamed the war for their poverty. One exception can be seen indirectly in veteran David Dyer's wry comment that if he got a loan, "I think I would be set until the next war." More common scapegoats for diverting responsibility from the petitioners—and thus hopefully for demonstrating the applicants' own worthiness—were their deadbeat neighbors. Several of the applicants told Sutherlin that they had worked hard but to no avail because they found themselves unable to collect money from people who owed them. As one man put it, "the best efforts now . . . don't pay my house rent, baker & butcher. Those I work for cant pay me." Another veteran explained to Sutherlin, "All I had except my little farm was invested in the merchantile business [but] I found collecting impossible."[25]

When petitioners asked for Sutherlin's assistance in finding a job, demonstrating worthiness included proving oneself qualified for the position, a claim most applicants made readily. "I beg leave to offer my services believing myself fully competant of fulfilling the duties required," argued Charles Redd. When applying for a job at the Danville Railroad Depot, George Linthicum based his allegation of qualification on his "long experience as a collector and Clerk in the Commerce community."²⁶ Applicants offered references to back up their qualifications. One applicant who wanted to work on a Sutherlin farm explained that references "can be given of industry or manage ment." Veterans such as William Harraway used wartime officers as their references, indicating that the ties that bound officers and men survived the war, at least through the immediate postwar years.²⁷

While many applicants explained why they deserved Sutherlin's help by demonstrating their worthiness, some justified asking for his assistance by pointing to the relationships they had with him, which they believed obligated him to fulfill their requests. These applicants reminded Sutherlin of the responsibilities laid on him because of the ties of friendship, family, and previous promises. Almost uniformly, these petitioners expressed regret for taking advantage of those bonds in asking the Major for help, but just as often, they articulated a notion that such requests were part of those relationships.

Petitioners who could claim friendship with Sutherlin attempted to base their requests on that relationship. David Dyer's appeal began, "The time has come when I must call on my old friends for small favors." One widow justified her request for aid by restating the extent of her connection with Sutherlin: "as an old friend of my parents as well as myself, I have presumed to ask a favor of you." Another petitioner eloquently reminded Sutherlin of the responsibilities that friendship could entail: "It grieves me much to be under the necessity of troubling my friends upon any matter what ever, and especially on money matters. But, then what is friendship for, or of what use is it, if it cannot afford us a little help in time of real pressing need?"²⁸

A few petitioners were related to Sutherlin and played up their family connection to justify their requests. Two veterans, in looking to Sutherlin for help, acted as many other ex-soldiers did in turning to family members for assistance in surviving and rebuilding their postwar lives. Robert Baugh, a distant cousin of Sutherlin's, attempted to use those ties to gain a $25 loan. Several times in Baugh's letter he called the former mayor "cousin William," reminding him of their relationship and the basis on which Baugh was making his claim. Robert's brother, William Baugh, also petitioned Sutherlin for help, referring to him as "cousin" as well.²⁹

A small number of applicants justified their requests by calling on Sutherlin to fulfill the promises of assistance that he had previously made to them. Madison Millner reminded the tobacco magnate, "Now Major you promised you would stand by me & aid me & let me have the use of your name & said the notes could be renewed.... I thought you would aid & not let my land be sold[;] you said you did not intend any such thing."³⁰

Another strategy used by petitioners was an attempt to reinforce or create a connection with Sutherlin that they believed would justify their request and make him more likely to assist them. Whereas the Major's family and friends could just remind him of these relationships in their appeals, people whose connections to Sutherlin were much more tenuous needed to find some way of strengthening their link to this man whom they asked for help. In M. T. Lanier's request for money, he spent a significant portion of his letter discussing how much the "young beaux" in Danville missed Sutherlin's teenage daughter Jennie while the Sutherlin family was in the mountains at White Sulphur Springs. This attempt to bring an intimacy and familiarity to the letter seems intended to force a sense of friendship, and thereby obligation, on Sutherlin.³¹

In a similar way, Edwin Redd did anything he could to reinforce any connections with Sutherlin that he believed would obligate the man to help him. Redd ended his appeal by trying to force Sutherlin to recognize the relationship between them and thereby the obligation Sutherlin owed Redd: "I hope you have not forgotten me[;] I was frequently in Danville ... while my daughter was at school." He added in a postscript, clearly intending to capitalize on any possible organizational connection, "I took my Knights Templars in Danville."³²

Both Lanier and Redd had met Sutherlin at some point, but even strangers making their appeals attempted to create connections that they believed would obligate Sutherlin to help them. Loula Terry tried to link herself into the local support network through William Sutherlin. After mentioning having read about his generosity, her petition for Sutherlin to pay for her education ended with, "I feel as if I were applying to a friend, instead of a stranger."³³

Given the many attempts by petitioners to connect with Sutherlin, why did few veteran applicants explicitly emphasize that status in their requests? Those who knew Sutherlin or lived in Pittsylvania County probably figured that he already knew of their service and sacrifice to the Confederate cause. It is also possible that many of these veterans just wanted to put the war behind them and thus were not interested in identifying themselves by their service. The latter explanation is supported by combining two facts: first, Confederate veterans organizations were not generally popular in the South until the 1880s, and second, all but two petitioners to Sutherlin wrote before 1880.³⁴

Another common component of most petitions to Sutherlin was an articulation of shame. These expressions seem sincere and not just standard phrasing for appeals. For many supplicants, the process of asking for help proved embarrassing. Robert Baugh's request for $25 from his "cousin William" included a statement indicating Baugh's concern for how he appeared to Sutherlin: "I am very sorry for what I have got to say and I hope you will not think hard of this." Another petitioner seemed loath even to mention the loan he wanted: "My dear Sir," he declared, "'tis with feelings of great diffidence & delicacy I am constrained to renew the subject mentioned to you in the city." Although Adie Ferguson asked the Major for money, she made clear her discomfort with having to do so: "I dislike exceedingly to make such a request."[35]

Often linked to these expressions of shame were apologies to Sutherlin for bothering him and for having to ask for assistance. Petitioners commonly used phrases such as "I trust you will excuse me for taking an unusual liberty" and "Excuse the liberty I take in addressing you." Several people hoped Sutherlin would "forgive my troubling you." Applicants also indicated their awareness of the many other appeals made to Sutherlin and the potential irritation they could cause: "I know your calls of a similar kind have been so numerous. If you have been much annoyed in that way, do not, I beg you, entertain mine, for one instant."[36]

Veteran Thomas Jones asked Sutherlin, "Please excuse me for any apparent bluntness in making the request so pointedly[;] in dealing with candid & practical men *blarney* is not necessary." Although Jones claimed "blarney" was not a required part of an appeal for aid, his asking for Sutherlin's pardon for his "bluntness" implies that the reverse was true, that such petitions were typically couched in flowery language and included flattery of and even deference to the person being asked for help. In fact, almost every letter asking for aid contained some kind of flattery of Sutherlin. One Danvillian told Sutherlin, "You see, Major, we cannot do without you either in Church, or State, at home or abroad." Another petitioner ended his appeal "with high appreciation of your admirable character as a gentleman and a christian."[37]

The number of appeals that made clear their respect for Sutherlin and their acknowledgment of their debt to him (albeit only if he fulfilled their request) support the notion that flattery and deference were generally part of this process of getting aid. Most petitioners deferentially indicated that they would owe Sutherlin a kind of "personal capital" for his involvement in their problems. David Dyer respectfully wrote Sutherlin, "Sir it will do me a great favor if you can conveniently aid me in this case and oblige your friend." Sutherlin's disabled cousin, William Baugh, conveyed the kindness that the Major would be doing for him in helping him achieve a lease on the toll bridge: "I shall take it as a great favor if you will see the Parties concerned about this matter. By so doing, you will very much oblige your humble servant." In a similar tone, a number of letters ended with polite closings such as "Very respectfully" or "respectfully yours." The similarity in words—"favor" and "oblige" and "respectfully"—indicates a common language for appeals, but the similarity does not mean that the words—or the debts incurred—were merely symbolic. Rather, the use of a language of respect and obligation should be taken for what it appears to have been, an acknowledgment that the debt owed Sutherlin for his assistance went beyond monetary sums.[38]

By "personal capital" I mean broadly the perceived reciprocal obligations that existed between people in this Southern hierarchical, unequal society. These obligations, in this case, came about when Sutherlin assisted those who needed his help. Although not only a part of interactions between socioeconomic classes (e.g., personal capital could be exchanged as favors between members of the same class), personal capital bound upper and middling/lower classes together in a network of debts paid off in money or in political or societal support.[39]

A few applicants attempted, albeit half-heartedly, to keep their exchanges on the level of independent individuals helping each other out, rather than merely accepting their role as the supplicants that their need forced them to be. These limited attempts at putting themselves on a more equal footing with Sutherlin are exemplified by one petitioner's framing of his request for assistance as an offer of reciprocity: "Please be so kind as to lend me $10, or even $5 for a few days in which time I should return you the money with many thanks & all the favors that is in my feeble power." Another petitioner was more tentative in her effort to claim her own independence when she suggested, "will perhaps someday be able to return the favor."[40]

At or near the end of petitioners' letters, many of them attempted to play on the Major's sense of guilt or obligation in order to improve their chances of getting money from him. Some applicants referred to Sutherlin's apparent wealth, pointing out his financial success, most likely with the intention of making him feel guilty for having it. In a multi-layered phrase, containing flattery and guilt for Sutherlin while revealing the writer's own bitterness, one applicant remarked, "Providence seems to smile on all you do financially." After saying that helping was what friends were for, another petitioner then laid on the guilt: "But I will not argue the case with you for I know if you can, and I think you can, you will afford me the very small amt. of help I ask." Another petitioner added a similar postscript to his letter: "Somehow or other, I have strong faith that I will something get. My wife has not clothes to wear respectable." This technique was used even after getting some money from Sutherlin. After Charles Ball had received $300 of the $600 he had asked for, he responded in another letter of appeal, "it is not enough, but I know you will let me have more if you can & have it, and Hope you will be able to do so."⁴¹

There is a sense of urgency evident in these letters that makes readers—even separated by nearly 150 years—feel the desperation and need of the petitioners. No doubt, the applicants hoped that conveying that urgency would motivate Sutherlin into helping them. Some letters are particularly intense: "I am in immediate need.... Please to answer this note immediately as I shall be very anxious to hear from you." Appeals commonly ended with some variation on a sentence that reflected the petitioners' immediate needs: "Please let me hear from you as soon as possible." The repeated absences of Sutherlin from Danville caused increased anxiety in some of the people who appealed to him for assistance, and they attempted to convey their concerns to him: "I have been to Danville twice lately to see you, have written twice & can neither see or hear from you.... I must see you about the matter in a few days[;] let me know what day to meet you in Danville[;] I am restless, uneasy, & know not what to do[,] what shall I do[? L]et me hear from you at once & save me from destruction."⁴²

Ultimately, these petitioners turned to Sutherlin for assistance for the same reasons that people all over the South turned to the upper-class men and women in their local support networks. For some, it was the pre-existing connection they had to him. William and Robert Baugh were family, and David Dyer and others were named among his friends. It was natural for these petitioners to look to the Major for help. Other factors included his prominent position, his wealth, and his known charity to others. Some petitioners appealed to Sutherlin because there was no one else to whom they could turn. Almost everyone approached Sutherlin for aid for some combination of these reasons.

Within the local support network of Pittsylvania County and Danville, Sutherlin would have been an obvious person to approach for support, in part because of his prominence in town, county, and even state politics, economy, and society. That prominence was a result of his perceived power and influence. When William Rison asked Sutherlin to express publicly his support of the Pittsylvania Bank during the war, he did so because he believed that Sutherlin's endorsement would meet the bank's needs: "I apply to you with confidence, knowing your practical experience in Banking."⁴³

One area of particular prominence for Sutherlin was with the local railroads. His wartime position as quartermaster in Danville and as one of the commissioners, as well as his later positions as president of several local railroad lines, prompted many others to appeal to him for positions. So George

Linthicum asked Sutherlin for a job at the Danville Railroad Depot, explaining that he looked to Sutherlin for help "knowing your influence as director of the Richmond & Danville Railroad."[44]

People also looked to Sutherlin for assistance because of his wealth, especially in the hard economic times of the postwar South. A widowed petitioner asked for Sutherlin's help "knowing you have an abundance of this world's goods." Another petitioner, seeking $800, applied to Sutherlin because he "thought that probably you might have that much money on hand to loan out." Given the size of some of these requests (as high as $2,000), families and churches would likely not have been able to help the petitioners. Local banks, especially in the immediate postwar period, also had problems that made it difficult for them to loan money to all the people who needed it. In such financial straits, Sutherlin or other members of the region's upper class would have been the only recourse. Such informal banking networks were popular in the agricultural antebellum South and probably expanded in the wartime and postwar world.[45]

People also applied to Sutherlin for help because he had already helped others, and word of his generosity had spread. If people wanted to get what they felt they needed, it only made sense for them to approach someone who they believed could and would help them, and William Sutherlin seemed to fit that profile. To petitioners, not only did Sutherlin have wealth and influence, but apparently he was also willing to use both to help people. One petitioner wrote in her appeal to Sutherlin that she knew of "your kindness and your willingness to assist those in need." Others had heard of his "liberal and generous heart." "So often have I read and heard of your deeds of magnanimity," wrote one woman, that she decided to ask for some of it for herself.[46]

Some applicants claimed that Sutherlin was the only person in the postwar world to whom they could turn for help. One desperate petitioner emphasized, *"I have no other friend in the world to whom I can apply in this the time of my extremity and sore need."* Another pleaded with the Major, "I am more & more convinced every day, that you[—]before and above all others I know any thing of—can render me the aid I desire—I mean pecuniary." Perhaps the best summary of the reason many people looked to William Sutherlin for help to survive or get back on their feet came from veteran Grief Lampkin: "I have no friend whose assistance I have a right to claim, and cannot call to mind any one who would be more likely to have it in his power to lend me a helping hand such as I ask for."[47]

The Results of the Petitions

Sutherlin's responses to these requests for his assistance suggest that the war created a new category of elite obligation, that owed to Confederate veterans. Unfortunately, determining the result of these petitions is possible in less than one-third of the appeals. Overall, Sutherlin agreed to help almost three-fourths of the applications whose outcomes can be determined. Although I acknowledge the limitations of a small sample, two comments can be made about what factors played a role in who Sutherlin helped. First, local people do not seem to have had a significant advantage in achieving a successful application. Of the people whose appeals were approved, 76 percent were from Danville or Pittsylvania, almost the same percentage as that of people from the area in the applicant pool. More significant, Confederate veteran families seem to have had a greater chance of getting assistance from Sutherlin than non-veteran families. Over 82 percent of the approved appeals came from veteran families, as compared to the 57 percent of veteran families within the overall applicant pool. Veteran families appealing to Sutherlin for assistance were more likely to get their aid than non-veterans.[48]

Sutherlin's assistance would have made a difference in the lives of veteran families and non-veteran families alike. Help getting a job could have a long-term, significant impact, providing a means of making a living or supplementing an income enough to support a family. The impact of financial assistance is a little more complicated. Only six of the successful applications detailed how much money Sutherlin gave: $300 in Confederate money in 1865 and postwar loans or gifts of $300, $100, $35, $25, and $16. The limited information on the amount that was given to people makes it difficult to assess the impact that monetary assistance had on veteran families. Certainly $300 or even $100 would have been very helpful in meeting the daily expenses of a family trying to survive. Three hundred dollars would have been at or greater than a year's wages for many occupations in the postwar period. Amounts less than $50 would have helped, but like the aid from churches and later aid from pensions, this money from Sutherlin would have to have been only part of the larger financial struggle to survive and rebuild, although an important part.[49]

It is also possible to get a sense of the emotional impact of Sutherlin's aid. The people who received assistance from Sutherlin made clear that they had been given something of great importance to them. Alfred Barbour showed his immense gratitude for the assistance Sutherlin had rendered his family: "I thank you from the bottom of my heart for your kindness.... I shall never forget you or cease to be grateful to you." Charles Ball, after receiving money from

Sutherlin, wrote back, "Your letter of the 8th reached me tonight, and it has so touched my heart & filled it with ... gratitude and thankfulness that I hardly know what to say to you."[50]

Several factors motivated Sutherlin to help out many of the people who asked for his assistance. Sutherlin probably felt some pressure, some sense of obligation, to assist those petitioners who were his family or his friends. His apparent favoring of veteran families in need probably came from an awareness of their sacrifices and a belief in their worthiness. Sutherlin may have believed that as a member of the financial and political elite of Danville and Pittsylvania, his role was to be a key part of the local support network.

Sutherlin's actions were not entirely selfless, however. While acknowledging his generosity toward some of his applicants, we must not overlook that Sutherlin himself gained from his assistance of others. Sutherlin succeeded as both a businessman and politician in the region. As an astute leader, he would have been well aware of the benefits to himself of these acts of assistance. If these gifts, loans, or uses of his influence met his perceived obligations, so much the better. His acts of charity can be seen as reciprocal actions that took place within a hierarchical Southern class system. In assisting people during and after the war, Sutherlin built up "personal capital." Sutherlin's acts of assistance created and maintained a fund of loyalty and gratitude in the region (and the state) that he could spend in his other roles as businessman, politician, and civic leader. When he loaned a horse to a soldier so that the young man could go see his newly married wife on a furlough, Sutherlin gained one family's kind feelings: "I will always feel grateful for the favor," wrote the soldier. When Sutherlin gave money to needy soldiers' wives and when Confederate army companies from Pittsylvania or Danville "received many kindnesses at [his] hand," he earned the respect and thanks of many veterans for years to come. Sutherlin's postbellum charity further secured people's friendship and loyalty to him, supporting not only his business work but also his political ambitions. His election to the Virginia legislature in 1872 was helped, no doubt, by the votes of the people to whom he had provided assistance.[51]

Along with other members of the upper class of Danville and Pittsylvania, Sutherlin probably also helped needy veteran families and other whites who applied to him for assistance in an attempt to maintain white solidarity. For the upper class in the post-emancipation world, the need for such racial unity must have seemed essential. Sutherlin's gifts, loans, and influence also served to bind lower- and middle-class whites to him and to the region's upper class.[52]

Although Sutherlin had good reasons for offering some measure of aid to those who asked him for help, he also refused some people's appeals—almost one-fourth of those for whom a result can be identified and perhaps three-fourths of all requests—suggesting that there were significant limitations to the number and type of people he could or would help.[53] Very few letters from Sutherlin to those who appealed to him have survived, but an extant letter from 1867 written by his assistant, S. R. Neal, reveals some of the reasons Sutherlin may not have helped people. Neal wrote, "He, no doubt, esteems you highly as a friend and would, if convenient, be gratified to comply with your request: But the present stringency of money matters is very great: and Besides this fact, the Major has been for some time past loaning out and otherwise useing large amounts of funds and as yet has been receiving nothing in return. Therefore under these circumstances, I am sure it will not be convenient for him to accommodate you at present." There is a formula for rejection here: Sutherlin thinks highly of you, and if he could help you he would, but he has already helped a number of people and his funds are not limitless, and so he cannot give you what you have asked.[54]

There are two basic reasons Sutherlin would not have helped people who applied to him for assistance. First, as indicated in the Neal letter, the petitioner asked for more than Sutherlin could give or wanted something he could not give. Second, he felt little or no connection or obligation to that particular applicant. For an applicant in the first group, Sutherlin could not fulfill the request. But for an applicant in the second group, Sutherlin would not fulfill the request.

As Neal stated, Sutherlin just did not have the money to help everyone. Sutherlin had significant assets during and after the war, but he would not always have had a great deal of currency available to him at any given time. He probably had enough to loan or give small amounts of money to some applicants, but even if he were willing, he was less likely to be able to access large sums without difficulty. Sutherlin turned down requests of $2,000, $800 and $600, writing the applicants that he had "no money." In fact, all the failed requests for money (that we know of) were for at least $600.[55]

The second reason Sutherlin did not help people who requested aid from him was that he did not want to help them. Put another way, Sutherlin did not help those people for whom he did not feel a strong enough connection or obligation. Sutherlin would probably not have told people that this was the reason he would not help them. If he replied to their requests at all, he almost certainly told them that he did not have the money (as Neal told Thomas Jones for Sutherlin), that the job was not open, or that there was nothing he could do. As a result, it is difficult to assess the extent to which this lack of connection motivated his refusal to help certain applicants for his aid.[56]

How typical was Sutherlin in terms of his assistance to others? Crandall Shifflett has found patron-client relationships in postwar Louisa County, Virginia, that involved limited assistance to the poor. Steven Tripp has found Lynchburg elites attempting to replicate antebellum trends that would bind laboring whites to the powerful. This evidence suggests that Sutherlin was not alone among the state's elite in continuing (to some extent) prewar trends of noblesse oblige. Neither historian, however, has looked specifically at the attitude of those members of the elite toward veterans, so a direct comparison is not possible. Sutherlin's typicality in his apparent favoring of veteran families is hard to place without a similar (or even more detailed) set of records from another member of the elite.[57]

On the other hand, certainly there was some religious and secular sentiment in the postwar South about the sacrifices that Confederate soldiers had made that would have encouraged wealthy men and women to help veteran families. Popular perceptions of veterans as deserving of recognition (and perhaps support) can be seen in Southern white public support for commutations and memorials in the immediate postwar years. Later, this sentiment can be seen even more strongly in the movement toward soldiers' and widows' pensions and even a home for former Confederate soldiers.[58]

Finally, it is appropriate to examine Sutherlin's typicality with regard to postwar wealth. Were other members of the county's elite in a position to grant loans or gifts? Evidence suggests that such was not the case. Sutherlin was among the top-twenty residents in total wealth in the 1860 manuscript population census for the county. (He was eighth.) By 1870, Sutherlin was the richest man in the county, but only three others from the top twenty in 1860 were still in the top twenty in overall wealth. Sutherlin was the only one of them to increase in total wealth from 1860 to 1870. In fact, the overall average individual loss in total wealth of those who had been in the top twenty in 1860 (including Sutherlin's gains) was over $170,000 (about 75 percent of their 1860 wealth).[59] So, although needy Southerners almost certainly asked for assistance from the elite, many formerly rich (or even well-off) Southerners would have been less able to help people in the postbellum period than they had been before the war. This fact, along with the clear problems faced by those who asked Sutherlin for help, suggests that the old system was insufficient to cope with the increased demand and financial consequences brought about by the war and emancipation.

Ultimately, people turned to William Sutherlin for help because he had money, power, and influence, and they thought he would help them. They turned to him because he was part of the local support network of Danville and Pittsylvania County at a time when their families and churches (and perhaps other upper-class members of the community) were failing to provide them with the help they needed. People looked to a few of the elite members of that network for assistance before, during, and after the Civil War. Elites such as Sutherlin who managed to retain some of their wealth after the war continued to play an important role, if limited in scale, in helping the needy of their area when they could, not just in Pittsylvania County and Danville but also all over the South. Their motives in assisting these people were not entirely selfless, since their charity could bind people to them politically and socially. Still, they probably also felt the tug of obligation to help their family and friends, as well as a general sense of responsibility that motivated them to help out others. Although elite aid to local needy people was nothing new, Sutherlin's choice of whom to distribute that aid to suggests that perhaps veterans and their families were becoming seen as a new category of people worthy of assistance. As later chapters show, the state of Virginia, through its assistance to veterans and their families, indicated that it came to accept this notion as well.

Veteran families turned to wealthy men such as Sutherlin as another way to survive and rebuild their lives in the postwar era. As with many of the other sources of aid outside the family, the money or influence received from Sutherlin would not have been enough, by itself, to solve an impoverished family's problems, nor could Sutherlin help all the veteran families of Pittsylvania County and Danville who needed help. The fact that relatively few appeals were successful indicates the limits of depending on such assistance for people in wartime and postbellum Virginia. Although Sutherlin's assistance would have partly filled a gap in the community's support of its veteran families, those families would have also had to look elsewhere for other assistance.

5

Veteran Families, Mental Illness, and the State

Dealing with the "Blue Devils"

> Ever since 1863 [he] has been a little irregular in his mental condition though of late the attacks have been more marked.... He used to call his attacks the "Blue Devils."
>
> —Case file of William H. White, Western Lunatic Asylum, 1896

THE VETERANS of Danville and Pittsylvania and their families turned to sources of aid other than their local support networks and relatives. Many Southern Civil War survivors required significant assistance from their home state to rebuild their lives and sometimes just to survive. Virginia provided a variety of services and types of aid to its veterans and their family members. By using the records of the Western Lunatic Asylum (later Western State Hospital), this chapter examines the connections between the war and mental illness and the role that the state's mental institutions played in "curing" or as caretakers of some of its soldiers and their families after 1861.

Although many Virginians seem to have suffered from what was considered mental illness, not everyone with apparent psychological problems went to an insane asylum. Relatives usually attempted to care for family members with psychological disorders. Only if the behavior of the mentally ill was violent, if they wandered off, or if their family could not take care of them would they be put in the local jail and would commitment to an asylum be considered. Although in some extreme instances an insane person would be taken straight to an asylum, someone, usually a family member or a county court, would apply to the asylum on his or her behalf. Upon acceptance, the mentally ill person would be taken—sometimes by force—to the asylum for admittance.[1]

Mid-nineteenth-century asylums had two goals in accepting insane patients. First, they attempted to cure mental illnesses, if that was in their power, and send patients back to their families. Second, they took care of those for whom such a cure exceeded their ability, sometimes for decades after admittance.[2] Virginia's insane asylums, Eastern Lunatic Asylum in Williamsburg and Western Lunatic Asylum in Staunton, although built well before the Civil War, served an important role in state assistance to Virginia's veterans and their families.[3]

Historians of the institutions of mental illness during this era have focused on two significant trends. First, they have detailed the way in which, by the late nineteenth century, the emphasis of asylums had shifted more toward the long-term care or "warehousing" of patients and away from the curability of people with mental illnesses, though the latter goal remained important. Second, historians have begun to explore the differences and similarities between Southern and Northern mental institutions, with a focus on the apparent post-emancipation rise in black mental illness. But neither of these approaches addresses the potential role of these asylums as state assistance to white Southern (or in this case Virginian) families severely affected by the war.[4]

Before the war, the support system of white families had been able to cope with most mental illness, leaving only the most extreme cases of insanity to be dealt with by the state institutions. An examination of Western Lunatic Asylum and the Civil War soldiers and family members who stayed there indicates that the war and its aftermath had a significant psychological effect on some veteran families. The antebellum support system broke down under the stress of the conflict and its consequences, and veteran family members with mentally ill relatives turned to the state for help. Virginia's asylums took their place as part of a postwar system in which the state took on responsibilities that families were unable to fulfill, caring for, or even "curing," men and women apparently affected by the war.

At the time of this writing, only Western Lunatic Asylum has substantive records accessible for the second half of the nineteenth century, but these medical charts, patient registers, and annual reports are enough to assess the significance of the institution to Virginia's Confederate veterans and their families.[5] Of the 455 patients admitted to Western State between 1861 and 1868, fifty-seven of them entered because of psychological problems attributed to "The War." In addition to these fifty-seven patients, this chapter includes the nineteen patients from the Pittsylvania-Danville area who could be shown to be part of a veteran family and were admitted between 1861 and 1900. Almost all these people had been Confederate soldiers or were related to one, and the state institution provided them and their families with much-needed support.[6]

The Civil War and Mental Illness

For most of these patients, their medical records directly link their mental problems to some kind of involvement in the Civil War. That is not to say that the conflict necessarily "caused" all these mental illnesses. Even today, our understanding of the causes of mental problems remains less than perfect. This section, however, examines the explanations assigned by the patients' relatives and by the doctors at Western State Hospital; these explanations linked the Civil War and its consequences to the mental problems that these Virginians suffered during this period.

For some men, conscription into the Confederate Army brought on (or exacerbated) some kind of mental disturbance. When John Reed learned that he had been conscripted, he suffered a severe attack of some undeterminable nature. He "slept none and ate nothing for three weeks and his whole conversation was a dread of the war." He announced that he would "rather kill himself than for others to kill him." Charles White serves as an example of what would happen if the Confederate government forced such men to serve. After purchasing substitutes for himself in 1862 and 1863, White was conscripted into the army in 1864. Despite his non-fighting position (battery sutler for the 8th Virginia Infantry), his doctors at the asylum and his wife believed "the anxiety & excitement of his new occupation" and his conscription had brought on his "insanity."[7]

Certainly we must acknowledge the possibility that men such as Reed and White only acted as if they were mentally ill to get out of, or stay out of, the Confederate Army. In fact, the number of admissions at the asylum increased in June, July, and August of 1862, as the first Confederate draft from April was enforced. Most of these patients stayed only briefly (an average of three months), long enough to ensure that they would not hurt themselves and long enough to reassure them that they would not be conscripted. Still, even if some men played at being mentally ill as an attempt to escape military service, it is much more likely that they had no interest in actually making it to the asylum, which was often not a place people wanted to be. In addition, getting into the asylum meant fooling the doctors at the state hospital. In fact, many of these patients admitted to Western State did suffer from mental disturbances brought on by their (potential) involvement with the Civil War.[8]

For other patients, medical records show that fighting itself could bring on mental problems. William Granville Gray served as a lieutenant for two years, but in late 1864, after being "ordered into the trenches, . . . he had an attack of paralysis." According to witnesses, he "lost the use of his tongue entirely for half an hour." Being routed in battle left psychological as well as physical casualties. "A member of the company of Hampden Sidney boys lately scattered by McClellan," William Miller came to Western State disoriented and confused. His chart indicated that he "tears his clothes and is uncontrollable." John Kerlin joined the Confederate Army in August 1862. According to his medical records, his first assignment put him into "a squad detailed to shoot some deserters, which frightened him out of his senses." After the shooting, Kerlin immediately jumped into a nearby river, in an apparent attempt to drown himself, resulting in his being sent to the asylum.[9]

Other Confederate soldiers admitted to Western State suffered from mental problems caused more generally by life in the army. Joseph Noel served in the Virginia Cavalry until July 1864, when he became "insane & violent." Upon his admittance to the asylum, his doctor recorded that Noel "can give no account of himself, can not even answer yes or no to questions." He tore his clothes and trashed his room. Although the doctors at Western State were not certain of the cause of his insanity, they believed that Noel's problems stemmed from anxiety over fighting against his brother, who had joined the Union army.[10]

Time as a prisoner of war also had psychological consequences for some Confederate veterans. According to James Langhorne's asylum admission information, he was "taken prisoner at the battle of Kernstown. Became insane and was sent by the Federal authorities to an asylum in Baltimore whence he was brought by his father in August 1862, he then being dyspeptic and melancholy [depressed]." In December 1863, however, Langhorne's father, unable to deal with him anymore, brought him to Staunton, because Langhorne had become "maniacal" to the point of violence and showed a violent "antipathy to his friends." At Western State, the staff recorded his behavior as "excited & incoherent, tears clothing.... He is dyspeptic and has a cough, is feeble and very lean." Simon Hornsberger and Richard Moran also spent time in Northern prisons, and both began to show signs of "insanity" after "6 months" as "prisoner[s] of war."[11]

As with these soldiers, Western State's medical charts reveal the war's potential psychological impact on men and women who had sons, husbands, and brothers involved in the fighting. Caleb Rector had four sons serving in the Confederate Army and "anxiety about [his] family and country" brought on a "deranged" episode that lasted a year. Catherine Bailey began to show her "first indication of insanity ... at the time her son was ordered into the Army." Bailey, a widow, feared both the loss of her son and being left alone. Her mental disturbance manifested as a severe depression, to the point that she "attempted violence to her self on several occasions."[12]

Although men made up thirty-nine of the fifty-seven people admitted to Western Lunatic Asylum with their cause of admission listed as "The War," the eighteen women admitted for this reason make clear that there remains a great deal of work to be done on the psychological impact of the Civil War on women. The medical records of these eighteen women indicate that their "mind[s were] unsettled by the war," although in a variety of ways. For women such as Polly Shank, it was the conscription of her husband, along with the "insolence & depredations of [Union] soldiers" near her home, that pushed her into a severe depression. For other women, anxiety or grief over the absence or death of loved ones seems causative. For still others, mental problems came from a particularly traumatic encounter with Northern troops.[13]

Other patients' charts indicate that anxiety over the absence of and possible danger to enlisted family members brought on or exacerbated the mental problems of many Civil War wives, mothers, and sisters. A number of women admitted to Western Lunatic Asylum during the war apparently worried to the point of mental illness. Catherine Nicholson's husband served as a physician in the Confederate Army, which was the "supposed cause" of her mental difficulties. Polly Shank's mental balance became "unsettled" in part because her "husband [was] called into the army." The doctors of the asylum attributed Mary Calfee's maniacal behavior to the "absence of her brother in the army." Such anxiety, not surprisingly, could increase when the Union forces caught and imprisoned an enlisted relative. Elizabeth Ann Pittman's "attack commenced suddenly . . . upon hearing that her son had been captured by the Federal Army." The depression under which this widow suffered continued after the war.[14]

Family members could also help bring on mental anguish. After Richard Whitehead, a Confederate soldier, ended up in Castle Thunder Prison in Richmond (because he forged a transfer to the signal corps), his father came to see him in jail. His father told "him that he had rather see him in his grave than in that place, which seem[ed] to mortify and wound his [son's] feelings very much." Apparently Whitehead's excited mental state began after this parental visit.[15]

Not surprisingly, the death of an enlisted relative could also trigger mental "attacks" and did so in 15 percent of the cases in the sample. Adam Thompson's mania began when he received word "of a brother who was killed in battle," after which he became "much excited when the condition of the country [was] brought up." Maria Harris had two sons, both of whom Union troops captured at the battle of Gettysburg. When she heard that "one of [them] died in a northern prison," she became severely depressed, confused, and occasionally delusional, symptoms that remained for years after the war ended.[16]

Some of the people admitted to Western State clearly had been bombarded by a combination of anxieties about, and real blows to, their families and their world. Mary Woodell began to suffer from "melancholy" as early as 1862 because of her belief that "the war would ruin the country, that she & her family would be separated, & she feared that her sons then in the Army would be killed." Unfortunately for Woodell, her husband died of smallpox in 1863, and "from that time [she] grew gradually worse." She "would sit & cry the greater part of the time." Then, in 1864 one of her sons in the Confederate army deserted to the Union side. "This greatly excited her, & she became much more unmanageable" and was committed to Western State.[17]

In fact, the asylum staff believed that the mental problems of a number of patients admitted to Western State stemmed from an inability to deal with the chaos and intensity of life in wartime Virginia as well as specific war-related problems. These "troubles incident to the war" affected Virginians such as R. B. Stratton in negative ways. At the beginning of the war, Peter White, a farmer and doctor, became "a refugee on account of the political battles of the country." He was unable to deal mentally with his new status and the war, and "he became insane." He "raved on all subjects" but especially on "the state of the country." Amos Pierce's mania apparently grew out of "the losses and distresses incident to the state of war."[18]

Of course, mental problems related to the war did not end with Lee's surrender. In fact, the end of the war itself proved too much for some of Virginia's soldiers to take. William Granville Gray, after recovering from his paralysis, gained release from the asylum to fight for Richmond in its last defense. The city's fall in April 1865 made Gray "almost frantic and after that event . . . [he became] perfectly demented." At his admission to Western State in September 1865, Gray could not dress or feed himself, eventually only saying, over and over, that he was "very small."[19]

For soldiers who received head wounds, the physical impact of the war could affect their mental stability for the rest of their lives. James Elliott, admitted to Western State almost twenty years after the war had ended, suffered from an extended mental and physical breakdown probably "caused by a wound received during the war on the head." Christopher Columbus Hedrick had been too close to an exploding shell at the battle of Malvern Hill, and thirty-five years later he still had problems with a "disease of the head" that "rises periodically giving much pain and discharge of matter through the nose," as well as forcing him "into insane" behavior.[20]

Western State's medical records also reveal that after the Civil War ended white Virginians (especially veterans' families) found themselves forced to deal with the unpleasant legacies of the conflict, especially the daunting task of caring for one's family in a postwar world dominated by economic hardship and poverty. Faced with such familial financial frustration, some people began to suffer emotional and psychological problems severe enough to bring them to the asylum. Of the patients in the sample, 15 percent were veterans with economic hardship listed as a causative factor of their admission. William Herndon, a major in the 8th Virginia Cavalry, a physician and a member of the General Assembly of Virginia, "became maniacal" soon after he returned home to find himself financially ruined and unable to take care of his family because Union soldiers had taken or destroyed all his property. The asylum staff partly blamed Edward Newcomb's attempted suicide on "the condition of his affairs" and the fact that he "has no property." William Dix, a member of Pittsylvania County's 38th Virginia Infantry, also tried, unsuccessfully, to kill himself. His attempt apparently was "developed by poverty."[21]

For veteran POWs such as James McCue and Benjamin Carder, postwar poverty was compounded by other problems, related to the war and its aftermath, which pushed these men past their mental breaking point. McCue, imprisoned and ill for the last three months of the war, came home to find that although he had been a moderately wealthy man before the conflict, he was now broke. McCue then "exhausted his energies by working very hard [and] his mind began to give way," showing signs of "indecision, loss of energy, neglect of business, seclusion, causeless fear [and lack of] sleep." Carder returned from his time in Northern prisons to find that two of his children had died and that he had been left with the responsibility of caring for his ill mother and two impoverished sisters, one of whom had five children. Unfortunately, his military service left him disabled and incapable of performing his prewar occupation of stonemason. Carder became delusional, believing that God spoke through him and told him to preach to the North.[22]

Poverty and the postwar world to which veterans returned put them under more mental strain than some could take. Simeon Hernsberger had been a soldier and a prisoner of war. When admitted to Western State in December 1865, his file read, "Cause, the war—its exposure, deprivations & excitement.... His derangement is evident on the subjects of the state of the country & his financial affairs." Simeon Hernsberger was not alone. The immediate postwar period (late 1865 through 1866) proved to be an extremely difficult time for most Virginians, especially veterans and their families. Contemporary accounts indicate that a number of Confederate veterans across the South suffered from a form of depression or melancholia in this postwar period. One-fourth of the sample entered the asylum during this period, apparently unable to cope with the trauma of the defeat of the Confederacy, the "state of the country," and the postwar economic problems.[23]

J. Hampden ("Ham") Chamberlayne serves as a good example of these depressed Virginia veterans. A lawyer in antebellum Richmond, Chamberlayne served time in the Confederate Artillery, achieving the rank of captain but spending over eight months in a Union prison. Chamberlayne returned from the war with no money and attempted to make his living as a farmer in Louisa County. According to his son (and editor of his letters), he spent "eighteen months ... of hard work and extreme poverty ... in the hopeless effort to extract from the none too generous soil of a small farm a living for his mother and one of his brothers as well as himself." Apparently poverty, hard work, and the Confederacy's defeat brought on "a complete physical and nervous breakdown, which for a whole year incapacitated him for effort of any sort." When Chamberlayne was admitted to Western State in May 1867, the asylum's doctors recorded that "he had been much depressed and saw little in the present condition of the country encouraging." They explained "that the late war in which he was engaged and was thoroughly identified with the cause" contributed to his mental problems. His friends told the asylum staff that "he was pretty mortified by the result [of the war]." Chamberlayne stayed at Western State for just over a year, a period that his son later described as "the darkest of his life."[24]

Almost all the patients discussed so far were committed to Western Lunatic Asylum with the cause for their admission listed as "The War."[25] For other veterans and members of veteran families, the linkage between the impact of the Civil War and their mental illness was not quite as obvious to the staff at the asylum. We can make a case, however, that the war-related problems already discussed—especially the postwar economic and political situation—had a psychological impact on Pittsylvania-Danville veteran family members that showed up in ways that were not explicitly linked at the time.

White reaction to postbellum race relations represented one such possible source of mental stress. Pittsylvania veteran Marcellus Cousins found himself committed to Western State almost fifteen years after the war ended because of his violent behavior and "antipathy to the negro race." This violence stemmed partly from his inability to rebuild his business after the war, a fact that he apparently blamed on African Americans. The staff noted that Cousins "has shown a disposition to commit violence to the negro." Cousins told asylum doctors "that God desire[d] him to kill them [black men and women]." He also attacked the asylum's attendants (mostly black) and had to be restrained.[26]

Excessive use or abuse of alcohol, tobacco, and drugs also brought a number of Pittsylvania County veterans (47 percent of those admitted) to the asylum.

To the medical staff of Western State, intemperate life styles could cause mental illness. J. J. Nuckols's episode of violent behavior was "believed to be caused by Intemperance." William M. Tredway, Jr., a prominent lawyer in postbellum Chatham, "after a time became addicted to Debauches." Although "intemperance" or "dissipation" could perhaps be blamed simply on the conflicting contemporary understandings of the proper uses of alcohol, some historians have argued more generally that Northern and Southern Civil War veterans abused alcohol (and other drugs). Whether these veterans tried to forget the war, escape their current problems, or just have a good time, the use (and abuse) of mind-altering substances by Nuckols and these other Western State inmates was unusual among veterans only in that it resulted in their being committed to an asylum.[27]

For 20 percent of the Pittsylvania-Danville veteran patients, their admission to the asylum stemmed from physical diseases or illnesses with a mental impact. Patients such as James McCue seemed to be suffering from a mental and physical breakdown related to exhaustion and overwork. The linkage of others' mental and physical illnesses to the war was more tenuous, although not necessarily absent. James P. Sykes, a Pittsylvania veteran and pensioner, was admitted in 1869 with "all the symptoms of cerebro-spinal disease," because of which he "had several fits and died." Sykes's widow connected the illness to his "exposure in the war between the states" when, in her successful pension application, she linked his military service to his admission to Western State and his death.[28] To the asylum staff, William Tredway's postwar life of debauchery had caused his "Paresis," an ailment characterized by "enlarged pupil of right eye, complete paralysis of tongue, and very considerable paralysis of lower extremities, all accompanied with complete imbecility." (He may have had a stroke, or perhaps he was suffering from tertiary-stage syphilis.) After several months in a stupor, Tredway died.[29]

For some patients admitted to the asylum from veteran families, heredity or previous mental illness were seen as more significant causative factors than the war. Genealogy played a primary explicative role for asylum doctors in 5 percent of the cases in the overall sample. The doctors at the asylum knew that mental illness ran in families, and they always asked about the mental-health background of patients' family members. When they found out that Samuel Davis had "two brothers insane, one in this asylum now" as well as "2 first cousins & one second cousin insane," they believed they had also found the cause of Davis's suicidal tendencies. They also knew that when close blood relatives produced offspring, those children were more likely to have mental and physical problems. Typically, a notation of "father & mother are third cousins" or "father and mother 1st cousins" served as all the explanation of cause that the asylum staff needed.[30]

In a few cases (4 percent of the sample), however, people who had shown signs of mental illness or who had actually spent time in the asylum and had been released before 1860 were admitted to the asylum after 1860 with diagnoses linked to the Civil War. In other words, although these men and women, having already been committed to the asylum or exhibited such symptoms, were certainly more likely to end up at Western State than the average Virginian, they might not have gone to the asylum (again) without the push of some highly stressful event or series of events, such as the Civil War. Not surprisingly, the act of conscription into the army seems to have been a key traumatic event for some of Western State's returning patients. James Burruss suffered from mental "attacks" in 1848 and 1849, but he had been fine since then, until "the calling out of the militia by Gov. Letcher." Of course, it was not just men being conscripted who were readmitted to the institution in this way. Women who were in asylums before the war were also readmitted partly based on diagnoses linked to the conflict. Catherine Nicholson spent time "in the Philadelphia Asylum" in 1859, and she entered Western State in 1862 for maniacal behavior when her husband went off to serve in the Confederate Army.[31]

Finally, for some patients at Western State, the records fail to reveal the reason for their commitment. For example, Cynthia Ann Gray, the wife of a Pittsylvania veteran, was admitted in September 1878 without any mental explanation, and she stayed at Western State for close to thirty years. She occasionally had problems with "tonsilitis of a grave character" and a "bronchial disturbance" but no apparent mental difficulties. Perhaps life in the postwar world was too stressful for Gray, or perhaps she suffered some specific problem. Without more information, we cannot say more about Gray or others like her.[32]

Of course, not everyone with apparent psychological problems was sent to an insane asylum. Relatives (and occasionally neighbors) usually attempted to care for family members with psychological disorders at home. These mental problems could result in demands on the ill person's relatives and friends ranging from just tolerating someone who had minor behavioral quirks to caring for someone who required constant care, attention, and supervision.

Commitment to Western State or other asylums occurred most often when families (or communities) found themselves unable to deal with the behavior of the mentally disturbed individual. Sometimes the problem was something as simple as the person's not staying at home, making it impossible to care for him or her. Mary Woodell's friends watched over her after her husband died and while her sons were absent in the Confederate Army, until one son deserted to the Union. Woodell "became much more unmanageable & requiring a greater degree of vigilence on the part of her friends to prevent her from going off after her son." Unable to care for her themselves and without any family to send her to, her friends had her committed to Western State.[33]

For some veteran family members, their commitment resulted from a perception that they were dangerous to others or to themselves. Marcellus Cousins attempted to "commit violence to the Negro." Simon Hornsberger threatened his family members with "violen[ce] when excited. On one occasion knocked down his brother." Edward Newcomb tried to hang himself, and his admission report indicated, "he had to be constantly watched and occasionally tied to prevent suicide." Catherine Bailey "attempted violence to her self several times" before her admission to the asylum. Under such conditions, the family and friends of these people could hardly be expected to take care of them.[34]

Sometimes when veteran family members showed signs of mental illness, their relatives attempted to care for them, until something happened that forced the relatives to acknowledge that they could not do so. After several months of depression and mental instability during which Polly Shank was cared for by her family, she "attempted suicide by hanging." Her family realized that they could not care for her any longer and sent her to Western State. Samuel Davis's family went through a similar experience. Davis showed signs of mental illness for six months—"manifested in his neglecting his business & talking religion"—but his family cared for him at home until he "attempted suicide … by taking Hydrat Chloral [chloral hydrate]." After that incident, he too went to the asylum.[35]

Some people admitted to the Western Lunatic Asylum had not wandered off and had not attempted to hurt themselves or others, but their families and communities still had them committed. One of those people was Elizabeth Ann Pittman. She suffered from "religious melancholia" for over a year (stemming from her son's wartime capture as a prisoner) before she arrived at Western State. Unlike in the other cases discussed, she does not seem to have been a danger to herself or others. So then, why was she committed? One possible clue lies in a comment she made just before she was released; she explained "that when at home she [had] never permitted her children to get out of her sight." She apparently became excited and frantic when they did not stay nearby, behavior that was impractical in the extreme for her children. It may have been this problem that drove her family to have her brought to the asylum. The commitment of Pittman—and other seemingly harmless but mentally disturbed people like her—to Western State may have happened because their families and communities had grown tired of caring for them or perhaps believed that the state mental institution could cure them.[36]

Diagnoses and Individual Results

The first step in any possible cure of veteran family patients was the initial formal diagnosis made by the medical staff at Western State. In order to make such a diagnosis properly, the doctors talked to the people who brought the new patient to the asylum or to the family and friends who sometimes came to visit loved ones soon after they arrived. Occasionally an interested party would write a letter to the asylum staff giving helpful background regarding the patient's mental condition. The significance of such information in the staff's psychological diagnoses should not be underestimated, because a lack of information could mean a faulty assessment of what was wrong with the patient. (Asylum doctors diagnosed Marcellus Cousins as delusional—"he imagines that he has a suit in court"—and treated him as such. As it turned out, however, Cousins did have a lawsuit in the courts back home.) Western Lunatic Asylum's staff members made the best possible assessments of their patients' mental condition, given the amount and quality of background information they received and the state of the mental-health profession in the second half of the nineteenth century.[37]

Although the nineteenth century was a time of change for the system of diagnosing psychological disorders, the diagnoses made at Western State for most of the patients in the sample came from the long-used three-part classification of insanity into "mania," "melancholia," or "dementia." Occasionally variations on these three diagnoses were used (such as "delusional" or "idiotic"), but the development of the complex and more sophisticated *Diagnostic and Statistical Manual* (*DSM*) grew out of the work of twentieth-century psychiatrists. For the most part, the staff at the Western Lunatic Asylum classified patients by this significantly simplified nosology.[38]

"Mania" was the most common medical diagnosis both for Pittsylvania-Danville veterans and their families and for the men and women admitted to Western State from other areas because of "The War."[39] Of the patients in the sample group whose diagnosis could be identified, 72 percent were placed in the "manic" category. When the staff diagnosed someone as being "manic" or suffering from "mania" or exhibiting "maniacal behavior," they meant that the patient seemed overexcited or overly talkative, was unable to keep still or quiet, and often suffered from insomnia or perhaps violent episodes. The medical staff often characterized William Granville Gray's mental status as "restlessness & impatience." Polly Shank's chart notes that she entered the hospital in an "excited" state and unable to sleep. Asylum doctors diagnosed Charles White as "maniacal" shortly after his arrival, pointing to his "restlessness, excitement, needless trading, loquaciousness, [and] unreasonable demands." The diagnosis seemed confirmed when, soon after the initial assessment, White "tore up his bed & part of his clothing" and could not fall asleep for several nights. Of course, maniacal behavior varied in its intensity from patient to patient, and the severity of some patients' mania varied over time.[40]

Often a patient's maniacal behavior was linked to some specific topic or issue. Not surprisingly, during and after the Civil War, discussion of the conflict or the state of the nation or even just a mention of politics could set off some patients. The staff noted that Adam Thompson became "much excited when the condition of the country is spoken of in his hearing." Thompson's sensitivity to that topic and the mentioning of it by others resulted in this notation in his medical chart: "Several times violent during stay in the hospital."[41]

Doctors also diagnosed about 9 percent of those admitted to Western State as "delusional," referring to the fantastic, improbable, or just inaccurate claims that these patients made. Benjamin Carder believed toward the end of the war that God had appointed him to talk to the president of the United States and finish the war by his fighting a champion appointed by Lincoln. If "Abe" did not accept his proposal, then Carder believed that he could end the war simply by preaching to the Union troops. Richard Moran thought that he was "just a skin stretched tight upon bones" and did not think he "weighed more than ten pounds." William Herndon believed at various times that he was "Adam, Christ, Lincoln, King, generalissimo" and that he had "squadrons of flying horse, infinite sums of money, won great battles." The staff said that he remained unaware of people around him and that he "holds conversations with the absent and dead."[42]

Herndon was far from alone in having delusions of wealth. J. Hampden Chamberlayne claimed that he was "very wealthy" despite being "little less than a pauper." A number of patients admitted to the asylum during and after the Civil War had severe financial problems. In that context, it is not surprising that Herndon, Chamberlayne, and others wanted to believe that they had "infinite sums of money." Their impoverishment was clearly a factor in such delusions.[43]

Delusions could also be accompanied by paranoia. William Herndon, "King" and "generalissimo," constantly informed the staff that he "suspects there is poison in the food." To be fair to Herndon's paranoid delusions, about fifteen years later there was an incident at Western State in which eight patients were poisoned. Herndon was not one of them, having died from heart disease long before.⁴⁴

Not all the patients admitted suffered from delusions or mania. About 11 percent of the veterans and veteran family members admitted to the asylum were diagnosed as having "melancholy" or "melancholia," what today might be called depression. The description given of Louisa Powell's "case of melancholia" is typical: "A striking feature of [her case] is an unwillingness to converse, a dislike to changing her clothes & an utter disregard to cleanliness of personal habits." Other patients, diagnosed as "melancholic" and in a "stupor," just sat and stared. Patients such as Powell kept to themselves, not participating (willingly or not) in the world around them.⁴⁵

Some 9 percent of the patients in the sample also suffered from "dementia," a confused state characterized by significantly disordered mental processing. Mary Calfee's "symptoms indicate[d] dementia." Her doctors thought she was "harmless & quiet, except occasionally also indulges in fits of laughter." In making a diagnosis of William Granville Gray at his second admission after the fall of Richmond, his doctor noted, "He is now perfectly demented.... The characteristics of his present state is confusion of ideas."⁴⁶

Why were so many patients diagnosed with mania (72 percent of identifiable classifications)? The asylum generally dealt with mentally ill people whose loved ones could not adequately take care of, or control, them. The ability of family members and friends to deal with a mentally ill person would have been directly related to that person's behavior. Logically, since maniacal behavior often included wandering around, restlessness, insomnia, and even violent or self-destructive behavior, and since it was more possible to provide at least minimum care in the home for someone suffering from depression or even dementia, more of the cases admitted to the asylum should have been those with symptoms of mania.

Beyond formal diagnoses, many Virginians at the time thought that the Civil War and its aftermath caused postwar mental illnesses, and clearly the staff members of the asylum saw a significant impact of the war on many of the Virginians who came through their doors. First, Western State doctors obviously believed that military service had affected the mental status of some of the men who fought for the Confederacy, because they made that causation explicit. In admitting a patient in September 1865, after discussing symptoms that included "indecision, loss of energy, ... causeless fear," the doctor who was recording information added, "Was, of course, a soldier." Second, fifty-seven men and women were admitted to the asylum with "The War" listed as the cause for their mental difficulties.⁴⁷

We should, however, be skeptical of these diagnoses, which are the product of a mid- to late-nineteenth-century medical world often still using a diagnostic system and treatment protocol for mental illness that is extremely different from that of the early twenty-first century. These differences also mean that any discussion of mental disorders in the past must be cautious about applying present-day psychological concepts to people in the past, especially when using brief and cryptic nineteenth-century medical charts.[48]

That caution, however, should not prevent us from analyzing the beliefs about madness and the war at the time or from using current knowledge—some gained from the traumatic effects of the wars of the twentieth century—to help understand those people seemingly most disturbed by the Civil War. Skepticism and caution do not preclude acknowledging the significant impact on these patients' mental health of the economic, political, familial, and medical stresses and demands related to the massive conflict and the postwar Reconstruction.

One use of current knowledge suggests the possibility of post-traumatic stress disorder (PTSD) among Civil War soldiers. Eric Dean's 1997 book, *Shook Over Hell*, focuses on the psychological impact of the Civil War viewed through a group of Northern veterans in mental institutions. Dean comes to the conclusion that many of the men in his sample suffered from long-term psychological effects of the war in ways similar to the condition now known as PTSD, but they also suffered from short-term responses to traumatic events seen in wartime diagnoses of "combat fatigue," "shell shock," and "irritable heart." It is possible to take the criteria for PTSD and examine the symptoms of the veterans admitted to Western State for matches. Although not definitive, such an exploration need not conclude absolutely that these men had PTSD. After all, the attempt simply illuminates one more aspect of the impact of the war on Confederate veterans and their families.[49]

One set of criteria for PTSD begins with "an event outside the range of usual human experience that would be markedly distressing to almost anyone." It is not much of a stretch to describe the experiences of most Civil War soldiers as "markedly distressing." The other symptoms of this "delayed-stress disorder" include fear, sometimes to the point of paranoia, sometimes of tragedy; insomnia, from anxiety, recurring nightmares, or physical ailments; depression; isolation and detachment from people; "difficulty concentrating"; apathy or "markedly diminished interest in significant activities"; anxiety, as "irritable heart" or "soldier's heart," irritability, or violence; and "duration of at least one month."[50]

There were several veteran patients at Western State who exhibited a number of symptoms of PTSD. In the 1880s, William Tredway over "some 3 or 4 years, developed symptoms of insanity, such as impatience, fretfulness, violence of temper, & loss of mental power." In 1896, the asylum admitted William H. White and explicitly linked his mental troubles to the war in ways that seem indicative of PTSD: "Ever since 1863 has been a little irregular in his mental condition though of late the attacks have been more marked though until recently has been able to discharge his duties as cashier of a Bank. He used to call his attacks the 'Blue Devils'[;] has shown no tendency to do others any harm. Evidences of insanity are that he thinks people are plotting against him to injure him & is noisy & quarrelsome." Of course, the diagnosis of PTSD or any mental disorder in people long dead is problematic, but it seems likely that these men had some kind of stress disorder at least partly brought on by the war.[51]

Regardless of the origins of these patients' mental problems, eventually they left the asylum. The goal of nineteenth-century asylums was to cure or care for the mentally ill, but veterans and veteran family members who were patients at Western State left in three ways: they ran away from the asylum; they improved enough that the asylum released them to return—temporarily or permanently—to their families and friends; or they died at the asylum.

About 14 percent of the patients whose fate could be identified attempted escape, all men. Some veterans tried to leave Western State because they saw it as a "slaughter pen" or just wanted some time away, and others ran away from the asylum out of a perceived need to help out their families financially. Richard Moran told asylum physicians that he wanted to go home to his family and that he was "man enough to go into the woods and maul rails." Even suffering from delusions, Moran (and other mentally ill men) felt the tug of masculine duty to support his family. Although female patients also felt the pull of family and the need to get back to those families—for example, Mary Woodell's willingness to work with the staff "to get well & return to her children"—they apparently did not attempt to escape.[52]

A few patients—two of eight escapees from the sample group—managed to evade recapture. For these patients, their time at Western State ended with their escape. For most other residents of the asylum, however, leaving the asylum meant either improving enough to be released or dying.

About 64 percent of the sample patients' mental conditions improved to the point that the medical staff believed they could be discharged. Four months after being admitted to the asylum in an excited state, John Kerlin "improved sufficiently to be moved to the 4th floor [for relatively calm patients] and put to work." One month later, Kerlin's "mother came to see him ... & took him home" with the physician's approval. The final entry in Charles White's file indicates his dramatic improvement from the maniacal patient he had been at admittance: "Discharged. Has become perfectly tranquil, and rational in his conversation and conduct. Has gained flesh considerably." White returned to his wife and two children and job as a clerk after six months.[53]

Even some of the patients who attempted to flee Western State eventually improved from the perspective of the asylum's medical staff and received discharges. Joseph Noel, who had escaped to return to his unit and who then came back to the asylum after the war, spent almost a year with no apparent improvement, until over a four-month period he "began to improve ... & is now orderly and industrious." About two months later, the asylum released him. James Burruss, who escaped so many times that the staff drugged him, began to improve after three months (and a couple more escape attempts), "his excitement ... considerably abated." Six weeks later, Burruss was released because he "behaved sanely."[54]

Occasionally a patient seems to have recovered but was not released. Initially emaciated and delusional, Maria Harris improved after about six months but was not released for two more years. Perhaps the initial recovery turned out to be temporary and the physicians simply failed to record her relapse, or perhaps they initially believed Harris's children could not care for her at her advanced age of seventy-one. Eventually though, the asylum discharged Harris to her son and daughter as being "much improved."[55]

Some patients improved to an extent that the medical staff believed they could be temporarily released to their friends and family although not completely discharged. Normally these "furloughs" lasted about one or two months and often served as trial runs at home. Polly Shank's delusions and depression faded after four months at the asylum, and she "work[ed] about the [asylum]." Soon after, the assistant physician recorded that she was sent "home to day on furlough." Shank's husband, a veteran, came to the asylum about two months later and "report[ed] his wife industrious, cheerful, sociable, in good bodily health & free from delusions." For many of the patients on furlough, the time among friends and family suited them and improved their mental status. For Mr. Shank and the couple's six children, Western State had apparently restored their wife and mother to them. Patients such as Elizabeth Pittman believed that home was what they really needed to feel better. She told asylum physicians that "she was confident that they [her delusions] would [go away] as soon as she reached home. Is very anxious to go home." Pittman received her furlough and went home, where she apparently thrived. Western State officially discharged her seven weeks after she left.[56]

The asylum often officially discharged patients such as Shank and Pittman after doctors received a letter or a visit from friends and family indicating that their loved one was doing well at home. Mary Bird received her discharge from Western State after a three-month furlough when her father wrote indicating that Bird seemed "now better physically and mentally than at any period.... [She] is cheerful & has quite a zest for social enjoyments." In other cases, the furloughed patient's doctor at home wrote to the asylum explaining that he had examined the patient and declared him or her sane (at least sane enough to stay with family). About ten weeks after Samuel Davis went on furlough, Western State "discharged [him] as cured" based "on [the] certificate of Dr. B. D. Downey, Boydsville, Pittsylvania."[57]

Sometimes, however, the furloughs did not seem to work out or help the patients. After fifteen months at Western State, Gertrude Handy was "taken home by father on visit. Has not evinced the slightest interest in the visit." Five weeks later, she "returned in same condition." The furlough had not changed her mental status at all. James Millner had a similar experience. He "went home with his son on furlough. [R]emained about a month & was brought back unimproved."[58]

If discharging patients is any indication of success, then Western State and other asylums did their job. Western State discharged 64 percent of the sample group, more than double the rate found by Peter McCandless in his study of the State Asylum of South Carolina during the Reconstruction era (31 percent). According to Gerald Grob's survey of institutions from Massachusetts, New York, and California in the mid- to late nineteenth century, it was common for asylums to discharge most patients after three to nine months. The people in the Western State sample followed a similar pattern, with over half of them released after a stay of a year or less and with the most common length of stay at three months. Whether or not these discharged patients had actually been cured is much more difficult to assess, but the fact that most patients (over 75 percent) did not return after being released is a factor in the asylum's favor.[59]

Still, some discharges reveal the fairly limited expectations of the Western State doctors for their patients' mental recovery. They discharged Mary Woodell after six months, noting, "In a few weeks after admission [she] recovered her spirits, and though weak minded and ignorant, exhibited no delusion or other evidence of disease. Physical state good for her age." Caleb Rector was released after fifteen months of delusions and emaciation with this notation: "Discharged ... a little better." Neither case leaves the impression that "discharged" from Western State meant "cured."[60]

The third way that people left Western State was by dying. Sixteen people in the sample died in the asylum (almost 28 percent of patients whose fate it was possible to identify). Some of the patients who died at Western State apparently expired with a much-improved mental state as compared to their admission. The staff treated James Langhorne's mania with varying doses of morphine for two months. Eventually the staff noted that the young former POW had become "composed," but at the same time his health had become "very feeble." About three months later, Langhorne died, having been rational for the last quarter year of his life. After ten weeks at Western State, Catherine Bailey seemed to be getting better. The assistant physician recorded that she "ha[d] been more quiet & composed for last few days; more rational than at anytime since her admission." Unfortunately, her improving mental status was accompanied by a "visibly declining ... Physical health" as well as a loss in "appetite." She took a turn for the worse, dying after only four months at Western State, but "mentally much improved."[61]

The physicians claimed that these patients were getting better mentally, even while their bodies were failing. Closely examined, however, claims of "mentally much improved" for Langhorne and Bailey ring overly optimistic, if not actively deceitful. By making these claims, asylum physicians could argue that they were helping their patients, even if the patients did not live to be discharged. After all, no one was likely to argue with the physicians' assessments of dead patients. To be fair, there is no evidence of any conscious intent to deceive on the part of physicians. Their assessments of the dying may have been accurate, or they may have been overly optimistic claims made by caring men who wanted to believe that they had made some difference in their patients' lives before they died.

Other patients at Western State did not improve mentally and after their admission physically deteriorated until they died. William Granville Gray died of what his doctors labeled "cerebral disease" after ten months of unsuccessful treatment in the asylum. He had "slowly gotten worse. . . . Died this morning while eating his breakfast. His condition has not improved, on the contrary grew worse." Although the asylum had not helped patients such as Gray, many of these deaths were caused by physical ailments unrelated to their mental condition. James Millner spent two years at the asylum with little psychological improvement, but one night he "suddenly fell on the Ward . . . and on examination was found to be paralysed on left side." The fifty-two-year-old veteran, husband, and father failed to recover from his apparent stroke and died two days later.[62]

Despite the stated goal of the asylum to discharge as many patients as possible—or to return them to their families—some patients stayed for decades, often until they died. Since many of these "chronic" patients whose physical and mental health remained the same were passive and rarely caused problems, their medical records often reveal little about them. They apparently passed their days, months, and years like Martha J. Lewis: "Very quiet and well behaved—no mind." Almost ten years after the war (and her husband's death), Lewis entered Western State exhibiting signs of dementia. That entry on her medical chart was only the third of four total entries in a ten-year period of her stay. Four years later, the next and last entry in Lewis's file reads, "Demented. Quiet and nice." She apparently never recovered from her dementia. Randolph Shelton spent over twenty years as a resident of Western State for "masturbation." Admitted in 1868, Shelton actually escaped in 1886 but returned two weeks later after he "visited his friends after an absence of 16 yrs. passed" in the asylum. Shelton stayed at Western State until he died. These two long-term cases at Western State reveal the caretaking role that the asylum played for some patients. Martha Lewis was calm and could have been fairly easily cared for at home; Randolph Shelton (unlike his nephew, Wilson Shelton) does not seem to have been violent or even excited. Patients such as Lewis and Shelton may have had no willing or capable relatives or friends to take care of them.[63]

Another possible factor in these long stays is that by the turn of the century asylums or mental institutions had become seen as the places to which mentally ill people should go and, if necessary, stay until they got better or died. This change often resulted in larger hospitals as people were admitted who previously would have stayed with their families (or perhaps in local jails). Western State fit this pattern, growing in size substantially in the postwar years—from 335 patients in 1870 to 954 in 1900—and the asylum increasingly was treated as a long-term care facility (see table 5.1). The state thus took over a caretaking role that had been predominantly seen as the responsibility of the family.[64]

The Impact of Mental Illness on Veteran Families

Thomas Mathews's medical chart notes that he was admitted to Western State Hospital because he was "disposed to do injury to his family." The dispassionate, clinical tone of one of the asylum's assistant physicians masks what must have been an incredibly emotionally wrenching experience for Mathews's wife and two children. How horrible for a family to have a husband and father act violently toward them, potentially without having any explanation why. Even if not expressed in violence, the mental instability of relatives caused a great deal of pain for family members.[65]

Most cases of insanity placed marriages under some kind of emotional strain. James Burruss wrote to his wife soon after he arrived at Western State; he complained that she never visited him and "charge[d] her with wanting to get rid of him" for his money. Two days after that letter, he sent another one

TABLE 5.1
WESTERN LUNATIC ASYLUM POPULATION, 1870–1900

Year	Number of patients
1870	335
1875	356
1880	479
1885	569
1890	604
1895	737
1900	954

Source: Compiled from Virginia, *Annual Reports of the Board of Directors and of the Superintendent of the Western Lunatic Asylum of Virginia*, 1869–1900.

calling for his "wife to come for him or he will repudiate her &c." Since Burruss was manic, delusional, and quite poor, it seems likely that his wife suffered a great deal from her ill husband's words, although there is no indication that he actually ever repudiated her (or she him). Mental illness was hard on the children of the mentally ill as well. Maria Harris "could not make up her mind whether it was her son or a spirit" who came to visit her at the asylum. It must have been difficult for her son who lived to be mistaken by his mother for his dead brother.[66]

A couple cases illustrate the important role that mothers played in taking care of mentally ill adult sons. Ham Chamberlayne's mother tried to get him to work after the war, but when it was clear that he suffered from psychological problems, she sent him to the asylum. John Kerlin's mother came to Western State to pick up and take home her son, no longer maniacal but still "delicate" and needing her attention. Although Kerlin's and Chamberlayne's mothers clearly felt emotional ties to their sons, a part of their concerns probably came from the women's dependence on their sons for financial support.[67]

The time spent by veterans in the asylum itself could have a significant financial impact on dependent family members. Married with several children, James Elliott was "a[n agricultural] laborer without property" who suffered from "great poverty and deficient physical ability." The fifteen months he spent away from Pittsylvania County and his family could not have helped the family's financial situation. Benjamin Carder was the sole financial provider for his poor mother, a blind sister, and a widowed sister with five children. The stress of his position probably brought about his mental trouble, but the time spent at the asylum almost certainly worsened his family's financial status.[68]

Not only did the family of an asylum inmate lose that person's labor and financial support, but it was also expected to pay part of the cost of keeping the person at the asylum. According to the section of the 1871 code of Virginia dealing with "Lunatics," the patient's estate, the patient's parents, or the cured patient were supposed to pay the costs of transporting the person to and from the asylum, as well as "his [or her] maintenance and care" once there. Fortunately for these families, the directors of the asylum could decide at "their discretion, [to] release the whole or any part of any claim of such asylum ... for the expenses attending the removal, maintenance or care of a lunatic, if he have a family dependent on his estate for support ... or if in their opinion, it be just and equitable, that the said claim should be so released." In this way, the state of Virginia directly took on a financial burden that families were responsible for but that not all could shoulder.[69]

Families who had men at the asylum faced practically the same problem in the loss of those men as families whose men did not come home at all from the war, but with some important differences. First, if a husband or father was committed to an asylum, his property (the family's property) came under the control of a court appointed "committee," not the female household head. Second, it was difficult (although possible) to get a pension for mental illness, but no one in state institutions such as the asylum could receive one (on the theory that the state already picked up the tab for his care). Finally, the family member was not actually dead but was at the insane asylum, a fact that most people in the home communities knew.[70]

William Miller spent time at Western State, but his father came and took him home for about twenty months. In justifying his veteran son's return to the asylum, his father explained that William "ha[d] not been considered altogether sane during stay at home." It is possible to speculate what "not [being] considered altogether sane" meant for William Miller and his family within their community. The perception of the asylum patients (and their families) in their community before, during, and after their time in the asylum was probably a strain on these families because of the social stigma attached to mental illness. That stigma may also have undermined a family's chance at economic support from the community (especially when that community took into account the cause of the family's financial need).[71]

Although a veteran physically wounded in service to the Confederate cause would have been recognized as a hero—or at least given the benefit of the doubt by many members of the community—the same would not have applied to the insane. Most Americans (much as now) did not understand the causes of insanity and found the mentally ill disturbing. At least some members of communities would have been uncomfortable being around people with psychological problems, even those who had served and sacrificed during the war. Some of those feelings probably shaped the community's reactions to the family and friends of the mentally disturbed.

As a result of this stigma, some people found themselves embarrassed by their insane relatives and associates. In the early 1880s, William Tredway, Jr., a prominent Pittsylvania veteran and lawyer, began to display "impatience, fretfulness, violence of temper, & loss of mental power." For a number of years, Tredway had shared a legal practice in Chatham with Langhorne Scruggs, but Scruggs broke it off in early 1884, only months before Tredway was sent to the Western Lunatic Asylum. Starting in April 1884, Scruggs, in continuing to use the stationery from the partnership, scratched out Tredway's name wherever it appeared. The marking out of Tredway's name may have been nothing more than a practical result of the breakup of their partnership (and not wanting to waste stationery), but the scratching out and the ending of the partnership together at least partly reflected Scruggs's attempt to distance himself from a man whose behavior had become increasingly erratic.[72]

Such feelings did not necessarily mean that all friends abandoned someone who began to show signs of mental illness. Several of William Granville Gray's friends accompanied him to the asylum. They explained that they had seen "a restlessness & impatience which his friends now consider as evidence of mental disorder." Their friend's behavior had become erratic, but they did not shun him; rather, they took him where they believed he could be helped.[73]

Still, some asylum patients worried about rejection from the community and family. Mary Bird expressed concern, in a letter to her sister a couple of weeks before she was to come home on furlough, over how she would be received by her friends, family, and community: "Sometimes I think I want to come home. Then again when I think how much better all my school mates have grown up I feel as if I did not want to come. I do not think you have forgot me." Bird made clear that she feared some kind of stigma from the community for her time in the asylum. "O that I had never come, that I had striven harder to overcome my bad feelings."[74]

Being related to someone who was mentally disturbed potentially affected a veteran family's financial success. The emotional and psychological impact of the Civil War and Reconstruction on the veterans of Pittsylvania County and Danville and their families could significantly affect postwar veteran families' economic status, as well as their relationships with one another and with their neighbors. From the community's perspective, grief, depression, and maybe even strange behavior among these people would have been understandable, but veteran family members would have been expected by people near them in Pittsylvania County to contribute to their family's economic survival unless physically hurt or weakened in some way. An additional burden for these veteran families with mental issues was that veteran families who suffered in poverty because of the physical, human damage of the war would likely have gotten first priority for financial aid. Although mental illness, whether or not it required commitment to an institution, probably contributed to the failure of some veteran families to support themselves after the war, it would not necessarily have been sufficient to gain them aid.

Trying to assess the value of the Western Lunatic Asylum for veteran families reveals a weakness of using the family as a unit of analysis. Since families consist of individuals, the ability to put a family member in the asylum did not mean the same thing for all members of the family. The most obvious of these different possible perceptions of the impact of being committed involves the difference between the patient and the other family members. In other words, some family members might have believed it was in the best interest of the family and the "ill" individual to commit another member to the asylum, while the person actually spending time at Western State may have felt differently.

It is worth looking at the possible benefits of commitment for both the families and the patients of the asylum. Some people may have been embarrassed or befuddled by their mentally ill family members. To these people, asylums such as Western State might have represented an escape, a way to get rid of a problem. A few commitments may have even had a more sinister aspect, serving as a way to get a particular person out of the way.[75] For most veteran families, however, mentally ill relatives simply turned out to be much more than they could handle, despite some societal expectations that families should care for their own mentally ill members. For these families, the option of a state institution whose avowed purpose was to cure the sick and return them to their homes must have been a sizable load off their shoulders. Even if their relative stayed for decades at the asylum or died soon after arriving, they could tell themselves that the person received care they could not give him or her.

For the patients themselves, it is hard for us to know how they experienced their time in the asylum. For some patients, the structure and order that the staff attempted to impose and the medical explanations and treatments that the doctors offered for their conditions brought a sense of calm to their lives. For others, the strange surroundings, the limits on their freedom, the treatments, and the odd assortment of other people made their time in the asylum traumatic.

Unfortunately, from our distance, in many cases we do not know much more than what the doctor recording William Tredway's case file tells us: "Does not suffer in slightest degree apparently. Takes nourishment regularly." That "apparently" is significant, but it is about all we have to go on for some patients.[76]

We do know, however, that some veterans and veteran family members recovered and continued to have "normal" lives after their time at Western State. Polly Shank seems to have been happy back with her family after her time as a patient. J. Hampden Chamberlayne went on to have fourteen fairly successful years of post-asylum life as a journalist and editor.[77]

Although not all the people discussed in this chapter may have had mental problems directly related to the war—at least from our perspective—almost all of them were admitted with problems that physicians attributed, in whole or part, to the Civil War or its aftermath. Even if ascertaining what proportion of the inmates of the asylum was actually there because of the war is difficult, certainly as a whole the residents reflected some measure of the war's damage.

These asylum records also provide insight into more than just those people judged mentally ill by their day's standards. The war and its psychological impact affected all Virginians and all veteran families. The issues cited by patients and doctors in these accounts were issues that many Southerners faced in the postbellum period. One Western State inmate was certainly not alone among veterans when he told the asylum staff that they "cant cure conscience & that is all that is the matter with [my] mind." Certainly, not everyone reacted to the war and its aftermath with such force that friends, family, and neighbors had the person committed to an asylum, but the tales of depression and violence seen in men and women across the South in the postwar period indicate that Southerners paid a significant psychological and emotional toll.[78]

Western State and other asylums were part of a postwar system in which the state took on more responsibilities in light of the failure of families to carry burdens that traditionally had been theirs to carry. Although not always successful, Western State Hospital helped some veterans or veteran family members reintegrate into society after the war or cared for those unable to do so. The state of Virginia thereby provided an important service to some of its most needy residents.

6

State Aid for Veteran Families

Artificial Limbs, Commutations, Pensions, and Confederate Homes

> He was discharged from the army . . . and has been a very delicate man ever since.
>
> —Dr. W. A. Brumfield, in John C. McHaney's 1905 pension application

IN AN 1895 application for a pension, Confederate veteran W. H. Power attempted to explain how wartime wounds to his right arm and leg had affected him: "there are many things I can't do now, that I am prevented from doing by the lameness which are necessary and which I used to do in laboring."[1] In the aftermath of the Civil War, many of Virginia's veterans and their families needed help. Some of that help came from relatives, friends, churches, or local members of the elite. Veterans and their families who needed more than those groups could provide them turned to the state of Virginia for additional assistance. Whereas the last chapter addressed the mental legacy of the war, this chapter explores the physical impact of the war and aging on veteran households and the ways, often financial, by which the state addressed the effective loss of many veteran families' ability to engage in manual labor. Though the aid served political and racial purposes, it responded to the needs of these veteran families in the decades after the war.

Through a series of postwar acts passed by Virginia's General Assembly, the state built on its wartime relief efforts to provide financially for the soldiers and families who had most severely borne the burden of the Civil War. It began in a limited way with aid for amputees, those survivors most physically harmed by the war. Over time, Virginia legislators widened the scope of financial assistance to include all veterans disabled by war, women widowed by war, veterans disabled by age, and widows whose veteran husbands died after the war. Eventually, Virginia provided homes for elderly and disabled veterans, veteran widows, and even veteran daughters. In doing so, the state of Virginia created a limited social-welfare system where one had not existed before, albeit only for white, "worthy" veterans and their families.

Most of the historical scholarship on Civil War pensions and homes has focused on the North and on the extensive financial and other aid offered to Union soldiers.[2] In recent years, however, several scholars have begun to examine Confederate pensions, as well as the creation of homes for Confederate soldiers and widows.[3] Still, there is work to be done in this area, most notably in placing damaged veteran families at the center of the story of increasing state involvement.

Although aid to Confederate veterans started immediately after the war in the form of artificial limbs and the one-time monetary payments known as commutations, the most significant expansion in Virginia came in the post-Reconstruction, post-Readjuster period of political turmoil often associated with the rise of the Lost Cause movement. Pensions and homes built on earlier attempts to address the demographic hole left in soldiers' families by the war and allowed white Conservative Democratic leaders to celebrate Confederate veterans and their families and to create a faint reflection of the robust federal system of veteran aid, all while funneling limited state financial aid toward whites.[4] Many veteran families took advantage of the state-based aid offered after the war in the form of artificial limbs, commutations, pensions, and homes for veterans and their widows. This veteran-specific assistance and the process of applying for it responded to and reinforced the legacy of the Civil War as the central event in the lives of many of Virginia's veteran families; this was especially true if one's last days were spent in a home built for participants in "The War." For most veterans and widows, the financial benefits supplemented, rather than replaced, the networks of family and local support discussed in earlier chapters. Still, the state's assistance was badly needed, avidly sought, and gratefully welcomed by veterans and their families.

The Laws

Wartime wounds hampered many former soldiers as they aged: the aches and pains, the twinge in a poorly healed knee or a stiff arm, the scars left by bullet holes and shell fragments, reminded veterans of the sacrifices they had made in their failed cause. Other veterans, weakened by diseases caught during their time in the army, died sooner than they would have or, in their weakened condition, attempted with great difficulty to eke out a living as they got older.

Some ex-soldiers worked with destroyed or amputated limbs, with damaged eyes or empty eye sockets. Families whose soldiers did not come back struggled on without them. Like other former Confederate states and the federal government, Virginia took steps to offer its veterans and their families some financial help to deal with the human damage done by the war.

As Virginia's aid to Confederate veteran families expanded from artificial limbs to commutations to pensions to homes for elderly veterans and widows, the state's goals become clear. From the end of the war, the state was most interested in helping those veteran families whose men had lost the ability to engage in manual labor. Practically, that meant procuring artificial limbs or money for the men most physically damaged, but eventually the state recognized the losses of veteran widows as well. Though pensions for widows and disabled veterans offered more regular funding, income and wealth limits reveal legislators' desire to respond to the neediest of veteran families and not to create a general fund for all Confederates. The number of people made eligible for pensions expanded as aging further reduced veterans' ability to engage in manual labor and widows' ability to subsist. State assistance (as money or care in state homes) lightened veteran families' burdens, increasingly providing functions of financial support and caretaking previously the bailiwick of familial households.

Artificial Limbs and Commutations

Postwar public discussion of assisting the state's maimed veterans in Virginia began with Governor Francis Pierpont's 1866 call to the General Assembly to provide artificial limbs to Virginia veterans who had lost an arm or leg during the war. Pierpont argued that by providing amputees with the means to work, the state of Virginia would not have to support these men for the rest of their lives. The General Assembly passed an artificial-limb law on January 29, 1867, setting aside $20,000 to provide replacement limbs to eligible veterans and "every citizen of this commonwealth who has lost a limb in the late war." Though not the panacea that Pierpont had hoped, this law became the first of more than twenty laws concerning artificial limbs for veterans that the Virginia legislature passed before 1894.[5]

The 1867 law also created a Board of Commissioners to control the application and distribution process for claims. Based in the county courts, this procedure became the standard routine for applying to the state for veteran claims. Men who believed they were eligible for a disbursement would go to their local county or corporation (city) court to be certified. They could bring witnesses who would testify to their current condition, their Virginia residency, and the circumstances that had led to their loss of limb or disability. Their certified claim would be sent to the Auditor's Office in Richmond for final approval.[6]

Despite the legislature's apparent belief that the initial appropriation would be more than enough—the 1867 act read, "if so much is required"—$20,000 proved inadequate to meet the needs of all Virginia's wartime amputees. Between 1870 and 1886, the General Assembly repeatedly passed new artificial-limb appropriations totaling $343,000 in a series of attempts to try to meet the ongoing demands of the state's disabled veterans. The appropriations were clearly insufficient to satisfy all the applications; several of the acts specifically mentioned applicants who had been approved but had not yet been paid. The appropriations failed to meet the growing demands from applicants in large part because of the gradually expanding number of people eligible to receive state aid. Starting in 1872, Virginia's General Assembly passed laws providing for commutations, one-time financial payments. Initially the commutations were offered to veterans with amputations whose artificial limbs did not fit or work properly, but later acts allowed commutations for veterans whose limbs had been permanently disabled or paralyzed, even if they had not been amputated.[7]

As historian Jennifer Davis McDaid has pointed out, during the war many soldiers had received "resections," surgery aimed at preventing amputation by removing damaged bones or bone fragments and resealing wounds. Although this procedure often saved the soldier's life, unfortunately it also usually resulted in the limb's "withering" away, leaving it virtually useless to the veteran. Pittsylvanian Joseph Boyd later complained that after being wounded by a "minnie ball shot through [his] left arm," the Confederate surgeons had performed one of these resections, "rendering [his] arm useless [and] causing ... paralysis." Men such as Boyd needed something other than artificial limbs.[8]

Following the logic behind artificial-limb legislation as proposed by Governor Pierpont, in 1876 the state linked commutations with the ability of veterans to work. The law offered $60 to any Virginia veteran whose wartime wounds "prevent the use of his limbs in manual labor." The commutation was "in lieu of the [artificial] limb heretofore provided by law." An 1882 act extended eligibility for commutation to all veterans permanently "disabled from performance of manual labor, induced by [their wartime] wounds" and not just to those who had lost the use of their limb(s). The ability of an applicant to perform manual labor proved to be the essential determinant for the success or failure of a commutation claim.[9]

One group that benefited during the 1880s from Virginia's developing commutation laws, albeit in limited ways, was the families of veterans. In March

1880, the General Assembly passed a special act granting commutation money for Josephine Robinson, a Culpeper County woman whose husband died after he had applied for an artificial arm or commutation. For the first time, the state addressed (however cursorily) the issue of veterans' families, and a widow received compensation for her husband's wartime wounds. Interestingly, however, Robinson received only $40, when the standard commutation by this time was $60. In 1886, the state of Virginia specifically codified the procedure to be followed in cases like Josephine Robinson's. If a veteran died after successfully applying for a commutation, then his widow (if alive) would receive the money. If his widow had also died, his children would be the recipients. Implicit in these acts lies an ironic acceptance that widows and families should get the commutation if their husbands or fathers had been disabled and successfully applied for it, but families whose male household head had died during the war got nothing. Either this was a case of following the letter of the artificial-limb laws, without following the spirit, or the legislators saw the spirit of the law differently from the Northern perspective that government had a responsibility to help support both wounded veterans and family members of soldiers who never made it home. Not until the 1888 Pension Act did Virginia eliminate this distinction and recognize the need for financial support of widows whose husbands had died during the war.[10]

Although the basic procedure set down in the first artificial-limb act of 1867 remained largely the same—applicants went to their local county or corporation (city) court to be certified, and their certified claim was sent to the state Auditor of Public Accounts for final approval—as more and more legislation appeared, getting an artificial limb or commutation generally became more complex. By 1884, applicants such as Danville's Joseph T. Miller had to testify under oath, had to prove that they were Virginia citizens and that their Confederate military service caused the loss of their limb or their permanent total disability, and had to provide "a certificate of a competent physician." An 1887 law added more medical supervision by creating in each county or city a "board of [three] competent physicians" to examine the local applicants. In addition to previous requirements, an applicant had to prove "that he [was] dependent on his physical labor for the means of subsistence." In adding this requirement, the General Assembly made three things clear. First, it reemphasized the notion that these artificial-limb and commutation laws were linked with the ability of Virginia's ex-soldiers to work; this money was supposed to help veterans who could not work. Second, the General Assembly had begun to reduce the number of people eligible for a commutation by effectively allowing to apply only men who had been disabled by wartime service from doing manual labor and those who depended on manual labor to survive. Finally, Virginia linked financial need to commutations, a trend that continued with later pension legislation. This change departed from earlier legislation that allowed people still capable of earning a living without the use of a limb (e.g., lawyers or politicians) to receive commutations from the government. Federal pension legislation of the 1880s did not require this link between need and veterans' benefits. In other words, to be eligible for a commutation in Virginia, a veteran had to be a citizen of the state and had to have been disabled by wounds received while in service, and his disability had to prevent him from supporting himself and his family with manual labor.[11]

The state intended artificial limbs and commutations to be one-time disbursements to its disabled veterans. Indeed, the appropriations of money from 1867 to 1879 attempted to meet the demands of veterans who had received neither artificial limb nor commutation. These acts clearly stated that successful applicants could not have previously received artificial limbs or commutations, thus preventing, for example, a man who had received an artificial limb in 1867 from getting a commutation in 1879 or from getting another commutation after a first one. Starting in 1876, the maximum commutation amount was set at $60 per veteran.[12]

By 1884, however, the General Assembly decided that a need existed among Virginia's disabled veterans for more than $60 or an artificial limb. The appropriations bill passed that year set up two classifications for the Auditor's Office: men who had "never received any aid from the state" would be "a preferred class," and "Class two" would be those who had already received money or an artificial limb from the state. Allowing second commutations for veterans opened the door to multiple and even regular cash payments to those who had borne the battle for Virginia during the Civil War.[13]

Pensions

With artificial-limb and commutation legislation from 1867 to 1887, the Virginia General Assembly had taken steps to provide economically for some of the more disabled veterans and had begun to move toward providing financial assistance to families who had lost their men during the war. It became clear to legislators, however, that some of these veterans and their families (especially widows) needed more than just one or two payments in order to stay out of the poorhouse. In addition, the state found that it needed to help a steadily increasing number of the men who had been "hampered" by their war wounds or weakened by diseases they had caught during their Confederate military service and required financial assistance to survive during their later years. To meet the financial needs of this growing class of veterans and their families, the Virginia General Assembly turned to pensions, annual payments to qualified impoverished applicants.

Pensions made sense for a number of other reasons. Beyond the immediate example of the Union pension system, annual payments had been offered to soldiers and their widows for earlier American conflicts, including the Revolution and the war with Mexico. Another reason, however, lay in the political context of Virginia in the late 1870s and 1880s. Although for much of the 1870s Virginia Conservatives cut funds to state programs such as schools in order to pay off state debts, in the aftermath of the biracial Readjuster movement (1879–83) Democrats saw the need to embrace state social-welfare spending, at least in targeted ways in order to retain white voters. Ultimately, pensions allowed the state to care for an aging, often damaged, needy population of veteran families, to create a system that built on earlier and Union examples, and to embrace the Lost Cause and Confederate memory in racially and politically useful ways.[14]

The Pension Act of 1888 marked both the culmination of the small steps taken with commutations and the beginning of a series of generally expanding pension laws in the commonwealth, laws that worked to assist the most damaged veteran families. The 1888 act provided annual support payments for Virginia's resident veterans who were "maimed or disabled in the war between the states" and for Virginia's widows of soldiers "who lost their lives in said war in the military service." It clearly stated that the benefits were meant only for people that the war had most intimately affected. Only men who had been severely wounded during the war and only widows whose husbands had died during the war could receive these annual benefits. (Not coincidentally, the ongoing resources dedicated to veterans in the 1888 act diverted to "worthy" whites funds that might have otherwise gone to the state's needy black residents or to the public schools had circumstances been different.)[15]

For the first time, legislators also dictated explicit financial poverty qualifications—income less than $300 per year and total personal property valued at less than $1,000—revealing their interest in helping only the neediest veteran families. These income and property maximums were extensions of the 1887 act's requirements that limited benefits to veterans whose injuries prevented them from working. They indicate that in 1888 the General Assembly was most concerned with supporting the state's poor veterans and veteran widows, rather than seeing this bill as a reward for all those who had served Virginia's Confederate military forces or even all those who had been wounded during the Civil War.[16]

The amount of the pension awarded to veterans depended on the severity of their wartime wounds (see table 6.1) and reinforced the linkage between manual labor and veterans' benefits that was made in earlier legislation. Applicants received $60 per year for the loss of two limbs or eyes or for complete and total disability (as determined by the examining doctor), $30 per year for the loss of one limb or eye, and $15 per year for partial disability. The General Assembly defined "total disability" as "such as wholly incapacitates the applicant for manual labor." It explained "partial disability" as "such as incapacitates the applicant for obtaining a livelihood by his manual labor, and to be equivalent to that which would be occasioned by the loss of a limb." The standard of disability equal to "the loss of a limb" caused problems for a number of Pittsylvania and Danville veterans.[17]

The 1888 Pension Act finally recognized the needs of Virginia's women widowed by the Civil War. Widows of veterans could apply for a pension of $30 per year if their husbands had died in service during the war, if they had not remarried, and if they had remained in Virginia. Such widows retained their pensions for as long as they remained unmarried and Virginia residents. Although the new pension legislation included widows, it did nothing for the children who had lost their fathers in the war. Since twenty-three years had passed since the war ended, those children were now adults. According to contemporary understandings of gender roles, the sons were expected to support themselves and the daughters were assumed to be married or engaged, and therefore, neither needed support from the state.[18]

Virginia's requirement that veterans' widows remain unmarried was not unusual. Union widows' pensions had similar requirements (although a remarried Northern woman could still receive lump-sum back payments for money due her from her first soldier husband's death until her remarriage). In fact, until recently, U.S. military widows lost their benefits if they remarried. Although apparently not alone in their perspective, by limiting pensions to widows who remained unmarried, the men in Virginia's General Assembly suggested that the state's responsibility to these women existed only as a surrogate husband (or perhaps as another male family member). If a veteran's widow remarried, then the woman's welfare stopped being the state's responsibility.[19]

Although many Virginians applied for aid under the 1888 Pension Act, not all of them succeeded. If Pittsylvania and Danville were any indication, there were quite a few disallowed pension applications in 1888. Of 313 applicants, 63 were not awarded a pension. Unsuccessful pension applications, not surprisingly, usually failed because they did not meet the requirements set forth by the 1888 act.[20]

TABLE 6.1
VIRGINIA'S MAJOR CIVIL WAR PENSION LAWS

	1888	1900	1902	1912
Veterans				
Two limbs/eyes	$60	$100	$100	$150
Total disability	$60	$30	$30	$36
One limb/eye	$30	$50	$50	$65
Partial disability	$15	$15	$15	$24
Annual income limits	$300	$300	$150	$200
Property limits	$1,000	$1,000	$500	$750[a]
War widows	$30	$40	$40	$40
Postwar widows		$25	$25	$25
Hospital matrons				$40

Source: Virginia, Acts (1887–88): 469–74; (1899–1900): 1257–59, 1261; (1901–2): 472–97; (1912): 385–87.
[a]Except for amputees ($1,000) and veterans over age eighty ($1,500).

The case file of David Shields, whose request for a partially disabled pension failed in 1895 but succeeded in 1897, highlights the important role that one's ability to labor and support a family had in successful veteran pension applications. In 1895, Shields provided a minimum amount of information on his application: he had been wounded in the hand at the battle of Gettysburg. The auditor declared that Shields's wound did "not equal [the] loss of [a] limb." In his 1897 application, Shields testified that the wound had been received in a "charge upon the position of the Federal troops." He also explained in detail the disability under which he now suffered because of his wounded hand. Finally, although initially he wrote that he was disabled "more than half of my time," he scratched that out and replaced it with "I can not do any work." The changes worked, and the Auditor's Office awarded him a partially disabled pension. Shields's case is, of course, not definitive. Other factors may have been at work in his change of luck: political pressure from Pittsylvania's representatives in the General Assembly, different staff in the Auditor's Office, or an official in the right mood. Yet it would be a mistake to overlook the requirement of the inability to work that lay at the heart of Virginia's 1888 Pension Act.[21]

The 1888 Pension Act began a series of expanding and modifying pension laws in Virginia.[22] By the late 1890s, the impact of old age began to take its toll on the state's Confederate veterans and their widows. The restrictions of the

1888 act prevented from getting pensions veterans who were disabled but not by war and widows whose husbands died after the war ended. A number of unsuccessful bills to meet the needs of these two groups of Civil War survivors can be seen in the records of the late 1890s General Assembly. Although these bills failed, a number of special resolutions passed the General Assembly, awarding pensions to individual veterans and widows who had failed to achieve pensions under the 1888 act. In 1899 and early 1900 alone, the Virginia legislators passed 462 of these exceptions that allowed veterans and their families yearly financial support, not just for those suffering from old age but also for those whom the politicians believed to be deserving.[23]

The attempts to expand the pension and the hundreds of special exceptions coming from the General Assembly eventually led to the passage of another major pension bill, the Pension Act of 1900. The special acts previously passed had indicated that the state was gradually increasing the number of veterans and veterans' widows for whom it took responsibility. For example, Elizabeth Hagood, a war widow, received a special act because she was "old, feeble, and penniless." An expanded sense of responsibility for all veterans and their widows—especially as they aged and grew less able to support themselves—shone through in the new act. The Pension Act of 1900 changed the application process by adding a local review board, increased the annual payments made for some pensioners (see table 6.1), and allowed more of the state's veterans and their widows to gain pensions by easing definitions of disability and accepting claims from women widowed since the war.[24]

Although amputees were still considered the most deserving veterans—which can be seen in the difference in pension amounts—many ex-soldiers became eligible as partially or totally disabled, even if they had been unsuccessful applicants before. Reuben F. Hankins had failed in two previous pension applications—in 1894 and 1897—because the Auditor's Office had felt that his injured foot did not equal the loss of a limb. Hankins applied under the Pension Act of 1900 just two months after it passed the General Assembly and succeeded in achieving a partial disability pension of $15. Hankins's application, like many others, shows that the 1900 act moved away from a standard of "equal to loss of limb" and thus allowed a number of veterans to get pensions who had not had access to them before. The 1900 act also made provision for veterans who had "not been wounded, but base[d their] application upon the fact that [they were] disabled from disease and infirmities of age." This change not only recognized the needs of the many veterans made ill or vulnerable to disease by their wartime service but also by eliminating the requirement that an ex-soldier's disability had been caused by his wartime service, it effectively made the state responsible for old age, chronic illness, and postwar injuries.[25]

The 1900 act also allowed those women such as Harriett G. Hodnett from Pittsylvania County whose husbands had died since the war to receive pensions, although they received less money. These postwar widows had to demonstrate more severe financial need by proving that their annual income was not more than $100. (Veterans and widows of soldiers who had died during the war only had to show the court an annual income of less than $300.) As before, all widows had to show that they had remained unmarried since their veteran husband's death.[26]

The Pension Act of 1902 refocused pensions on the neediest of the state's veterans and veteran widows by setting more severe property and income restrictions (see table 6.1) and by further complicating the application process. Applicants could not make more than $150 per year and could not own more than $500 of real and personal property. They also had to bring "at least two disinterested and reputable witnesses" who lived in their city or county, "the affidavits of at least two of [their or their husband's] comrades in arms" to testify to their loyal service, the "certificate of some reputable and practicing physician," and "also the certificate of [approval by] some camp of Confederate veterans" from their county or city.[27]

The 1902 act also redefined what the General Assembly considered worthy Confederate widows. In doing so, the state further limited the applicant pool for the widows of veterans and involved itself in defining veteran households. It denied pensions to widows who had married their husbands after May 1, 1866, and to those who had remarried, divorced, or separated from their veterans. These restrictions suggest that the General Assembly believed that the state's responsibility toward veterans' wives extended only to certain widows and reinforces the perception of the state as a surrogate husband.[28]

The restrictions of the Pension Act of 1902 suggest that Virginia's legislators intended it as an attempt to pull back from the opening up of pensions that had occurred in 1900. The significant widening of eligibility under the 1900 act meant that the number of Virginia's pensioners increased over 300 percent (from 3,475 to 11,601). The 1902 act, with its reduction in property and income maximums, its restrictions for eligible widows, its stress on loyalty, and its warning against giving false or perjurious information, indicates a desire to verify that the over eight thousand new pensioners truly deserved the state's money. Ultimately, the 1902 act failed to restrict significantly the number of existing pensioners, since by 1905 the number of pensioners actually grew to 12,200.

The 1902 act was the only time that a pension law in Virginia restricted—rather than widened—the bounds of eligibility.[29]

Another major pension law in 1912 proved beneficial to Virginia's female Civil War survivors. Most significant to the widows of veterans, especially to women such as Cassandra Burch and Mary Blake, the new act provided pensions for women who had lost a husband to military service, "although [they] may have married again" and then lost that husband as well. Having remarried, both Burch and Blake had been denied pensions before, but the 1912 act allowed re-widowed women to reapply and receive annual pensions as long as they remained unmarried.[30] As part of this 1912 act, Virginia began to offer pensions ($40 per year) to "any woman who served as a matron in a Confederate hospital for a period of twelve months during the war between the States." This provision for hospital matrons did not affect widowed pensioners, however, because the act specifically excluded women "already receiving a pension as the widow of a Confederate soldier."[31]

Other changes in the 1912 act continued to provide important financial help to veteran families and increased the amount of money that the state spent on individuals. Annual pension amounts increased for amputees and disabled veterans, although not for widows. The property and income maximums allowed also increased for all categories of pensioners, including a special property limit for veterans age eighty and over that was double that of disabled veterans or widows. Finally, the state began to pay the funeral expenses of all pensioned veterans.[32]

With all these acts, the General Assembly took steps to provide financially for the soldiers and families who had most severely borne the burden of battle during the Civil War. Later acts continued this trend, though they broadened definitions of eligibility. In 1915, the state implemented a county-level property tax to provide an additional county pension for veterans and widows. Virginia also continued to increase gradually both the amount of pensions and the income and property maximums. The state could afford to increase its spending per veteran or widow or to increase the number of eligible veterans or widows (through raised financial limits or by relaxing the timing restrictions on when a widow had to have married a veteran) or to add new categories of Civil War pensioners (ex-slaves who had worked in the army and unmarried daughters of veterans) because the number of eligible people decreased each year as more of those who had lived through the war died.[33]

Confederate Homes

In April 1883, a group of ex-soldiers in Richmond organized the Robert E. Lee Camp of Confederate Veterans. Part of this group's stated purpose was to build a poorhouse and retirement home for needy and deserving Confederate veterans. After raising funds in both the North and South, the Robert E. Lee Camp Confederate Soldiers' Home opened in Richmond at the start of 1885. Beginning in 1886, the state of Virginia began to give the home yearly financial support in increasing amounts, peaking at $90,000 in 1918. Despite contributions from private citizens and the City of Richmond, by 1904 almost 80 percent of the funding came from the state.[34]

There were many impoverished or disabled Confederate veterans in Virginia in the late nineteenth and early twentieth centuries for whom a commutation or a pension would not have been enough to meet their needs or whose families could (or would) not care for them. As with pensions, however, the need of these veterans was not the sole driving force behind the creation and state support of this home for Confederate veterans. Many of the same factors behind the expansion of the Confederate pensions in the 1880s, 1890s, and 1900s can be seen in the state's support for the home. This first Confederate Soldiers' Home had earlier precedents in Europe and the United States. It imitated the National Homes established for Union veterans, and it grew in part out of the linkage of the Lost Cause, the powerful image of the disabled, Confederate soldier, and the politics of the late-nineteenth-century Southern Democrats. In a speech given at the opening of the home, Col. Archer Anderson reminded the crowd of the sacrifices that Confederate veterans had made, the worthiness of their needs, and the example they set: "wherever the good soldier's service called, there followed and enveloped in him an atmosphere of consecration, of self sacrifice, of a life exalted above the ordinary life of men, of a life which existed only for duty." Finally, the home grew out of an increasing willingness on the part of the state to take over roles traditionally seen as familial.[35]

In 1900, for many of the same reasons, the Home for Needy Confederate Women opened in Richmond. This home was started with the support of a Ladies' Auxiliary to a group of Richmond Confederate veterans, but the state of Virginia soon became involved. An 1898 General Assembly act incorporated an organization that would create and run a "Home for Needy Confederate Women," offering care and a place to stay to a broad range of impoverished female relatives of Confederate soldiers. Though supplemented by aid from other sources, such as the Richmond chapters of the United Daughters of the

Confederacy, the home for Confederate spouses, sisters, and daughters also received significant funds from the state of Virginia.[36]

Taking Advantage of the State's Benefits

According to historian Jennifer Davis McDaid, "By 1894, more than six thousand veterans, either amputees or those otherwise disabled, had received artificial limbs or commutations ... from the commonwealth." In 1890, there were 48,713 Confederate veterans living in Virginia, so roughly 12 percent of those veterans took advantage of commutations or artificial limbs. In 1888, after the first pension law was passed, only 2.4 percent (1,167) of veterans had signed up for the annual payments. By 1900, with the Pension Act of that year widening eligibility, at least 17 percent (8,514) of Virginia's living veterans took advantage of the state's yearly financial assistance.[37]

The Lee Camp Home admitted over three thousand Confederate veterans between 1885 and 1941, more than any other Confederate state home. These veterans, called "inmates," came mostly from Virginia, although men from all over the nation successfully applied. Virginia's home for veterans had about 250 residents for most of the 1890s, peaked at close to 300 between 1912 and 1914, but by the 1930s had fewer than 60 residents. The last four veterans living in the home died in 1940 and 1941. A conservative estimate using the 1890 veteran census numbers suggests that 5 percent of Virginia's surviving Confederate soldiers entered the home at some point. There is no reliable set of overall numbers for the Home for Needy Confederate Women, though historian Susan Hamburger notes that "hundreds of women" were "cared for in the home" by the time the institution finally closed in 1989.[38]

It is possible to see what percentage of Pittsylvania's soldiers who survived the war tried to take advantage of the state's commutations, pensions, and homes. (The 1890 manuscript census was destroyed in a fire, so there is no easy way to determine which Pittsylvania-area veterans were still alive in 1890 and to make a direct comparison with Virginia soldiers as a whole.) In Pittsylvania County and Danville, about 10 percent (246) of veterans who survived the war applied for commutation benefits. Over 33 percent (822) of the area's veterans who survived the war eventually applied for a pension from the state. Only about 4 percent (98) of Pittsylvania veterans who survived the war applied for admittance to the Lee Camp Soldiers' Home.[39]

Looking more broadly at government aid, although Virginia was one of the first former Confederate states to give pensions to its veterans and their widows, it was far from the first to give financial aid to Civil War soldiers and their families, nor was it the most generous. The federal government started pensions for disabled Union soldiers and the families of deceased servicemen before the Civil War had ended. From the end of the war until the Dependent Pension Act of 1890, the federal government expanded the numbers of eligible Union veterans and family members (including widows, orphans, parents, and under-age siblings), added special categories of disability and payment for amputees, and made it easier to apply. By 1890, the federal government had awarded over seven hundred thousand Civil War pensions.[40]

The federal government was also a great deal more generous and timely than states such as Virginia could afford to be. Pensions paid $8 to $30 a month, depending on rank, for total disability. A "totally disabled" Union ex-private in 1900 received over three times the amount his counterpart in Virginia did, and the Northerner could have been receiving it for over thirty-five years. After 1879, it became possible for Union veterans or their families to receive retroactive payment of pensions (averaging $1,000) from the point of disability or death, even if applied for decades later.[41]

The federal government's provisions for Union soldiers and their families dwarfed Virginia's pension system. At the peak of the federal system of pensions in the 1890s, it cost between 40 and 50 percent of the entire income of the national government. Virginia's pensions never required more than 8.5 percent of annual state expenditures and typically were closer to 4 percent. In 1900, over 74 percent of Union veterans received pensions, compared with just 17 percent of Virginia's veterans.[42]

Beginning with the end of the war, the federal government eventually established homes for disabled Union veterans. The nine branches of the National Home, combined with state homes set up in twenty-eight states, eventually became "de facto old-age homes for soldiers," according to Theda Skocpol and other scholars. In addition, unlike in Confederate homes, Union residents of veterans' homes kept their pensions.[43]

On the other hand, the aid provided by Virginia to its veterans and their families was comparable to that of most other Southern states. In the years after the war, some Southern states provided artificial limbs and limited commutations to their disabled veterans. In the last two decades of the nineteenth century, all the former Confederate states created pensions for the neediest of their veterans. Most states, like Virginia, kept their pensions limited to seriously wounded or disabled ex-Confederate soldiers and to the truly impoverished veterans and widows. In the early twentieth century, the other ex-Confederate states also gradually expanded their notion of "disability" to include old age, although poverty continued to be an essential requirement. Fifteen other

Southern state soldiers' homes were formed in the other ten former Confederate States, and other Confederate women's homes arose in Texas and North Carolina. Historian Elna Green emphasizes the immense fiscal commitment by Virginia and other Southern states to the various forms of care for Confederate families. Ultimately, however, most Southern states offered small payments and limited bed space when compared to the largesse of the federal pension and National Home system. Still, the pensions and other direct aid to veteran families from Virginia (and the other ex-Confederate states) mattered a great deal to the people who received them.[44]

Pittsylvania's Pensioners and Home Inmates

Understanding fully the significance of the state aid received by the veteran families of Danville and Pittsylvania requires first an examination of the long-term impact that war wounds and deaths had on these men and women. Here the focus is on the economic impact for veteran families as seen in commutation and pension applications made decades after the war had ended. The most serious economic impact for wounded, disabled, or diseased veterans' families grew out of the inability of many veterans to work in the postwar period.

Wartime wounds left many men unable to work as they had before the war, forcing them to depend more on their wives and other family members. D. P. Marshall's gunshot wounds to his right hand and left shoulder left him incapable of "perform[ing] manual labor without great pain." John Henry Riddle claimed his war wounds made working, or even walking, difficult: "I have to make a long step & then a short one & my leg frequently gives entirely out." As of 1888, John H. Towler's thigh bone, broken at Petersburg in 1864, still "disables me to great extent from traveling, standing or laboring."[45]

For veterans who had lost a limb amid the fighting, postwar manual labor was particularly difficult. Reuben Powell, shot in the left elbow at Antietam, lost his left arm above the elbow joint. In his pension application he explained, "[I] Can do but little with one hand & arm." Succinct and to the point, Powell's sentence reveals the attitude of many veteran amputees and the most significant economic problem they and their families faced. Virginia's politicians clearly recognized this economic need, since the greatest financial compensation they offered at any time went to amputees.[46]

Diseases caught during wartime service, often combined with lingering wounds, left many veterans weakened and unable to support themselves. Isaac A. Keesee's doctor testified that his patient had "chronic diarrhea lasting for twenty years," which made it impossible for him to work. By 1900, Henry Davis had been coughing up blood for thirty-six years, caused by wartime wounds but exacerbated by apparent lung infections, leaving him with "great shortness of breath." He too found himself incapable of working, especially as he got older, leaving him dependent on his wife and their three adult children still living at home.[47]

Not surprisingly, wounds and debilitating diseases had their most significant impact on men who had earned their living before the war as manual laborers. Roughly three-quarters of white men and veterans in Pittsylvania worked as farmers or farm laborers. For men who worked in agriculture, a wounded (or amputated) leg, foot, arm, or hand could make it hard, even impossible, to perform common farming tasks. Thomas Cook claimed, "I cannot plow or hoe, but a short time as my hand gives out." Abram Crews's frustration with his inability to work shines through in his application: "[I] cannot plow, nor plant tobacco or hoe tobacco. In fact, I can do no farm work which requires me to use the said right foot." Many of the area's veterans with legs wounded during the Civil War would have identified with B. H. Lewis, who declared in his application, "[I] cannot walk but very little & can not plow any at all nor plant tobacco and I am a farmer by occupation & dependent on it for support." It is likely that Lewis's and Cook's sons (and perhaps wives) had to replace the veterans in the fields.[48]

Some veterans became completely disabled, even to the point of becoming invalids, leaving their wives and families in a bad spot. John Douglas was disabled by "paralysis and confined to my bed and have been for 4 years." Pension applications indicate that Douglas's wife, Nannie, had to care for him and could not support the two of them by herself. James C. Wilson's commutation application reveals that his chest wound received in the Battle of the Wilderness continued to completely disable him in the 1880s: "said wound is very severe. . . . it seriously incommodes him in breathing and . . . in the performance of manual labor."[49]

For all of Virginia's veterans, the constant march of time only exacerbated old wounds and brought new health problems that prevented them from working and supporting themselves and their families. Pension applications trace the health decline as these aging veterans' bodies succumbed to a variety of diseases or ailments. Many ex-soldiers found themselves in straits similar to those of Samuel Robertson, who filed a series of pension applications indicating that, in addition to a wrist wound that he received during the war, his health began to suffer as he came down with rheumatism, then consumption (tuberculosis), then kidney disease; the combination of medical problems completely disabled the former soldier from making a living, leaving him in 1900 a burden on his wife and his five young children at home.⁵⁰

Many wives and children of veterans also needed more economic help than they could get from local sources of aid. For the families of veterans who had died or who were incapacitated by wartime wounds or disease, or old age, financial support was a serious problem. These veteran families had to figure out some way to replace the income lost in the disability or death of their men, usually the main economic breadwinner of their households. Despite the initial postwar strategies of widows of Civil War soldiers, they often found themselves in desperate financial straits by the 1880s and 1890s. Amelia Riddle's husband was killed "by a gunshot wound" at Drewry's Bluff in 1864. Mary Hubbard's and Nancy Mullins's husbands died years after the war ended. By the time veteran widows became eligible for state pensions in 1888, these women and many others in Virginia needed that money to help support themselves or to help take that burden from their children.⁵¹

Not surprisingly, given the financial problems that many veterans, widows, and their families faced, many of the first formal applications to the state for commutations mentioned the petitioners' economic need. Enoch Farmer applied multiple times for commutation in the 1870s and 1880s, including several letters to the Auditor of Public Accounts indicating, "As I greatly need the money . . . please send me as early as practicable what the State allows." One of the people assisting John Robertson in filling out his commutation application added, "He is a man of family and of very limited means and stands much in need of any assistance the State may make him by way [of] commutation for the loss of his said limb."⁵²

As with commutation applications, pension claims filed by veterans and widows prominently mentioned their lack of money, partly because of the poverty requirements that started with the Pension Act of 1888 and partly because they probably assumed (correctly) that demonstration of need would make the local court and state Auditor's Office look more favorably on their claims. Martha Yeatts's application revealed that her husband died in the county poorhouse, leaving her and her six young children to fend for themselves. James Blanks's petition in 1888 describes his inability to work and included a letter of support from a friend who testified that "Blanks is a very poor man [who] has a large family." By 1900, older veterans such as David Adkinson found themselves forced to sell their property in order to pay debts because they could not work anymore.⁵³

Although most applications successfully demonstrated the financial need of the petitioners, the definitions of eligibility for both commutations and pensions required more proof until the Pension Act of 1900. Specifically, commutation and 1888 Pension Act applicants needed to prove that their disabilities or, for widows, the deaths of their soldier husbands were caused by their wartime service. Many veterans' disabilities or postwar deaths obviously stemmed from their wartime service, but not all commutation or pension applicants had such clear cases. This lack of clarity was especially true for cases in which disease crippled or killed veterans after the war ended. John Mann caught "scurvy [during the war], from which [he] never recovered and which render[ed him] unable to work," but his initial pension application in 1888 was denied since he had not been wounded. Martha Dodson argued that her husband died of "measles contracted during the war," but since he died about two weeks after Lee's surrender at Appomattox, the Auditor's Office heavily questioned and later disallowed her claim.[54]

Beginning with the 1900 Pension Act, however, applicants no longer had to prove their wounds or, if widows, that their husband's death occurred during wartime service. Still, many of those who attempted to gain pensions under the 1900 and later pension acts continued to link their injuries or their husband's death to the war. Starting in 1902, these attempts at linking increased, in large part because reapplying veterans had to indicate the cause of their disability. In other words, although it largely did not matter why the soldiers in question had been disabled or died, the applicants still had to decide how to answer that question. If a soldier died during the war, lost a limb, or sustained a serious wound, then the answer was obvious. Disease, time spent as a prisoner of war, accidental injury, exposure, and old age all were cited as causes of postwar disability and death for veterans.

An examination of how applicants and their supporters attempted to link the less obvious cases of disability or death with the wartime service of the men involved, however, not only reveals what they thought was important in their attempts at gaining financial aid from the state but also allows some insight into the way that the Civil War continued to be the central event for these veteran families' lives long after the fighting had stopped. Many pensioners claimed that diseases picked up in the army had caused their disabilities (or their husband's death). Richard Pugh "had pneumonia during the war which settled on my left lung; & have never recovered from it, suffer at times with general weakness & debility." John Gatewood also "had a severe spell of fever during the war which almost wrecked my health & have not been a strong man since." Francis Gibson testified that her husband died in 1898 of "disease contracted during the war." Gabriella Ricketts argued that her husband died in 1891 "of Dropsy which was probably a result of an attack of measles during the war."[55]

Some former POWs blamed their long-term health problems on their time in Northern prisons and thereby linked their suffering to their military service. Thomas Tucker claimed that his "asthma, rheumatism [was] contracted in prison 1865." Robert Biggs blamed his "chronic diarrhea, liver disease, and consumption" on his time spent as "a prisoner at Point Lookout, [Maryland]." Such claims were at least based in truth, since many prisons, North and South, lacked adequate sanitation.[56]

Some pension applicants linked disabilities or death to accidents that occurred while the soldiers were in the army. John Milam died "while on March from a fall accidentally in the Confederate service." John Ferguson lost his middle finger and use of his left hand when shot "while disembarking from the train by accidental discharge of musket." These claims linking accident to military service did not always work; James Shelton failed to get a pension in 1894 when he blamed his inability to work on an "accidental discharge" in camp that wounded his foot, but he succeeded five years later when his application mentioned wounds at Gettysburg and Yorktown and left out any reference to his accident.[57]

Many applicants under the 1900 and 1902 acts cited the "exposure" that soldiers had endured serving in the military during the war as the source of their current disabilities or the cause of the death of their husband. Joshua Towler claimed "great bodily infirmity occasioned [by] hardship and exposure during the war between the states." James Gosney argued that his "chronic Bronchitis, Stomach and Liver troubles[,] also Heart troubles" stemmed from "exposure during the Civil War." When applicants blamed "exposure," they usually meant the time spent outside in grueling conditions or the privations that Confederate soldiers endured, including shortages of food and clothing, extended difficult marches, and less-than-sanitary encampments.[58]

It is reasonable to question how many of these pensioners' health problems directly related to the soldiers' wartime service and how much can more accurately be attributed to old age. Many of these veterans were in their sixties and seventies by 1900. But it was acceptable for veterans to say that their disability came from the "infirmities of age" because, starting in 1900, pensions were approved for both war-related disabilities and old age. Some veteran applicants did acknowledge that their disabilities were the result of old age. Pensioner Hugh George described his health problems as part of the "general weakness of old age." Such claims were the exception, however, rather than the rule. Why were claimants so unwilling to acknowledge aging as a cause? Perhaps because they felt entitled to the money because of their sacrifices, or perhaps some of these men who claimed that their disabilities stemmed from wartime exposure actually were avoiding facing their own mortality.

Even if some of these applicants exaggerated the links between the disabilities or deaths and the war, physicians rarely disagreed with the claims made by applicants. In most applications for which the cause of the disability or death seemed unclear, doctors also linked petitioners' health problems to military service. Joseph Green's doctor testified that Green's "repeated attacks of kidney colic, a double hernia, shortness of breath & general weakness . . . is due to exposure during the Civil War."[59]

Except for a few obvious cases of postwar accidents and applicants who blamed their advancing years, almost all the applicants from Pittsylvania County and Danville truly believed that their disabilities or their husband's death had been caused by the war, that their family's financial problems stemmed from their service. The process of applying for artificial limbs, commutations, and pensions in Virginia certainly encouraged such thinking, both by requiring proof of military injury or death for commutations and pensions under the 1888 act and by paying more to widows whose husbands had died in the war. Such financial considerations may have persisted for veterans even after the 1900 act allowed veterans to make old-age-based claims. From this perspective, post-1900 applicants may have believed that they could still improve their chances of getting a pension by explaining that their disabilities were caused by exposure or wartime diseases. Seeing the war as the source of health problems and husbands' deaths, however, also stems from a continuing focus on the Civil War as a central event of these survivors' lives, so integral to their perspectives that they could not perceive their losses (of the ability to work or of loved ones) without linking them to that time.

The Impact of State Aid on Veteran Families

In measuring the impact of the various forms of "Confederate welfare," previous scholars have emphasized the importance of prospective recipients matching an idealized version of the Lost Cause soldier. Although such expectations had an impact, this approach overlooks the fact that this state aid was also about providing limbs for the most damaged veterans, about assisting the neediest of veteran families in rebuilding, and about supplementing veteran family functions with state resources. It is clear that this state aid, in all its guises, mattered to Pittsylvania's veteran families.[60]

Joseph T. Miller received a gunshot wound at Gettysburg as part of "Pickett's Charge" on July 3, 1863. The wound required the amputation of Miller's leg "midway between the knee & ankle." Two days later, the twenty-four-year-old Miller was captured, sent to military hospitals, and eventually shipped to the Union prison at Point Lookout, Maryland. In March 1864, he was exchanged and, that August, was allowed to retire from the army. In 1871, Miller applied for and received one of the artificial limbs that Virginia offered to its amputees. He wore the leg for thirteen years, although he "had to have it repaired" using $40 he received for that purpose from the state in 1880. In 1884, however, the wooden leg "had the misfortune to break" again, and Miller was too poor to get it fixed; but once again, the state approved his application for financial aid (although two years after he applied), this time awarding him $60 as a commutation and in order to repair the artificial limb. In 1897, Miller applied for a pension under the 1888 act, asking for the standard $30 annual payments allowed to single-limb amputees. Not only was his application approved, but the Auditor's Office granted him an unusual $50 annual pension, which he apparently received for the rest of his life.[61]

Joseph T. Miller took advantage of almost all the financial opportunities that the state of Virginia offered to its veterans (although he did not stay at the Lee Camp Soldiers' Home). The aid provided to Miller seems to have made his life after the war a little easier. The artificial leg probably allowed him some improvement in mobility, perhaps even in his labor. The commutation and money awarded him to repair his wooden leg aided him as well. The pension he received allowed him the chance to pay some of the debts undoubtedly accumulated by his young family after he could not do manual labor to any significant extent. (His three children were still under age thirteen when his artificial limb first broke in 1880.) Virginia's financial aid had made a difference in Miller's life. He and his family could have argued that the state for which he fought and sacrificed had not forgotten him. In fact, it celebrated his service. Many Confederate veterans and their families found that these artificial limbs, commutations, pensions, and homes had a similar impact.[62]

Impact of Artificial Limbs and Commutations

During and immediately after the Civil War, the standard artificial leg often consisted of just an unwieldy wooden peg, and manufacturers made the standard artificial arm out of a lighter wood. Given the nearly thirty thousand amputations in the North, and about that number in the South, it is not surprising that artificial-limb design improved as more and more amputees demanded better limbs. According to one historian, some of these new limbs were constructed from willow because this light wood proved "durable and able to absorb shocks and jarring, much like natural bone." Other artificial limbs used metal bolts, springs, vulcanized rubber, even ivory, or some combination to simulate joints.[63]

Governor Pierpont's argument that artificial limbs would enable these veterans to stay off government support by allowing them to engage in manual labor again proved optimistic. It is true that Joseph Miller, an overseer, used his wooden leg to enable him to do his job, even if he was less mobile after the war. Even with an artificial arm or leg, however, most amputees would have had trouble farming; plowing and hoeing required more agility and mobility than most veterans with artificial limbs could muster. Some amputees never found a prosthesis they liked, possibly the result of improperly fitted limbs, the awkwardness of wearing them, the fact that they wore out and broke, or that a particular amputation did not allow the fitting of a replacement arm or leg. John S. Robertson, a farmer, lost his left arm "about six inches from the shoulder joint" in the same charge in which Joseph Miller lost his leg, but Robertson apparently found an artificial arm unhelpful. His application for financial assistance argued that he remained "perminently disabled by said wound for doing manual labour and thus earning a livelihood for himself and family wherefore he makes application for . . . assistance." An artificial arm did not allow him to farm well enough to feed his family, even with their help. Despite Governor Pierpont's beliefs, wounded veterans such as Robertson needed different help from the state.[64]

Artificial legs, arms, hands, and feet had at least a chance of making amputees more productive, but men whose limbs had been severely injured but not amputated, as well as men who could not successfully use a prosthesis, needed some other form of assistance from the state. Starting in 1872, the state attempted to fulfill those needs through commutations. Veterans such as Robertson desperately needed any financial help available and certainly appreciated their commutations: "he is a man of family and of very limited means and stands much in need of any assistance the State may make him by way [of] commutation for the loss of his said limb."[65]

Ultimately, however, commutation payments were so small that they provided wounded veterans with a largely token recognition of their plight. During the 1880s, the $60 that most successful applicants for commutation received would have been less than half what a tobacco-factory worker made each year. By itself, a one-time commutation of $60 or $30 or $15 would not have made a significant change in the life of someone who could not work because of their wounds. Still, it would have been some extra money that the veteran could combine with the kinds of help discussed in earlier chapters.[66] In a broader sense, however, commutations were not long-term solutions.

Impact of Pensions

Pensions grew out of a need of families of wounded, disabled, diseased, or dead veterans for regular financial aid in the postwar period, stemming from the inability of these men to work for decades and from the lack of sufficient assistance from any other sources. Since Virginia's pensions required a certain level of poverty, pensioners were clearly in desperate financial straits. But pensions meant more to veteran families than just the money they offered. They also signified a public acknowledgment of the worthiness of families who had forfeited health and wealth for the Confederate cause.

Unfortunately for veterans and their families, the money provided by annual pensions failed to replace fully the income lost in the disability or death of these men. Commutations paid a maximum of $60, and under the 1888 Pension Act, double amputees received the largest pensions, $60 a year. To put such funding into context, white public-school teachers in Alabama in 1890 made only $215 a year, but that was still 3.5 times as much as the highest paid pensioner received. Between 1900 and 1912, pension amounts for double amputees (again the highest awards) rose to $100 per year. In 1904, however, spinners—among the most poorly paid Southern cotton-mill workers—made about $150 per year.[67]

The economic impact of these pensions would have varied by the amount of other income or aid to which each veteran family had access. A pension of $30 a year could mean the difference between complete abject poverty and just being poor, with the pension supplementing work done by other family members; it could be enough to support a wounded veteran living with his cousin, or an aging widow living with her adult child. Virginia's Civil War pensions never paid enough to replace the income of a healthy male agricultural laborer, but that does not mean that that money was not important to those who applied for it. For many recipients, it may have been enough to keep them out of the poorhouse.

Many wives and children of veterans needed financial help and benefited from one of two types of pensions. For the families of veterans who had been incapacitated by wartime wounds or disease, financial support was a serious problem to which their husband's or father's pensions became at least a partial answer. Worse-off economically were those families who had lost their male household head to the war or war injuries. Without the income earned by these men, many of these veteran families depended on the widows' pensions offered by the state to supplement other familial strategies, such as moving in with relatives. The death of Martha Yeatts's husband left her living alone with her six young children in 1870. By 1900, she had already lived at different times with two of her married daughters. The pension she received under the Pension Act of 1888 allowed her to contribute to her family's survival.[68]

Some of Virginia's veteran wives, such as Nannie Douglas, benefited from both types of state pensions. Her husband, John, had been paralyzed for years and finally received a pension in 1900, and Nannie benefited from the much-needed money. After he died in 1901, she managed to get a pension of her own, claiming, "I have no children who will support me." Nannie Douglas and many other poor wives and widows of Virginia's veterans were helped by the state's pensions, even if the money failed to meet all their needs.[69]

While the financial aspects of pensions had an important economic impact on veterans and their widows and families, having one's pension application accepted almost certainly meant more than just the money it awarded the petitioner. Although such money made life a little easier for desperately poor men and women, an awarded pension represented an acceptance and recognition of the sacrifices made by both the applicants and their family members during the Civil War. Because of the nature of the application process, successful pensioners would have received that approval from both their local courts and the state (via the Auditor's Office).

Pension-application files also reveal that Pittsylvanians and Danvillians believed that veterans and their families deserved such recognition and benefits. In a letter in support of S. M. Garrett's pension claim, a friend wrote to the auditor, "If you can do this, then justice demands that he should have this." Physician Questor George testified that widowed applicant Nannie Jane Mullins "is deserving" of a pension. Such approval from their neighbors probably meant a great deal to veteran families.[70]

Looking beneath the surface of some commutation applications may indicate that for some ex-soldiers, the importance of veterans' benefits lay more in their recognition of sacrifices than in monetary benefit. Even though income restrictions limited pension recipients to those who could prove financial need, not all veterans who applied for commutations needed that money to survive. Rawley Martin, a doctor in Chatham, Pittsylvania's county seat, applied for and received a commutation because "his right hip broken, his leg broken & is three inches shorter and flesh wounds through his left thigh[,] leg & foot."

Martin, although "disabled to manual labor," could still perform quite well as a physician and seems to have been financially sound. To veterans such as Martin, the money was a nice bonus, but the real importance may have been the state's recognition of their sacrifices.[71]

Another possible impact of pensions may have been produced by Virginia's requirement that widows could not receive or keep a pension if they remarried. Because of that rule, pensioned widows had a motive to avoid remarrying even if they had an opportunity to do so. Whether this desire to retain a pension encouraged women to be more independent of men or, as Megan McClintock has shown in the North, inspired women to live with potential mates outside the bonds of marriage, such consequences were almost certainly not intended by legislators in Richmond and all over the South. A number of Pittsylvania County and Danville women married just before or during the Civil War but lost their husbands in the conflict and never remarried for over twenty-five years. Jennifer Gross has argued that many of Virginia's Civil War widows did not remarry if their financial situation did not require it of them. Although there are a number of possible reasons for these women not to have remarried, Pittsylvanians such as Nancy East and Bettie Galloway may have decided not to remarry once they got their pensions, because they no longer needed to financially. Other women whose veteran husbands died after the war may have felt the same way. In any case, it is possible that at least a few Virginia pensioned widows found themselves declining remarriage opportunities, either to keep their pensions or because of the independence that the pensions gave them. Since the amount of money included in a pension would not have been enough to support single women by themselves, however, they would have needed a job or some other financial support.[72]

If a successful pension showed that the state (and local courts) remained aware of the sacrifices of veteran families, how disappointing it must have been for veterans or widows whose applications were turned down by the auditor. Under the 1888 Pension Act, 20 percent of applicants in the Pittsylvania and Danville area failed. Since there was a general sense that veterans and widows deserved these pensions, those who did not get that money or acknowledgment of their sacrifice would probably have been hurt and frustrated by their rejection, seeing it as a personal affront and a denial of their financial need.[73]

Some men were denied pensions repeatedly between 1888 and 1900, yet they continued to reapply. When men such as George Lynch applied multiple times for pensions that they believed they deserved, they showed both their financial need and their desire to be recognized. Lynch unsuccessfully applied in 1888, 1893, and 1897, repeating his claims that his wounded right foot "render[ed him] unable to work." Lynch kept reapplying though, as did Charles Owen, who sent the auditor five separate pension claims between 1888 and 1900.[74]

The persistence of some veterans paid off. Twenty-one men from the Pittsylvania area whose applications under the Pension Act of 1888 initially failed managed to achieve a pension before 1900. Charles Owen finally had his persistence pay off. Perhaps he (and other multiple applicants) just wore the Auditor's Office down: on Owen's fifth attempt in 1899, his pension was approved. For forty-two other applicants, however, their quest for financial recompense and recognition of status failed, despite multiple attempts.[75]

The length of time between eligibility and application on the part of widows and veterans serves as one more indication of the economic and psychological importance of pensions to these men and women. Unfortunately, timing of applications can be interpreted in a number of ways, but when people applied can indicate some notion of the needs and pressures they felt. Almost all widows applied as soon as possible, whereas most veterans eligible under the 1888 Pension Act did not apply until after 1894.

One obvious explanation for this difference in the timing of application submissions is that earlier applicants were worse-off economically. The speed with which widows applied—95 percent of female applicants from Pittsylvania and Danville who applied under the 1888 act filed their claims in 1888 or 1889—indicates the significant economic importance of pensions for these women. Almost 30 percent of the veteran applicants under the 1888 act also filed their claims in 1888 or 1889. Veterans' widows and some veterans apparently needed that money immediately.[76]

In general, however, most veterans (about 60 percent) who applied for a pension under the 1888 act waited to apply until 1894 or after, for a variety of reasons. The veterans who applied in the late 1890s, despite being eligible because of their physical condition, may not have met poverty requirements in 1888. Some men may have waited, thinking at first that they were not eligible under the 1888 act. Others applied after they deteriorated physically, as aging worsened war wounds. In 1895, John Gunnell testified about his arm that was wounded at Petersburg, "as I grow older the worse it gets."[77]

Many veterans of the war seem to have avoided applying for pensions until it was absolutely necessary, perhaps partly out of concern about the impact on their perceived status as independent men. After all, taking a pension revealed that they could not take care of themselves or their families anymore without the state's help. Robert Turner in 1894 admitted that his wounds had finally rendered him "unable ... to support my family." Robert Evans stated defensively in his application, "[I am] not helpless, but am not frequently able to do work." Societal expectations in this time and place required men to support their family. Inability to do so challenged their masculinity both to themselves and within their community.[78]

By 1900, however, age, wounds, disease, and financial hardships had caught up with most men and women. In a sample of claimants who petitioned for a pension under the 1900 act, both widows and veterans applied as soon as possible. In fact, about 85 percent of applicants under the 1900 Pension Act filed their claims in April and May of 1900. Whatever had delayed men from applying immediately for the 1888 pensions, it ceased being a problem by 1900.[79]

Impact of the Homes

Assessing the impact of the Lee Camp Soldiers' Home on Confederate veterans must begin with the high expectations set for the "inmates" by the administration and the Board of Visitors. The application for admission explained that only Confederate veterans "who served honorably during the War . . . and have borne a good character since, shall be entitled to admission . . . if they are indigent and infirm." As R. B. Rosenburg has argued generally for Confederate soldiers' homes across the South, the Lee Camp Home inmates were expected to live up to an ideal of the heroic Confederate veteran, to become "living monuments" to the Lost Cause. But Virginia's home also provided veterans with a place to go and a way to reduce the burden on their children or other relatives as the state offered to take on this traditional familial responsibility.[80]

Still, during the 1880s and 1890s, the home served mostly as a poorhouse for Confederate veterans. The commandant and the Board of Visitors (made up of members of the Lee Camp veterans organization and appointed state officials) attempted to run the home in a military manner, requiring inmates to act as if they had rejoined the army. They were expected to appear for roll call and drill, to serve guard duty, and to help in the upkeep of their rooms and the grounds, although resistance to such discipline seems to have been common. As part of residents' position as "living monuments," they were expected to wear their uniforms when visitors came and pose for photographs with their guns and in front of cannons on the grounds of the home.[81]

Inmates would be disciplined or expelled from the home for a number of violations, including drunkenness, stealing, leaving grounds without a pass, aggressive behavior toward other inmates or the home's staff, even cursing and rudeness. Mild punishments usually involved being restricted to the grounds of the home, and more serious or repeated offenses brought expulsion. After inmate James Redd, a veteran of the 18th Virginia Infantry, threatened "to kill the

Commandant of the Home" in 1902, he was "immediately dismiss[ed] ... from the Home" by the Board of Visitors.[82]

Even beyond the conflict between the administration and the veterans, life does not seem to have been pleasant for some residents of the home. Despite work assignments and limited recreational activities and day trips into the city, many inmates felt bored. Most of them had no spending money, since all the veterans who were accepted were impoverished and when they entered the home they had to give up any pensions they had. Given the chance, some residents retreated into the fog of alcohol.[83]

As the veterans' average age increased and the number of residents declined, however, the home increasingly took on the air of a hospital; the administration relaxed some of the strict rules for inmates, allowing disabled or weak veterans to have assistance in keeping their rooms clean and tidy, maintaining the grounds, and standing guard duty. During the 1910s and 1920s, the home went through a rough period, during which a state board assessed the living conditions at the Lee Camp Home as being considerably worse than those of the poorhouses of the state, in part because of "bedclothing that seemed to have been unchanged for months."[84] The state threatened closure of the home, administrators apparently succeeded in making the needed changes, and the home remained open until the death of its last resident in 1941.[85]

High expectations, strict discipline, and boredom, as well as later problems with adequate living conditions, made it hard for all residents to enjoy their time at the home. Residents at Virginia's Home for Needy Confederate Women seem to have had similar experiences to the men in the Lee Camp Home, including restrictions on behavior, conflicts between residents and administrators, and constant funding shortages. Still, the homes did generally meet the basic needs of food, shelter, and medical care for their residents, they did provide homes for those veterans and widows with few options or overburdened families, and residents' very presence there celebrated their service and sacrifice decades before. At the least, the homes gave Confederate veterans and widows a place to live out their last years.[86]

From early in the Civil War through the turn of the century, the human landscape of Pittsylvania County and Danville included the constant presence of wounded or disabled veterans: men missing arms, legs, or eyes, limping, some weakened by their time in the army, and the ever-increasing strain of age. As the end of the nineteenth century approached and the twentieth century began, more and more of the health problems of these men could be blamed on their age, but such rationalization would have been brought up short by the occasional visual reminder of the veteran whose arm or leg was no longer there. From the passage of the first artificial-limb law, the state of Virginia's benefits for veterans and their widows remained most generous for the families most physically impacted by the war. Gradually benefits widened from the amputees to veterans disabled by wounds to war widows to veterans disabled by age and to widows who had lost their veteran husbands after the war. Although assistance began with wooden arms and legs, Virginia's veterans' benefits came to be a social-welfare system focused on the poor, although only a select, "deserving," nearly exclusively white population. Although the services and financial help that were eventually offered by Virginia and other ex-Confederate states never came close to matching the massive aid given to Northern veterans, Southern veterans and their families took advantage of what the states offered.

Artificial limbs, commutations, pensions, or residence in one of the state's Confederate homes also helped to reinforce—or simply allowed veterans and their families to express—their belief that the Civil War had been the central event in their lives. This notion, seen in applicants' attempts to link the war to their disability, even when not required, was encouraged by the fact that one was only eligible as a veteran or through one and by the requirement until the 1900 Pension Act that such links be proven.

The impact of these artificial limbs, commutations, pensions, and Confederate homes on the veterans and their families in Pittsylvania County and Danville, Virginia, was economically and psychologically significant. Certainly the money or services did not solve all the veterans' (and therefore the state's) problems, as Governor Pierpont claimed artificial limbs would do. But the men and women who sacrificed for their state did receive some assistance that may have kept them out of the poorhouse and that maintained, if not improved, their condition. Finally, it is important to acknowledge the significance of pensions beyond financial needs and of residence in the Confederate homes beyond a place to stay, to recognize the emotional and intellectual satisfaction of receiving such Confederate welfare.

Conclusion

CLEARLY, THE consequences of the war and its aftermath for Pittsylvania's veteran families were significant. One-fourth of the soldiers sent by these families died during the conflict, and another half suffered wounds, diseases, or imprisonment. During and after the war, veteran families experienced significant financial declines in real and personal property because of emancipation, Southern economic depressions, and the temporary or permanent loss of the labor of men who had gone off to war. Emotionally and psychologically, members of veteran families also suffered from temporary wartime physical separations, permanent losses of family and friends, and tensions caused from economic woes or physical and mental war damage. At a minimum, these changes placed stress on Confederate veteran families; at worst, they left some of those families impoverished and dysfunctional and, in a few cases, put people in the care of a state mental institution.

This book contends that many Confederate veteran families were not just worried about the end of slavery but were occupied with the struggle to survive and cope with the human and economic impact of the war. Emancipation was certainly part of that impact for veteran families, but only part. In this sense, I argue that fully comprehending the impact of the Civil War and its aftermath on veterans, their families, Southerners, and Americans in general requires assessing the effects of white military service as well as the consequences of black freedom.

For the most part, the veterans of Pittsylvania County and Danville and their families tried to keep to a minimum the changes that war and all its consequences brought to their lives. That goal first meant surviving, then rebuilding their families using a variety of strategies, including finding all possible sources of income. The institutions and people to which those families turned for assistance in their attempt to prevent, minimize, or cope with the significant physical, economic, and emotional consequences of war reveal a postwar world fraught with difficult choices.

This book details a gradual shift from a reliance on family, friends, churches, and local elites to an expanded state-based system of support, at least for veteran families, which foreshadowed the rise of twentieth-century government assistance. Although families, churches, and local elites failed to meet all the needs of Confederate veteran families, these sources of aid continued to play an important part in their lives, even after pensions, mental asylums, and soldiers' and widows' homes came into the picture. Within both the older local networks and the newer state system, the needs of veterans and their families were acknowledged as worthy of assistance.

We should not overstate the effects of these options for assistance, however. Financial aid was limited in its scope, and non-financial forms of aid did not always work out for members of veteran families. Some families suffered from internal conflicts; church members were expelled; William Sutherlin did not help everyone who sought his influence; though William Dix was released from the asylum after nineteen months, others were there for years and in what seems to us today to be horrific conditions; and James Redd was kicked out of the Lee Camp Soldiers' Home just a few months after his admission. Even with all the various forms of assistance available to Confederate veteran families after the war, for some families their fight was a losing battle, particularly if family members had died or had been severely handicapped by wartime injuries or illnesses. Not surprisingly, the veteran families most likely to survive with the least amount of economic change were those whose soldiers came back healthy. In a world still largely organized around manual labor, unless a veteran family had alternative means of making money—lots of land to rent, professional skills to employ, a fortuitous remarriage—death or disability could financially cripple a family's rebuilding efforts.

Still, many of the county's veteran families survived the war and rebuilt their lives and their fortunes with the help of their relatives, their friends, their communities, and their state. As the preceding chapters have shown, there were multiple sources of assistance for the most needy of Pittsylvania's veteran families. In the end, these sources of aid did not fully replace the labor and money taken from many Confederate veteran families by the Civil War. But receiving aid was about more than just financial assistance. Pittsylvania's veteran families also found affection from family members, other relatives, and friends; spiritual and emotional support from church communities; a place to care for mentally ill family members; and recognition from their communities and the state for the sacrifices they had made to their "Lost Cause." Although the aid in all its forms failed to restore all veteran families to their prewar position, most of them adapted to the new postbellum world. Despite all attempts at minimizing changes or rebuilding antebellum homes, veteran families had been transformed by the war and its aftermath, shaped by the human, economic, and emotional impact in ways that affected their lives forever.

Appendix
A Note on Sources

Much of this book's argument is built on two large databases created for this project about the soldiers of Pittsylvania County and Danville and their families. The first database is the Soldiers Database, a collection of individual records of soldiers and their service and experiences. The second database is the Pittsylvania County Population Census, a massive database incorporating the entire 1860 and 1870 manuscript population censuses, as well as the 1860 slave schedules, for the county and town. The databases allow me to discuss both the individual and collective experiences of the area's veteran families. This appendix explores how these databases were created, linked, and used in the project. Smaller source databases were created specifically for the petition letters to William T. Sutherlin in chapter 4 and the commutations and pensions in chapter 6. They are explained further in the text and notes for those chapters.

The Soldiers Database is a Microsoft Excel spreadsheet compiling military service information available about the over three thousand Confederate soldiers from Pittsylvania County and Danville, Virginia. I created a separate entry for each soldier using the microfilmed Confederate Service Records (available at the Library of Virginia and the National Archives), Mike Williams's *Confederate Soldiers of Pittsylvania County and Danville*, and the unit rosters for twelve of the volumes of the Virginia Regimental Histories Series. These entries collate whatever (often scattered) information survives for each soldier about enlistment dates, residence, rank, company, physical appearance, age, presence on muster rolls, battles, wounds, illnesses, capture and time as POW, circumstances of discharge, desertion, or death, even small details about family and postwar life. The painstaking work done in collecting information about individual soldiers by the Virginia Regimental Histories Series authors on the 18th, 21st, 24th, 38th, 46th, 53rd and 57th Virginia infantry regiments, the 5th and 6th Virginia cavalry units, the Ringgold and Danville artillery units, and the Virginia Home Guards was particularly helpful in achieving a major goal of the Soldiers Database, namely, fleshing out the stories of collective and individual service of the Pittsylvania and Danville soldiers. After combing this broad range of sources and adjusting for men who served in multiple units and sorting through some issues of similarly named (or inconsistently spelled) individuals, the database contained 3,453 men from Pittsylvania County and Danville who served in some kind of Confederate military unit (including local defense forces). Of those 3,453 men, 3,283 served in what can be called "front-line" units, namely, those who saw some kind of combat during the war.[1] (Unless otherwise stated, statistics about "county soldiers" are calculated using the front-line number. For more on the soldiers themselves and the classifications of various illnesses and injuries, see the notes to chapters 1 and 2.)

The other database, the Pittsylvania County Population Census, includes the 1860 and 1870 manuscript population schedules for Pittsylvania County and Danville, as well as the slaveholder information from the 1860 slave schedule. This data, entered by hand from the microfilm into Microsoft Access, includes nearly eighteen thousand entries from 1860 and nearly thirty-six thousand entries from 1870 with some twenty data points for each entry, as well as nearly fifteen hundred slaveholders from the slave schedules.[2] I then linked the veteran family households in the databases together, a painstaking process that began with attempting to identify each soldier from the Soldiers Database and his familial household in the 1860 population census (linked with the 1860 slave schedules where applicable); I then did the same for the 1870 population census. (In the 1860 population schedule, I located 2,453 [future] front-line soldiers from the Soldiers Database in 1,808 families; in the 1870 population schedule for the county, I was able to find 1,165 front-line veterans and 1,348 families of veterans.) Finally, I identified the veteran families found in the censuses immediately surrounding the war. (There were 1,110 county veteran families who were recorded in both the 1860 and 1870 population schedules.) The linking process was done using names, family structures, soldier and family member ages, and any other information available about the individuals. Complicating factors in this process of linking families ten years and a war apart included overlapping or similar names, census-taker spelling mistakes or other errors, difficulty in finding widows and orphans in 1870 unless they kept their family name from 1860,[3] normal changes in family structure brought on by the life cycle (e.g., adult children moving out or getting married), and even the decision by some people to move out of the area. Given these complications, it is possible that some individual soldiers or families were missed or misidentified. Still, I have identified a substantive cross-section of the soldiers of Pittsylvania and Danville and their families, allowing me to explore their lives during and after the war.

The data provided by this detailed census work offers a rich and unique insight into the legacy of the war and the strategies employed by area veterans and their families. The Soldiers Database allowed me to discuss wartime experiences of individual soldiers throughout the time period, but it also allowed me to analyze the collective experiences of all county soldiers and of subgroups. When I combined the Soldiers Database with the Population Census, I was able to analyze the larger experiences of soldiers' families as well. For example, I can separate out the soldiers who were injured during the war. Then, because the soldiers are linked to their census entry and to that of their families, I am able to ask questions, as I did in chapter 2—such as, How would the wounding of a soldier affect the economic status of his family from 1860 to 1870 compared to those families who were fortunate enough not to have a soldier wounded in the war?—simply by sorting veteran families based on the "wounded" or "not wounded" status of their soldier(s). (For more on the process of identifying and classifying veteran family households and analyzing the impact of war and the strategies on those families, see the text and notes for chapters 1 and 2.)

As a final note, although ideally this study might have followed all these veteran families on through the 1880, 1890, and 1900 censuses, doing so was simply not feasible. Beyond the significant time required to enter and link census information, there are practical, often insurmountable, reasons for not using those censuses. Individual personal and real estate information was not included in the 1880 manuscript population census schedules as it was in 1860 and 1870, making many of the economic statistics I employ in chapter 2 more difficult or even impossible to calculate in 1880. Most of the manuscript population schedules of the 1890 census burned in a fire in 1921, much to the great regret of historians and genealogists.[4] By 1900, forty years had passed since the first census used here; those four decades made the complicating factors significantly worse. It was simply impractical to track thousands of veteran families and their members in that census. (I did, however, locate a few specific families in the 1880 and 1900 censuses in order to provide further context for their commutation or pension applications in chapter 6.) Ultimately, the 1860 and 1870 censuses, both extensive and rich, provided the foundation for a database that—in combination with the Soldiers Database—shed valuable light on a number of significant questions about the impact of the war on, and the strategies used by, these Confederate veteran families.

Notes

Abbreviations
CSR   Confederate Service Records
DU   Duke University, Durham, NC
ICPSR   Inter-University Consortium for Political and Social Research, Ann Arbor, MI
LVA   Library of Virginia, Richmond
NARA   National Archives and Records Administration, Washington, DC
SHC   Southern Historical Collection, University of North Carolina, Chapel Hill, NC
UVA   University of Virginia, Charlottesville, VA
VBHS   Virginia Baptist Historical Society, University of Richmond, VA
VHS   Virginia Historical Society, Richmond, VA
WSH   Western State Hospital Records, Library of Virginia, Richmond (formerly at the hospital in Staunton, VA)
WTS   William Thomas Sutherlin

Introduction

1. Pittsylvania County Population Census, 1860, 1870; Confederate Compiled Service Records, LVA; James S. Redd file, Robert E. Lee Camp Confederate Soldier's Home Applications for Admission, LVA; James Redd to WTS, May 26, 1862, WTS Papers, SHC; Mt. Hermon Baptist Church, 1884–1890, VBHS; Kentuck Baptist Church Minutes, 1867–1890, VBHS; William Dix File, Male Case Book #2, 310, WSH; Gregory, *38th Virginia Infantry*, 111; Joseph T. Miller file, Danville, Act of 1884, Auditor of Public Accounts, Confederate Pension Disability Applications and Receipts, LVA, and Act of 1888, Auditor of Public Accounts, Confederate Pension Applications, LVA.

2. For wartime experiences and motivations, see Robertson, *Soldiers Blue and Gray*; Mitchell, *Civil War Soldiers*; McPherson, *For Cause and Comrades*; Linderman, *Embattled Courage*; Sheehan-Dean, *Why Confederates Fought*. The classic accounts of Civil War soldiers are Wiley, *The Life of Johnny Reb* and *The Life of Billy Yank*. For scholarship on Northern Civil War soldiers' postwar lives, see McConnell, *Glorious Contentment*; Skocpol, *Protecting Soldiers and Mothers*; McClintock, "Binding Up the Nation's Wounds"; Truslow, "Peasants into Patriots"; Kelly, *Creating a National Home*; Johnson, *Warriors into Workers*; Marten, "Exempt from the Ordinary Rules of Life." The literature on Southern veterans is less robust, though that has been changing. For example, see Foster, *Ghosts of the Confederacy*; Gorman, "When Johnny Came Marching Home Again"; Gorman,

"Confederate Pensions as Southern Social Welfare"; Rosenburg, *Living Monuments*. For a look specifically at the generation of elite Virginia men who came of age just before the Civil War, see Carmichael, *The Last Generation*. One attempt to assess the overall postwar impact on veterans on both sides is Logue, *To Appomattox and Beyond*.

3. McCurry, *Masters of Small Worlds*; Rable, *Civil Wars*; Faust, *Mothers of Invention*; Whites, *The Civil War as a Crisis in Gender*; Edwards, *Gendered Strife and Confusion*; Mitchell, *The Vacant Chair*; Kenzer, "The Uncertainty of Life"; Gross, "'Good Angels': Confederate Widowhood and the Reassurance of Patriarchy"; Censer, *The Reconstruction of White Southern Womanhood*; Berry, *All That Makes a Man*.

4. Green, *This Business of Relief*; Green, ed., *Before the New Deal*; Green, ed., *The New Deal and Beyond*.

5. On one view of the terms, see McCurry, *Masters of Small Worlds*, 171–72; on changes to the Southern white household, see Whites, *Gender Matters*, 1–24, 85–111.

6. Making up roughly half the population of the county, former slaves also had lives truly changed by the Civil War. Yet the county's African Americans did not have access to the same sources of aid that veteran families did in the postwar period, despite equal or greater needs. They had to make their way in the postbellum world without the same benefits that veterans and their families received from the community and the state.

7. Among the most prominent of the many works placing emancipation at the center of the postwar story of the South is Foner, *Reconstruction*. On emancipation in this part of the South, see Kerr-Ritchie, *Freedpeople in the Tobacco South*; Edwards, *Gendered Strife and Confusion*.

8. See, for example, Blight, *Race and Reunion*; Foster, *Ghosts of the Confederacy*, 11–75; Blair, *Cities of the Dead*; Levin, "William Mahone, the Lost Cause, and Civil War History."

9. J. E. L. Holmes, quoted in Roanoke Baptist Association, *Minutes of the Annual Meeting*, August 1875, 18, VBHS.

10. A number of scholars have used a regional and community focus to great effect. See Kenzer, *Kinship and Neighborhood in a Southern Community*; Shifflett, *Patronage and Poverty in the Tobacco South*; Tripp, *Yankee Town, Southern City*; Ash, *Middle Tennessee Society Transformed*.

11. When I refer to the inhabitants of the county, I mean the residents of the city too, unless I explicitly indicate otherwise. This decision is based on both convenience and the legal status of the city at the time of the Civil War. In 1860, Danville was part of Pittsylvania County, although it later gained status as an independent city.

12. The figures presented in this paragraph and the origins of these figures are discussed further in chapters 1 and 2.

13. Due to a fire, few county newspapers have survived, making exploration of many local activities more difficult.

14. To explore the social and economic ramifications of the war for veteran families, I created two large databases. One contains the 1860 and 1870 manuscript population censuses for Pittsylvania County, including the 1860 slave schedules (a total of over fifty thousand entries). The second database is a master list of, and data on, the over thirty-four hundred soldiers from the county, taken from the Confederate Compiled Service Records

and several other military history sources. I tracked down as many veteran families as possible in the 1860 and 1870 population census and then linked them to the slave schedules and the list of soldiers. The first database is cited as "Pittsylvania County Population Census, 1860" or "Pittsylvania County Population Census, 1870," and the second is cited as "Soldiers Database." Confederate Service Records are at the Library of Virginia in Richmond and the National Archives and Records Administration in Washington, DC. The other sources of information used in the Soldiers Database are the unit rosters from twelve of the books in the Virginia Regimental Histories Series—on the 18th, 21st, 24th, 38th, 46th, 53rd, and 57th infantry regiments, the 5th and 6th cavalry units, the Ringgold and Danville artillery units, and the Virginia Home Guards—and Mike Williams's *Confederate Soldiers of Pittsylvania County and Danville*. See the appendix for further discussion of the databases and their creation.

15. For most of the nineteenth century, assistance to the needy was fundamentally local in nature. Typically, receiving assistance required extreme impoverishment and "good character." See Katz, *In the Shadow of the Poorhouse*; Trattner, *From Poor Law to Welfare State*; Green, *This Business of Relief*.

16. This system of perceived reciprocal obligations between people in this Southern hierarchical, unequal society existed before the Civil War and has been described by J. William Harris in his *Plain Folk and Gentry in a Slave Society*.

17. Several historians have described federal pensions for Union soldiers within a larger framework of governmental responsibility for individuals. See Skocpol, *Protecting Soldiers and Mothers*; McClintock, "Binding Up the Nation's Wounds"; McConnell, *Glorious Contentment*. For the general shift from local to governmental assistance and the general expansion of state or federal responsibility, see Katz, *In the Shadow of the Poorhouse*; Trattner, *From Poor Law to Welfare State*; Bremner, *The Public Good*. The most prominent exceptions to the Northern focus are Green's *This Business of Relief* and Rosenburg's *Living Monuments*.

18. Although the psychological impact of the war on women has been vastly understudied, there is some debate among historians of Civil War soldiers over the overall psychological impact of the war on veterans. Linderman, in *Embattled Courage*, and Dean, in *Shook Over Hell*, both argue that the war psychologically affected Civil War soldiers in dramatic ways, whereas Robertson, in *Soldiers in Blue and Gray*, and McPherson, in *For Cause and Comrades*, contend that it had little significant psychological impact on the men who served in the military during the conflict. See Mitchell, "Not the General but the Soldier." Given the evidence that I present in chapter 6, I am inclined to support the perspective of Linderman and Dean.

19. In a way, this project details a transition similar to the one Peter Bardaglio traces in his book on nineteenth-century Southern law and families, a shift from a world in which patriarchal households were the center of society to one in which a paternal state existed that preserved the family and family members by taking over some of the provider and protector roles previously fulfilled by (and reserved to) those individual patriarchs. Unlike Bardaglio, who details the transition in legal thought and practice, I trace the transition in what person or group was responsible for the financial support of individual needy families and emphasize the symbolic role of Confederate service in the late-nineteenth-

century South. Bardaglio, *Reconstructing the Household*. See also Katz, *In the Shadow of the Poorhouse*; Trattner, *From Poor Law to Welfare State*; Bremner, *The Public Good*; Skocpol, *Protecting Soldiers and Mothers*.

20. Elna Green makes a similar point as part of her larger study of Richmond's social-welfare system. Green, *This Business of Relief*, 68–127. Megan McClintock argues that the same shift happened for Northern veterans and their families. See McClintock, "Civil War Pensions and the Reconstruction of Union Families," 456–80.

1. The War Comes, 1860–1865

1. Please note that spelling, punctuation, and emphasis are in the original for all quotations unless otherwise noted. Siegel, *The Roots of Southern Distinctiveness*, 86, 105, 107–8; *Historical Demographic Data*, 1850, 1860, ICPSR. (ICPSR census data was accessed through the Historical Census Browser, Geospatial and Statistical Data Center, University of Virginia, http://fisher.lib.virginia.edu/collections/stats/histcensus/.)

2. Blair, *Virginia's Private War*, 12–17; *Historical Demographic Data*, 1850, 1860, ICPSR. The county's white and slave populations both grew by 12 percent from 1850 to 1860.

3. Siegel, *The Roots of Southern Distinctiveness*, 77–85 (quote on 83); *Historical Demographic Data*, 1860, ICPSR.

4. Siegel, *The Roots of Southern Distinctiveness*, 68–74, 84–88, 90, 93–135; Blair, *Virginia's Private War*, 13–15; 1860 Pittsylvania County Population Census.

5. Siegel, *The Roots of Southern Distinctiveness*, 100–106, 120, 132; Kerr-Ritchie, *Freedpeople in the Tobacco South*, 13–30; Tilley, *The Bright-Tobacco Industry*, 37–88. Slaves, predominantly male and frequently hired, did most of the work in Danville's tobacco factories, although some whites and free blacks worked in factories as well. Some plantations in 1860 were still doing basic processing of their tobacco using their own slaves, and non-slaveholding farm families did so using family and sometimes hired labor (see Siegel, *The Roots of Southern Distinctiveness*, 129–32, 184n11). Those families who processed their own tobacco, and maybe that of a few of their neighbors, are particularly difficult to track, since the Census typically lists their occupations as "farmer" or "farm laborer."

6. Siegel, *The Roots of Southern Distinctiveness*, 149–50; Pollack, *Illustrated Sketchbook*, 34.

7. Withers, *Autobiography of an Octogenarian*, 211–12 (first quote); "A True Friend" to WTS, February 5, 1861, election results for Virginia secession convention, February 4, 1861, and George H. Sutherlin to WTS, February 25, 1861, WTS Papers, SHC; Crofts, *Reluctant Confederates*.

8. Crofts, *Reluctant Confederates*, 308–23 (quote on 315).

9. Pittsylvania County Population Census, 1860, 1870; Soldiers Database. See note 14 of the introduction for a description of these databases, and see the appendix for complete information on how the data were compiled.

10. T. J. Patrick to WTS, March 25, 1861, WTS Papers, SHC.

11. William M. Tredway, in Clement, ed., *Recollections of the Confederate Veterans of Pittsylvania*, 13–14, quoted in Gregory, *53rd Virginia Infantry*, 8–9.

12. Powhatan B. Whittle to Lewis Whittle, May 20, 1861, Lewis Neale Whittle Papers, SHC. Pittsylvania-Danville men made up the majority of the members of at least one

company in each of these regiments: the 18th, 21st, 38th, 46th, 53rd, and 57th Virginia Infantry Regiments, the Danville Artillery and the Ringgold Artillery, and the 5th and 6th Virginia Cavalry Regiments.

13. Vinovskis, "Have Social Historians Lost the Civil War?" 9; Pittsylvania County Population Census, 1860; Soldiers Database. Gary Gallagher has suggested that Vinovskis's count underestimates the degree of Southern participation in the Confederate Army, which actually enlisted 75 to 80 percent of Southern white men. If so, the county's participation rates may be closer to the norm for the South. Gary Gallagher, email message to author, November 9, 2005.

14. The men in the area's local defense troops did actually participate in a skirmish, commonly known as the Battle of Staunton River Bridge. Wounded and furloughed soldiers from Danville, civilians from Halifax County, and local defense troops fought off a Union attempt to destroy this key railroad bridge in 1864. Withers, *Autobiography of an Octogenarian*, 204–5. Because these men did participate in this skirmish, I include them in my figures for total mobilization of the people in the area. But because the records that exist for local defense forces are scant (rarely indicating any more than a person's presence at some point in that unit) and because their service was not in front-line combat units, I have not included them in all other calculations (casualty rates and the like) or in the later economic statistics for veteran families (unless they served in a combat regiment at some other point in the war, in which case they are counted as regular soldiers). One more relevant demographic statistic: about 35 percent of all the front-line troops from the county (858 of 2,453 found in the 1860 census) came from slaveholding families. Pittsylvania County Population Census and Slave Schedule, 1860; Soldiers Database.

15. Withers, *Autobiography of an Octogenarian*, 129; Isaac Carrington to Langhorne Scruggs, November 15, 1861, Langhorne Scruggs Papers, DU.

16. Withers, *Autobiography of an Octogenarian*, 170; Diary of Richard Waldrop, July 23, 1861, Richard Woolfolk Waldrop Papers, SHC.

17. W. Dame, *From the Rapidan to Richmond and the Spotsylvania Campaign*, 190; Charles E. Lippitt Diary, June 17, 1863, SHC.

18. Jedediah Carter to Susan Carter, October 26, 1863, and November 8, 1863, Jedediah Carter Papers, DU. See also George Jones to Sarah Jones, October 15, 1862, and May 1, 1863, George W. Jones Papers, DU.

19. J. R. Cabell to WTS, August 16, 1861, WTS Papers, SHC; Richard Waldrop to his family, August 17, 1863, Richard Woolfolk Waldrop Papers, SHC.

20. Richard Waldrop to his family, August 17, 1863, Richard Woolfolk Waldrop Papers, SHC; Rebecca Martin to Rawley Martin, November 13, 1862, Rawley W. Martin Papers, SHC; Rawley Martin to the Ladies' Soldiers' Aid Society, December 25, 1862, Rawley W. Martin Papers, SHC.

21. W. Dame, *From the Rapidan to Richmond and the Spotsylvania Campaign*, 28, 72–73; Jedediah Carter to Susan Carter, November 22, 1863, Jedediah Carter Papers, DU; George Jones to Sarah Jones, April 12, 1863, George W. Jones Papers, DU.

22. S. J. Hopkins to WTS, April 20, 1862, WTS Papers, SHC. Veterans made these claims in their pension applications, which are discussed in detail in chapter 6. See, for example, Joshua Towler case file, Pittsylvania County, and James W. Gosney case file, Dan-

ville, and Garland McGhee case file, Pittsylvania County, Act of 1900, Auditor of Public Accounts, Confederate Pension Applications, LVA.

23. Jedediah Carter to Susan Carter, October 13, 1863, Jedediah Carter Papers, DU.

24. Vinovskis, "Have Social Historians Lost the Civil War?" 9; McPherson, *Battle Cry of Freedom*, 487. All statistics on Pittsylvanian-Danvillian disease come from the Soldiers Database. (Union rates of disease death were lower than Pittsylvania-Danville's: ~7 percent versus almost 12 percent. Comparable statistics for the Confederate Army as a whole are nearly impossible to ascertain. Steiner, *Disease in the Civil War*, 8–9.) The rosters indicate 1,518 out of 3,283 Pittsylvanian soldiers went to the hospital at some point during the war. There were almost certainly more sick soldiers, but the hospitals of the Confederacy did not always record who was there, and some soldiers remained sick in camp.

25. Steiner, *Disease in the Civil War*, 4–5; McPherson, *Battle Cry of Freedom*, 487–88. The "killer diseases" caused the death of 222 Pittsylvanian soldiers, out of 383 disease deaths and 696 deaths whose cause is known. Soldiers Database.

26. Joseph R. Cabell to WTS, August 16, 1861; George H. Sutherlin to WTS, September 14, 1861, and September 23, 1861, all in WTS Papers, SHC (emphasis in original).

27. Soldiers Database; George Jones to Sarah Jones, December 10, 1863, March 12, 1864, October 26, 1864, and January 2, 1864, George W. Jones Papers, DU.

28. Jedediah Carter to Susan Carter, December 3, 1863, Jedediah Carter Papers, DU.

29. Thomas J. Elliott to Sarah E. Elliott, March 31, 1863, and May 19, 1863, Thomas J. Elliott Papers, DU; Richard Waldrop Diary, September 4, 1863, Richard Woolfolk Waldrop Papers, SHC.

30. George Sutherlin to WTS, October 9, 1861, WTS Papers, SHC; Jedediah Carter to Susan Carter, October 4, 1863, October 13, 1863, and October 26, 1863, Jedediah Carter Papers, DU.

31. Jedediah Carter to Susan Carter, November 22, 1863, Jedediah Carter Papers, DU.

32. Abner Anderson to WTS, April 28, 1862, WTS Papers, SHC; Rebecca Martin to Rawley Martin, June 10, 1862, Rawley W. Martin Papers, SHC. For evidence of increased delays in mail service, see letters from George H. Anderson to WTS and the dates that Sutherlin received them. Also see McPherson, *For Cause and Comrades*, 132–33.

33. W. Dame, *From the Rapidan to Richmond and the Spotsylvania Campaign*, 113, 126–27. Civil War soldiers who had been in a battle spoke of having "seen the elephant."

34. W. Dame, *From the Rapidan to Richmond and the Spotsylvania Campaign*, 118, 149 (emphasis in original); Withers, *Autobiography of an Octogenarian*, 147–52.

35. McPherson, *Battle Cry of Freedom*, 661–62. The charge more accurately should be called the "Pickett-Pettigrew Charge." See Reardon, *Pickett's Charge in History and Memory*. The range of men in the charge and the excerpt comes from page 6.

36. Charles E. Lippitt Diary, July 3, 1863, SHC.

37. Ibid.; William Fitzgerald to Sarah Jones, July 11, 1863, George W. Jones Papers, DU; Jacob B. Click to Evaline G. Haney, July 17, 1863, Jacob B. Click Papers, DU. Four other units from Pittsylvania and Danville (the 21st Infantry, the Pittsylvania Dragoons of the 6th Virginia Cavalry, and two companies from the Danville Artillery) were at or near the battle but were not part of the charge.

38. Compiled from the company strengths and casualty rosters in Harrison and Busey, *Nothing but Glory*, 451–67.

39. Soldiers Database. Battle casualties typically include being wounded in action (WIA), being killed or mortally wounded in action (KIA/MWIA), and being captured and made a prisoner-of-war (POW).

40. Steiner, *Disease in the Civil War*, 9–26; McPherson, *Battle Cry of Freedom*, 486–87.

41. Steiner, *Disease in the Civil War*, 9–26; McPherson, *Battle Cry of Freedom*, 486–87.

42. Soldiers Database; Withers, *Autobiography of an Octogenarian*, 193–94. Of these nearly 250 discharged men, 51 had had a portion of a limb amputated.

43. Soldiers Database.

44. Soldiers Database. Overall, 1,241 out of 3,283 area soldiers had no record in the roster of being ill or wounded.

45. Soldiers Database. Overall, 683 out of 3,283 area soldiers spent time in Northern prisons during the war. In 1863, a new Southern policy refused to treat black soldiers as prisoners of war, leading the Union Army to suspend the exchange program. The number of POWs in military prisons ballooned in the North and South. McPherson, *Battle Cry of Freedom*, 791–95.

46. Peter F. Shelton, "A Veteran[']s Prison Experience," April 30, 1916, Elizabeth Seawell Hairston Papers, SHC; McPherson, *Battle Cry of Freedom*, 797–98; Benjamin Farinholt, "Narrative," undated, Benjamin Lyons Farinholt Papers, VHS.

47. Soldiers Database; McPherson, *Battle Cry of Freedom*, 801–2, 796–97n48. Over the course of the war, 108 of 683 area POWs died in Northern prisons.

48. Abner Anderson to WTS, September 5, 1861, and April 28, 1862, WTS Papers, SHC; W. Dame, *From the Rapidan to Richmond and the Spotsylvania Campaign*, 176–77; Dean, *Shook Over Hell*, 62–66.

49. Ash, *When the Yankees Came*, 76–107.

50. The Piedmont Railroad was privately built but heavily subsidized by the Confederate government in order to ensure a railroad line from Richmond to the supplies and troops further south. Siegel, *The Roots of Southern Distinctiveness*, 153–54; McFall, *Danville in the Civil War*, 38–47.

51. Withers, *Autobiography of an Octogenarian*, 191.

52. Siegel, *The Roots of Southern Distinctiveness*, 153–54.

53. Blair, *Virginia's Private War*, 68.

54. Robertson, "Houses of Horror," 333–35; Withers, *Autobiography of an Octogenarian*, 198. See also McFall, *Danville in the Civil War*, 49–63.

55. Faust, *Mothers of Invention*, 80–113.

56. Blair, *Virginia's Private War*, 73–74; George W. Jones to Sarah Jones, February 6, 1863, George W. Jones Papers, DU; WTS to J. H. Owen, March 16, June 1, 1862, WTS Papers, SHC; James M. Norman to WTS, June 1, 1862, WTS Papers, SHC.

57. John Hickman to WTS, May 14, 1862, WTS Papers, SHC.

58. Withers, *Autobiography of an Octogenarian*, 210; Soldiers Database; Shockoe Baptist Church Minutes, 1862–1864 (quote from September 11, 1864), VBHS.

59. Withers, *Autobiography of an Octogenarian*, 131; James M. Norman to WTS, January 26, 1865, WTS Papers, SHC.

60. Abner Anderson to WTS, June 5, 1862, WTS Papers, SHC; Jedediah Carter to Susan Carter, November 22, 1863, Jedediah Carter Papers, DU; Waldrop Diary, September 18, 1863, Richard Woolfolk Waldrop Papers, SHC.

61. Catherine M. P. Cochran Diary, December 25, 1863, VHS, quoted in DeCredico, "Hardships Most Bitter," 3–4.

62. Blair, *Virginia's Private War*, 69, 94; Thomas J. Elliott to Sarah E. Elliott, March 31, 1863, Thomas J. Elliott Papers, DU; Allen Womack to Charles Womack, May 8, 1864, Womack Family Papers, DU; Martin, *The Standard of Living in 1860*, 57–66, 418–21.

63. Blair, *Virginia's Private War*, 116; Martin, *The Standard of Living in 1860*, 65–66; Withers, *Autobiography of an Octogenarian*, 199.

64. William M. Perkins to WTS, August 9, 1861, WTS Papers, SHC; Withers, *Autobiography of an Octogenarian*, 209–10. These actions contradicted the Virginia General Assembly's directions for government impressment agents. Impressment was not supposed to include "any supplies laid in and necessary for the support of any family." Virginia, *Acts and Joint Resolutions* (1863): 23.

65. Blair, *Virginia's Private War*, 119–20; Withers, *Autobiography of an Octogenarian*, 209.

66. Henry E. Taurman to his wife, August 27, 1862, Henry E. Taurman Papers, DU; Rebecca Martin to Rawley Martin, June 16, 1862, Rawley W. Martin Papers, SHC. See also Bettie Penick to W. S. Penick, April 23, 1862, and Beckie [Rebecca] Martin to Rawley Martin, April 22, 1862, Rawley W. Martin Papers, SHC.

67. Rebecca Martin to Rawley Martin, January 19, 1863, Bettie Penick to W. S. Penick, April 23, 1862, and Mollie Martin to Rawley Martin, December 16, 1862, Rawley W. Martin Papers, SHC.

68. Bettie Penick to Rawley Martin, September 17, 1863, Rawley W. Martin Papers, SHC.

69. George Jones to Sarah Jones, October 21, 1862, George W. Jones Papers, DU; Jedediah Carter to Susan Carter, November 5, 1863, Jedediah Carter Papers, DU; Beckie Martin to Rawley Martin, November 1, 1861, Rawley W. Martin Papers, SHC (emphasis in original).

70. George Jones to Sarah Jones, June 27, 1862, October 13, 1863, July 26, 1864, April 3, 1862, October 13, 1863, and December 10, 1863, George W. Jones Papers, DU; Soldiers Database; Robertson, *18th Virginia Infantry*, 64.

71. George Jones to Sarah Jones, June 17, 1862, September 7, 1864, and May 23, 1863, George W. Jones Papers, DU.

72. W. Dame, *From the Rapidan to Richmond and the Spotsylvania Campaign*, 44–49 (quote on 48; emphasis in original); Soldiers Database.

73. Rawley Martin to Chesley Martin, October 5, 1863, and Rebecca Martin to Rawley Martin, January 19, 1863, Rawley W. Martin Papers, SHC; Jedediah Carter to Susan Carter, November 17, 1863, and November 25, 1863, Jedediah Carter Papers, DU; George Jones to Sarah Jones, September 7, 1864, and January 3, 1863, George W. Jones Papers, DU.

74. George Jones to Sarah Jones, April 3, 1862, June 17, 1862, and January 6, 1864, George W. Jones Papers, DU.

75. George Jones to Sarah Jones, October 9, 1864, and October 26, 1864, George W. Jones Papers, DU.

76. Elias Davis to Mrs. G. A. Davis, August 14, 1863, Elias Davis Papers, SHC, quoted in Blair, *Virginia's Private War*, 65–67, 89 (quote). See also Weitz, *More Damning than Slaughter*; Soldiers Database; Vinovskis, "Have Social Historians Lost the Civil War?" 10.

77. Timothy Stamps resignation quoted in Cavanaugh, *The Otey, Ringgold and Davidson Virginia Artillery*, 101; Gregory, *38th Virginia Infantry*, 84; Withers, *Autobiography of an Octogenarian*, 173–74; Soldiers Database. Over the course of the war, 49 out of 192 officers from Pittsylvania and Danville resigned.

78. See Murrell, "Of Necessity and Public Benefit," 77–99.

79. Jedediah Carter to Susan Carter, October 13, 1863, Jedediah Carter Papers, DU; Thomas J. Elliott to Sarah E. Elliott, May 19, 1863, and September 25, 1863, Thomas J. Elliott Papers, DU; George Jones to Sarah Jones, October 21, 1862, and January 3, 1863, George W. Jones Papers, DU.

80. George Jones to Sarah Jones, June 27, 1863, George W. Jones Papers, DU.

81. George H. Sutherlin to WTS, October 9, 1861, and October 18, 1861, WTS Papers, SHC; George Jones to Sarah Jones, November 2, 1864, George W. Jones Papers, DU.

82. Bettie Penick to W. S. Penick, April 23, 1862, Rawley W. Martin Papers, SHC.

83. George Jones to Sarah Jones, July 26, 1864, and August 17, 1864, George W. Jones Papers, DU.

84. George Jones to Sarah Jones, October 13, 1863, September 11, 1864, and October 26, 1864, George W. Jones Papers, DU; Jedediah Carter to Susan Carter, November 17, 1863, Jedediah Carter Papers, DU.

85. George Jones to Sarah Jones, August 17, 1864, and September 11, 1864, George W. Jones Papers, DU.

86. Withers, *Autobiography of an Octogenarian*, 210.

87. H. S. Carter to Susan Carter, January 10, 1864, Jedediah Carter Papers, DU.

88. McPherson, *Battle Cry of Freedom*, 846–50; O'Connor, *River City*, 73–79; Siegel, *The Roots of Southern Distinctiveness*, 158–59. See also Brubaker, *The Last Capital*; McFall, *Danville in the Civil War*, 80–96.

89. Withers, *Autobiography of an Octogenarian*, 218–20; Berry Benson, "Reminiscences of Berry Greenwood Benson, C.S.A.," Benson Papers, SHC; John Averill in *Richmond Dispatch*, July 4, 1897, quoted in Robertson, "Danville under Military Occupation," 331–33.

90. Robertson, "Danville under Military Occupation," 333–34, 337–42; Withers, *Autobiography of an Octogenarian*, 218–25 (quote on 223). For a detailed account of Danville in the last days of the Confederacy, see McFall, *Danville in the Civil War*, 100–113. Withers also managed to stop the departing Confederate troops from burning the one bridge over the Dan River, trying with logic first but eventually resorting to sending "a company of guards to the bridge with instructions to resist, by force if necessary, any attempt to fire the structure." The Confederate forces gave up and left town. Withers, *Autobiography of an Octogenarian*, 215–16.

91. W. Dame, *From the Rapidan to Richmond and the Spotsylvania Campaign*, 10.

92. See Chapter 2.

93. See Chapter 3.

94. Pittsylvania Ladies' Soldiers' Aid Society, letter, 1861, UVA. See also Chapter 4.

95. Murrell, "Of Necessity and Public Benefit," 77–100; Blair, *Virginia's Private War*, 7, 94–96; Virginia, *Acts and Joint Resolutions* (1863): 56, 21–23 (first quote); Virginia, *Acts and Joint Resolutions* (1864): 48; "Account of Commissioners for Soldiers' Families," in Pittsylvania County Public Schools, Financial Accounts, 1856–1864, UVA (second quote). See also Green, *This Business of Relief*, 68–84.

96. Blair, *Virginia's Private War*, 9. See also Chapter 6.

97. See also Chapter 5.

2. Loss and Reconstruction: The Impact of the Civil War on Veteran Families and Their Postwar Rebuilding

1. W. Dame, *From the Rapidan to Richmond and the Spotsylvania Campaign*, 58; Withers, *Autobiography of an Octogenarian*, 236. The *Religious Herald* was the state newspaper of the Baptist Association of Virginia.

2. Vinovskis estimated that 61 percent of military-age Southern white men (13–43) in 1860 served in Confederate forces. During the war, 18 percent of Southern white men of military age and over one-quarter of Confederate soldiers died (compared with the deaths of 8 percent of Northern white men of military age and one-sixth of white Union soldiers), while many more suffered wounds that affected the rest of their lives. Vinovskis, "Have Social Historians Lost the Civil War?" 5–10. If Gary Gallagher is correct that Vinovskis's count underestimates the degree of Southern participation in the Confederate Army, then the county's participation rates may be closer to the norm for the South. Gary Gallagher, email message to author, November 9, 2005. Out of 4,137 white men aged 13–43 in the county in 1860, 3,283 served in Confederate forces and 831 died in service. In this chapter, unless otherwise noted, statistics are calculated using the Soldiers Database and the database created from the 1860 and 1870 Manuscript Population Censuses (including 1860 slave schedules) for Pittsylvania County. See the appendix for more on these two databases.

3. Of the 4,137 white men aged 13–43 in the county in 1860, and the 3,283 front-line soldiers, 1,592 of those who survived the war were wounded in action, got sick, or were captured and imprisoned by Union forces, and 2,423 soldiers had something happen to them during the war (831 deaths plus 1,592 wounded, ill, or POW).

4. "Veteran family household" here refers to the households with veterans and veteran family members in them, removing those people clearly employing the veteran and his family or employees (or slaves in 1860) of the veteran and his family. "Real estate" meant the value of land and buildings, while "personal estate" referred to all other items owned by the person, which in 1860 included slaves.

5. This statistic actually overestimates veteran land ownership since it measures all real-estate-possessing households with any veterans in them, including those with landless soldiers who worked for landowning non-family-members.

6. I do not use the 1880 population census here for two reasons. First, I am particularly interested here in the immediate impact and initial strategies used by these families by 1870. Second, individual personal and real estate information was not included in the 1880 manuscript population census schedules as it was in 1860 and 1870, making many of

the statistics more difficult or even impossible to calculate. See the appendix for more on issues with the 1890 and 1900 censuses.

7. I do not know of any work that has addressed this question in a systematic way for a large sample of Confederate veteran families. Russell Johnson's work on the Union soldiers of Dubuque, Iowa, suggests that the overall economic impact of military service was to make them less upwardly mobile than their non-veteran counterparts. Johnson, "The Civil War Generation." See also Johnson, *Warriors into Workers*.

8. James S. Redd to WTS, May 17, 1862, WTS Papers, SHC; Judgment Orders from J. A. Lovelace, April 27, 1867, December 14, 1867, and December 14, 1867, David Harris Watson Papers, VHS. "Healthy" families included any family whose soldier's (or soldiers') records had no indications of any injury, illness, capture, or death. (It is possible that inaccurate records may have caused some miscategorizations, but at a minimum, this method provides some measure of differences in economic impact based on experiences.)

9. Soldiers Database; Pittsylvania County Population Census, 1860, 1870; Shockoe Baptist Church Minutes, December 1879, and January 1880, VBHS.

10. Rawley Martin to Bettie Penick, January 7, 1864, Rawley W. Martin Papers, SHC; W. N. Layne file, Pittsylvania County, Act of 1888, Auditor of Public Accounts, Confederate Pension Applications, LVA; Soldiers Database; Pittsylvania County Population Census, 1860, 1870. POWs are included in the non-healthy group because poor prison conditions had long-term health effects.

11. As discussed later, however, many widows did not have the opportunity to remarry, and others chose not to do so.

12. George Jones to Sarah Jones, August 17, 1864, George W. Jones Papers, DU; Jedediah Carter to Susan Carter, October 3, 1863, Jedediah Carter Papers, DU.

13. LeeAnn Whites demonstrates these difficulties for couples in postwar Georgia in *The Civil War as a Crisis in Gender*, 132–59. See also the discussion on the postwar limitations of the family as a support system at the end of this chapter.

14. George Jones to Sarah Jones, September 11, 1864, and December 13, 1864, George W. Jones Papers, DU; Pittsylvania County Population Census, 1860, 1870; Jedediah Carter to Susan Carter, November 5, 1863, and November 17, 1863, Jedediah Carter Papers, DU.

15. Marten, *The Children's Civil War*, 68–100, 204–7.

16. The more severe instances of psychological trauma are discussed in chapter 5.

17. Woodward, *The Burden of Southern History*, 19. LeeAnn Whites and others have discussed the appeal of the home to Southern white men returning from the Civil War. See Whites, *Civil War as a Crisis in Gender*, 132–59.

18. Bettie Penick to Rawley Martin, May 2, 1862, Rawley W. Martin Papers, SHC (emphasis in original). For death in Northern families, see Mitchell, *The Vacant Chair*.

19. New Hampshire soldier quoted in Robertson, "Danville under Military Occupation," 346.

20. Rawley Martin to Beckie Martin, February 3, 1863, Rawley W. Martin Papers, SHC; George Jones to Sarah Jones, July 26, 1864, George W. Jones Papers, DU.

21. Rawley Martin to one of his sisters, September 3, 1863, Rawley W. Martin Papers, SHC; George Jones to Sarah Jones, November 16, 1864, George W. Jones Papers, DU.

22. The mental impact of the war on the minds of veteran family members and the long-term physical impact of the war on veterans are discussed in chapters 5 and 6.

23. Edwin Redd to WTS, May 28, 1868, WTS Papers, SHC. In reconstituting households after the war had ended, some white families confronted a larger change. For those veterans and all whites who had owned slaves, black men and women had been at least part of their households, even, in some cases, part of their families. With emancipation, however, that changed, as ex-slaves asserted their freedom.

24. In 1870, 714 of the 1,348 veteran families living in Pittsylvania could be classified as living in single-family households. Calculated from Pittsylvania County Population Census, 1860, 1870, and the Soldiers Database. For comparison, in 1860, 845 of the 1,808 future veteran families could be classified as living in single-family households, revealing a slight increase from 1860 (47 percent) to 1870 (53 percent).

25. In 1870, 550 of the 1,348 veteran family households in Pittsylvania could be classified as extended-family households, homes in which the residents are related to one another but which are composed not only of parent(s) and children under age twenty-one. H. S. Carter to Susan Carter, January 10, 1864, Jedediah Carter Papers, DU. For comparison, in 1860, 813 of the 1,808 future veteran families could be classified as living in extended-family households, revealing a slight decrease from 1860 (45 percent) to 1870 (41 percent).

26. Pittsylvania County Population Census, 1860, 1870. Jane Turner Censer found this strategy to be more common after the war among families in the South that had been members of the antebellum elite. Censer, *The Reconstruction of White Southern Womanhood*, 51–54. See also Carmichael, *The Last Generation*. The average age for Pittsylvania veterans was 24.3 in 1860 and 35.3 in 1870. By 1870, the average and median age of the county's soldiers had clearly shifted well past the age at which the average man married (somewhere between twenty-one and twenty-seven, according to several different studies cited in Kenzer, *Kinship and Neighborhood in a Southern Community*, 189n33). Ages calculated from Pittsylvania County Population Census, 1860, 1870; Soldiers Database.

27. In 1870, 260 of the 1,348 veteran family households in Pittsylvania had hired workers or rented out space to boarders. Pittsylvania County Population Census, 1870. For comparison, in 1860, 134 of the 1,808 future veteran families had hired workers or rented out space to boarders, revealing a significant increase from 1860 (7 percent) to 1870 (19 percent) that can probably be attributed to the end of slavery and the fact that many of those workers were now counted in the population census. (For a fuller discussion of the economic transition from slavery to freedom in this area, see Kerr-Ritchie, *Freedpeople in the Tobacco South*.)

28. In 1870, out of 1,348 veteran family households in Pittsylvania, 48 veteran families were living in households of people to whom they were not related. For comparison, in 1860, 229 of the 1,808 future veterans were living in households of people to whom they were not related, revealing a significant decrease from 1860 (13 percent) to 1870 (4 percent). This change is probably related to the life cycle of the soldiers themselves. In 1860, many of the future soldiers were young enough (see note 26) to have not yet established themselves, and most of them were single at that time. (Only 3 of the 229 were boarders in 1860.)

29. In 1870, 54 out of the 1,348 veteran family households in Pittsylvania were single men living without family. For comparison, in 1860, 37 of the 1,808 future veteran families could be classified as living without family, revealing a slight increase from 1860 (2 percent) to 1870 (4 percent).

30. Pittsylvania County Population Census, 1860, 1870; Soldiers Database. The shortage of white men of marriageable age was significant. Looking at those whites in Pittsylvania between the ages of twenty and thirty-nine (roughly marriageable age), in 1860, there were 98.9 men per 100 women. By 1870, in that same group (now age thirty to forty-nine), there were only 81.8 men per 100 women. Pittsylvania County Population Census, 1860, 1870.

31. Gross, "'Good Angels': Confederate Widowhood in Virginia," 133–34.

32. Ibid., 137; Lebsock, *The Free Women of Petersburg*, 268n13. Percentage for Lebsock calculated from 1821 to 1850 widows (27 of 80 remarried). See also K. Wood, *Masterful Women*, 237n58. Out of 108 veteran widows found in the 1870 census, 8 were found to have remarried. Although it is also possible that some of the women in the group remarried after 1870, Kenzer notes in his study of Virginia's war widows that four-fifths of the widows who remarried did so before 1870. Kenzer, "The Uncertainty of Life," 125–26.

33. Gross, "'Good Angels': Confederate Widowhood in Virginia," 134; Pittsylvania County Population Census, 1860, 1870; Soldiers Database.

34. K. Wood, *Masterful Women*, 150–57; Lebsock, *The Free Women of Petersburg*, 24–27; Barber, "The White Wings of Eros," 127. Kenzer also notes that some widows did not want to remarry because their husbands' wills required them to give up their inheritance if they married again. Kenzer, "The Uncertainty of Life," 121–22.

35. Of the 108 veteran widows found in the 1870 census, 76 of them lived as independent household heads.

36. Of the 108 veteran widows found in the 1870 census, 18 were found to be living with family members.

37. Gross, "'Good Angels': Confederate Widowhood in Virginia," 151n15; Pittsylvania County Population Census, 1870. Only 4 of the 108 widows lived with apparent non-family-members; 3 of those lived in the county's poorhouse. See also Kenzer, "The Uncertainty of Life," 112, 129–31.

38. The farming statistics come from occupation classifications made in the 1870 population census. In 1860, 67 percent of white men and 69 percent of future soldiers worked in agriculture. Pittsylvania County Population Census, 1860, 1870; Soldiers Database.

39. Siegel, *The Roots of Southern Distinctiveness*, 156–62, Kerr-Ritchie, *Freedpeople in the Tobacco South*, 94–95; Tilley, *The Bright-Tobacco Industry*, 35–36, 124–25, 489–98. See also *Danville Times*, September 3, 1870.

40. Kerr-Ritchie, *Freedpeople in the Tobacco South*, 5, 93–156; Edwards, *Gendered Strife and Confusion*, 81; Siegel, *The Roots of Southern Distinctiveness*, 165.

41. Siegel, *The Roots of Southern Distinctiveness*, 94–95, 163, 187n3; David Dyer to WTS, March 10, 1866, WTS Papers, SHC; Wright, *Old South, New South*; Wayne, *The Reshaping of Plantation Society*, 202–4; Kerr-Ritchie, *Freedpeople in the Tobacco South*, 102–4; Edwards, *Gendered Strife and Confusion*, 80–106.

42. Hahn, *The Roots of Southern Populism*; Reidy, *From Slavery to Agrarian Capitalism*

in the Cotton Plantation South; Wright, *Old South, New South*; Grief Lampkin to WTS, February 22, 1877, WTS Papers, SHC.

43. Calculated from the Soldiers Database and the Pittsylvania County Population Census, 1860, 1870. The statistic is crude because it includes farming workers living with their landed employers as part of landowning households.

44. William Harraway to WTS, October 27, 1867, WTS Papers, SHC; Pittsylvania County Population Census, 1860, 1870.

45. Kerr-Ritchie, *Freedpeople in the Tobacco South*, 97; James Whittle to Mrs. Lewis N. Whittle, September 25, 1869, Lewis Neale Whittle Papers, SHC.

46. Pittsylvania County Population Census, 1860, 1870; Soldiers Database.

47. William A. Baugh to WTS, May 26, 1866, WTS Papers, SHC.

48. D. P. Marshall case file, Pittsylvania County, Act of 1886, Auditor of Public Accounts, Confederate Pension Disability Applications and Receipts, LVA.

49. James Gunn to WTS, March 13, 1865, WTS Papers, SHC.

50. Withers, *Autobiography of an Octogenarian*, 234, 237–39; W. Dame, *From the Rapidan to Richmond and the Spotsylvania Campaign*, 10–11, 51. See also Carmichael, *The Last Generation*, 217–18, 240.

51. E. D. Terry to D. H. Watson, December 6, 1861, undated; G. G. Giles to D. H. Watson, May 26, 1875; Farmers' Warehouse tobacco sales receipt, November 18, 1874; G. P. Herndon to D. H Watson, July 7, 1888; David Harris Watson file description, all in David Harris Watson Papers, VHS.

52. "For the Moral and Religious Improvement of Young Men," *Religious Herald*, October 1865, 25.

53. Jedediah Carter to Susan Carter, November 8, 1863, Jedediah Carter Papers, DU; Bettie Penick to Rawley Martin, June 5, 1863, Rawley W. Martin Papers, SHC. This work was unrecognized, in part, because only 17 of the 1,882 veteran women in the 1870 census were recorded as having a farming occupation, despite the extensive amount of farm-related work that many of these women did.

54. Rable, *Civil Wars*, 244–46; Pittsylvania County Population Census, 1870.

55. In 1870, seven of twenty-three veteran widows recorded with a "formal" occupation (not including "keeping house," "at home," or "without occupation") were listed as "farmer" and owned real estate of their own. Widows with no land seem to have stayed out of agriculture altogether or were forced out after their husbands died. For more on widows and farming, see Censer, *The Reconstruction of White Southern Womanhood*, 132–44.

56. In the 1870 census, out of the 1,882 women in veteran families age fifteen and over (the ages for which census takers were required to list an occupation), only 145 were listed with a "formal" occupation, meaning jobs separate from the work expected by female family members (listed under "keeping house" or "at home") and separate from the "without occupation" classification. Percentages in this paragraph are based on the census occupations listed for these 145 women. Out of 145, 107 were domestic servants, 11 were in clothing, and 4 worked as teachers, labored in a store, or ran a hotel.

The number and percentage of women in veteran families working as domestic servants for others increased significantly from 1860 to 1870, perhaps replacing black women as domestics in wealthier homes. In 1860, only 8 veteran women are listed as domestic servants (~7 percent of those with a formal occupation). By 1870, 107 veteran women are listed as domestic servants (~74 percent of those with a formal occupation). For a discussion of the use of white women as domestic servants by elite households and of postwar teaching opportunities, see Censer, *The Reconstruction of White Southern Womanhood*, 69–71, 159–83.

57. Stevenson, *Life in Black and White*, 41–51; Tilley, *The Bright-Tobacco Industry*, 489–521; Jedediah Carter to Susan Carter, November 8, 1863, Jedediah Carter Papers, DU; Rebecca Martin to Rawley Martin, January 28, 1863, Rawley W. Martin Papers, SHC. Out of 1,882 women age fifteen and over in veteran families, 1,536 were listed as "keeping house" or "at home"; another 205 were listed as "without occupation" or "no occupation." See also Gross, "'Good Angels': Confederate Widowhood in Virginia," 151n15.

58. Whites, *The Civil War as a Crisis in Gender*, 130–31. See also Censer, *The Reconstruction of White Southern Womanhood*, 59–65.

59. Withers, *Autobiography of an Octogenarian*, 191–92, 209–10.

60. Pittsylvania County Population Census, 1860, 1870, 1880; Collection introduction, Katherine Spiller Graves Moses Papers, VHS.

61. On the 1870 Pittsylvania census question of whether a person had attended school within the past year, 330 of 2,151 veteran children between the ages of five and eighteen and 731 of 3,994 non-veteran family white children between those ages were marked yes. Roanoke Baptist Association, *Minutes of the Annual Meeting*, 1874, 9, VBHS; Pittsylvania County Population Census, 1860, 1870; Soldiers Database.

62. Of the 1,808 veteran family households found in the 1860 census, 1,110 of them were found again in 1870. Without linking every white household in the 1860 and 1870 censuses, there is no easy way to compare veteran persistence numbers to whites as a whole. In Kenzer's study of Orange County, North Carolina, *Kinship and Neighborhood in a Southern Community*, however, he found that the persistence rate from 1860 to 1870 of white men age twenty to thirty-nine (in 1860) was only 36.8 percent (pp. 164–65). The persistence rate for a similar group of Pittsylvania's veterans (age twenty to thirty-nine in 1860) was 58.1 percent (of the 1,524 veterans found in the 1860 census, 885 were found in the 1870 census). Peter Carmichael's study of elite Virginia men of the "Last Generation" found that 80.3 percent of the men in his sample stayed in Virginia after the war. I include this statistic for the sake of comparison, though its usefulness for contrast is limited because of its smaller sample size, restriction to the elite class, and larger geographic boundaries. Carmichael, *The Last Generation*, 240, table 9.

63. Withers, *Autobiography of an Octogenarian*, 234–39; J. M. Hines to WTS, January 22, 1866, WTS Papers, SHC; Soldiers Database.

64. Stevenson, *Life in Black and White*, 7.

65. Samuel S. Bryant to WTS, February 26, 1866, WTS Papers, SHC; Whites, *The Civil War as a Crisis in Gender*, 151–57.

66. Bertram Wyatt-Brown has described this tension between fathers and sons in antebellum planter families in *Southern Honor*.

67. Logue, *To Appomattox and Beyond*; Faust, *Mothers of Invention*, 252–53; Carter, *When the War Was Over*, 269–71; Trelease, *White Terror*, xlii.

68. Kentuck Baptist Church, October 1867, November 1867, and June 1868; County

Line Baptist Church, June 1874, July 1874, June 1875, April 1881, January 1889, November 1895, and December 1895, all in VBHS. On the economic effects of "intemperance," see Edwin Redd to WTS, May 28, 1868, WTS Papers, SHC.

69. Kentuck Baptist Church Minutes, September 1876, and October 1876, VBHS. See also Bardaglio, *Reconstructing the Household*.

70. Kentuck Baptist Church Minutes, December 1866, January 1867, and July 1871, VBHS; Soldiers Database; Pittsylvania County Population Census, 1860, 1870. Evans was expelled from his church when his adultery was revealed.

71. Bettie Penick to W. S. Penick, April 23, 1862, Rawley W. Martin Papers, SHC; George Jones to Sarah Jones, April 3, 1862, June 17, 1862, and January 6, 1864, George W. Jones Papers, DU; Rable, *Civil Wars*, 50–51. See also Faust, *Mothers of Invention*; Whites, *The Civil War as a Crisis in Gender*.

72. Faust, *Mothers of Invention*, 250–54; Whites, *The Civil War as a Crisis in Gender*, 132–59; Rable, *Civil Wars*, 240–88.

73. Whites, *The Civil War as a Crisis in Gender*, 132–36.

74. Edwin Redd to WTS, May 28, 1868, WTS Papers, SHC. For more on the impact of lost limbs on Civil War veterans, see Herschbach, "Fragmentation and Reunion."

75. Whites, *The Civil War as a Crisis in Gender*, 160–98; Faust, *Mothers of Invention*, 250–54 (quote on 252). For a slightly different take, see Janney, *Burying the Dead but Not the Past*.

76. Kentuck Baptist Church Minutes, September 1876, and October 1876, VBHS.

77. Edwards, *Gendered Strife and Confusion*, 20–21, 107–83.

78. Ibid., 184–254; Bardaglio, *Reconstructing the Household*, 131–36. See also Dailey, *Before Jim Crow*.

79. Kenzer, *Kinship and Neighborhood in a Southern Community*; George Jones to Sarah Jones, June 17, 1862, September 11, 1864, November 16, 1864, and December 13, 1864, George W. Jones Papers, DU.

80. Edwin Redd to WTS, May 28, 1868, WTS Papers, SHC; Charles H. Owen file, Pittsylvania County, Act of 1888, Auditor of Public Accounts, Confederate Pension Applications, LVA.

81. Pittsylvania County Population Census, 1870. On the role of the local poorhouse in Virginia, see also Watkinson, "Rogues, Vagabonds, and Fit Objects"; Green, *This Business of Relief*.

82. Mt. Hermon Baptist Church Minutes, April 1884, March 1889, and April 1890, VBHS.

3. Local Support from Baptist Churches

1. Because of the sources available, most of the discussion in this chapter focuses on the county's Baptist churches. This focus is not unreasonable since Baptists in 1870 were the single largest denomination in the county, with 44 percent of the churched citizens (5,100 of 11,500) and 54 percent of the churches (23 of 42). U.S. Census Office, *Statistics of the Population of the United States at the Ninth Census*, 558. In addition, Baptists represented a significant force (along with Methodists) in the state, and in the South as a

whole, before, during, and after the Civil War. See Harvey, "'Yankee Faith' and Southern Redemption," 167–86; Woodworth, *While God Is Marching On*.

2. Chatham Baptist Church Minutes, VBHS. See also Woodworth, *While God Is Marching On*, 15; Schweiger, *The Gospel Working Up*.

3. First Baptist Church of Danville Minutes, April 1864, VBHS; Mt. Hermon Baptist Church Minutes, January 1863, VBHS; Pittsylvania County Population Census, 1860; Gregory, *38th Virginia Infantry*, 77–133. On other area churches providing financial assistance, see McFall, *Danville in the Civil War*, 19.

4. Shockoe Baptist Church Minutes, June 7, 1862, May 9, 1863, May 7, 1864, May 13, 1865, May 12, 1866, July 1867, July 11, 1868, and May 1869, VBHS; Pittsylvania County Population Census, 1860. The family is listed both as "Owen" and "Owens."

5. Ash, *When the Yankees Came*. For one example of the continuity of the county's religious institutions, see Kentuck Baptist Church Minutes, 1861–1865, VBHS.

6. Baptist General Association of Virginia, *Annual Meeting Minutes, June 1862*, 43–44, and *Annual Meeting Minutes, June 1864*, 6, VBHS.

7. Straight Stone Baptist Church Minutes, April 1863, and February 1864, VBHS; Kentuck Baptist Church Minutes, August 1864, and March 1865, VBHS. See also Blair, *Virginia's Private War*, 90.

8. Roanoke Baptist Association, *Minutes of the Annual Meeting*, 1861, 9–10, VBHS; "The Cost of War," *Religious Herald*, July 1862, 22, VBHS. Similar concerns have been common among civilian populations during many U.S. wars. For a World War II example, see Wecter, *When Johnny Comes Marching Home*.

9. Roanoke Baptist Association, *Minutes of the Annual Meeting*, 1861, 7, VBHS; Kentuck Baptist Church Minutes, September 1864, March 1865, VBHS; Roanoke Baptist Association, *Minutes of the Annual Meeting*, 1864, 6–7, VBHS. Conversion statistic from Barton and Logue, eds., *The Civil War Soldier*, 327. See also Woodworth, *While God Is Marching On*, chaps. 8, 9; Harvey, "'Yankee Faith' and Southern Redemption," 171–73; Faust, "Christian Soldiers," 327–53; Schweiger, *The Gospel Working Up*, chaps. 5, 6.

10. Roanoke Baptist Association, *Minutes of the Annual Meeting*, 1861, 17; 1863, 13; 1864, 11; 1865, 10–11, VBHS; Straight Stone Baptist Church Minutes, October–December 1863, VBHS. For one discussion of the wartime role of religion and churches for elite women, see Faust, "Without Pilot or Compass," 250–60.

11. Baptist General Association of Virginia, *Annual Meeting Minutes, June 1863*, 68–71, VBHS. See also Shattuck, *A Shield and Hiding Place*; Woodworth, *While God Is Marching On*, chaps. 7–14.

12. Greenfield Baptist Church Minutes, August 6, 1861, and September 26, 1861, VBHS.

13. Baptist General Association of Virginia, *Annual Meeting Minutes, June 1864*, 5, VBHS.

14. The Civil War did not change American churches' "devotion to social reform," a commitment that led those institutions in the postwar period to attempt to improve the world. Hill, "Religion and the Results of the Civil War," 360–75.

15. Harvey, "'Yankee Faith' and Southern Redemption," 174–75; Hill, "Religion and the Results of the Civil War," 366–67; Woodworth, *While God Is Marching On*, 287; Baptist

General Association of Virginia, *Annual Meeting Minutes, June 1865*, 26, VBHS; Ash, *When the Yankees Came*; Kentuck Baptist Church Minutes, September 1866, VBHS. Southern churches also had to deal in the postwar period with the decision by Southern black Christians to form their own churches. See Hill, "Religion and the Results of the Civil War," 364–68; Montgomery, *Under Their Own Vine and Fig Tree*.

16. Pittsylvania County Population Census, 1860; Soldiers Database; Kentuck Baptist Church Minutes, 1867–1890, VBHS. On the databases, see also the appendix.

17. Kentuck Baptist Church Minutes, July 1866, July 1867, and February 1868, VBHS.

18. Kentuck Baptist Church Minutes, June–August 1868, January and June–July 1869, and January 1870, VBHS.

19. Kentuck Baptist Church Minutes, July 1867, June–August 1868, May 1869, March–April, June, and October–November 1870, June–July, September, and November 1871, June 1873, June 1876, December 1880, August 1881, August 1883, June–July 1884, August 1888, and August 1890, VBHS.

20. Kentuck Baptist Church Minutes, July 1867, May 1869, April–October 1870, May and June 1874, April–May and November 1875, September 1877, July 1878, and March 1882, VBHS; Soldiers Database; Pittsylvania County Population Census, 1870. The Hay family was sometimes listed as "Hays."

21. Kentuck Baptist Church Minutes, 1874–1885, VBHS.

22. F. H. Jones, "Historical Sketch of Kentuck Church from May 1788 to May 1888," VBHS.

23. First Baptist Church Minutes, June 20, 1889, VBHS.

24. Mt. Tabor Baptist Church Minutes, 1869, VBHS; Mt. Hermon Baptist Church Minutes, October 1871, VBHS.

25. Shockoe Baptist Church Minutes, February 1885, VBHS; Mt. Hermon Baptist Church, April 1884, March 1889, and April 1890, VBHS.

26. Kentuck Baptist Church Minutes, June 1876, June 1874, and August 1875, VBHS.

27. Straight Stone Baptist Church Minutes, 1860–1861, VBHS. See also Shockoe Baptist Church Minutes, 1867–1890, VBHS; Riceville Baptist Church Minutes, 1866–1870, VBHS.

28. See chapters 1 and 2 for more on women's work and threats to Southern white male masculinity.

29. Straight Stone Baptist had a rule that women could not even vote for their minister. Straight Stone Baptist Church Minutes, 1860–1861, VBHS. See Heyrman, *Southern Cross*.

30. Shockoe Baptist Church Minutes, June 7, 1862, May 9, 1863, May 7, 1864, May 13, 1865, May 12, 1866, July 1867, July 11, 1868, and May 1869; Kentuck Baptist Church Minutes, April 1865, August 1870, April–May 1872, and April 1873, VBHS; Gregory, *38th Virginia Infantry*, 77–133; Pittsylvania County Population Census, 1860, 1870.

31. Kentuck Baptist Church Minutes, December 1872 and March 1873, VBHS; Pittsylvania County Population Census, 1860, 1870; Shockoe Baptist Church Minutes, October 1883, VBHS.

32. Chatham Baptist Church Minutes, July 13, 1867, VBHS; Kentuck Baptist Church Minutes, 1861–1880, VBHS. Chatham averaged 62 white members between 1861 and 1880.

Kentuck's 234 average members gave $294.94 in direct aid to poor members from 1861 to 1880. First Baptist's aid to the poor may well have been comparable for this period, but unfortunately its minutes from 1870 to 1886 are not at the VBHS. See also County Line, Greenfield, and New Prospect (Mt. Pleasant) Church Minutes, 1860–1890, VBHS.

33. Quote from 1880 First Baptist Church of Danville Constitution, VBHS; County Line Baptist Church Minutes, December 1878, July 1895, and December 1896, VBHS; Chatham Baptist Church Minutes, 1861–1870, VBHS; Roanoke Baptist Association, *Minutes of the Annual Meeting*, 1860–1880, VBHS.

34. Baptist General Association of Virginia, *Annual Meeting Minutes*, June 1871, 45, VBHS; Roanoke Baptist Association, *Minutes of the Annual Meeting*, August 1875, 6–7, 18 (emphasis in original), VBHS.

35. Roanoke Baptist Association, *Minutes of the Annual Meeting*, August 1883, 10, VBHS.

36. Kentuck Baptist Church Minutes, 1860–1890, VBHS; Derks, ed., *Value of a Dollar*, 10. For comparison, when adjusted for inflation, $20–$30/year in 1880 would equal approximately $400–$600/year in 2005. See "The Inflation Calculator," http://www.westegg.com/inflation.

37. Kentuck Baptist Church Minutes, 1860–1890, VBHS. The number of families is calculated based on the average white household size of 4.7 in Pittsylvania County Population Census, 1870.

38. Compiled from Minutes of Pittsylvania County Baptist Churches, 1860–1890, VBHS.

39. Roanoke Baptist Association, *Minutes of the Annual Meeting*, 1875, 6–7, VBHS.

40. Schweiger, *The Gospel Working Up*, chap. 6. Schweiger argues that "pastors did not intend these [financial] needs [of veterans' families] to become the primary focus of religious benevolence" (122).

41. Baptist General Association of Virginia, *Annual Meeting Minutes*, June 1864, 4–5, VBHS. The plan developed was modeled after Baptist programs in Georgia and Alabama to set up "Asylums for the orphans of soldiers" (5).

42. Roanoke Baptist Association, *Minutes of the Annual Meeting*, August 1864, 8, VBHS; Chatham Baptist Church Minutes, September 1864 and March 1865, VBHS; First Baptist Church of Danville Minutes, September 1864, VBHS.

43. Baptist General Association of Virginia, *Annual Meeting Minutes*, June 1865, 30, VBHS; Roanoke Baptist Association, *Minutes of the Annual Meeting*, August 1867, 10, VBHS.

44. Baptist General Association of Virginia, *Annual Meeting Minutes*, June 1867, 46–47 (emphasis in original); June 1868, 59; June 1869, 28–29; June 1870, 16, VBHS.

45. Baptist General Association of Virginia, *Annual Meeting Minutes*, June 1870, 16; June 1871, 16–17, 36–37, VBHS. It is worth noting that many of these soldiers' "orphans" still had mothers.

46. Unfortunately, the number of Pittsylvania children involved in the program could not be identified, except for the notations from the 1864 church minutes of Chatham Baptist and First Danville cited in note 42. Sunday schools and other missions of educational

benevolence also offered limited additional learning opportunities for children in veteran and other families (Schweiger, *The Gospel Working Up*, 121–27).

47. Mt. Tabor Baptist Church Minutes, 1869, VBHS; New Prospect (Mt. Pleasant) Baptist Church Minutes, July 1874, VBHS.

48. Baptist General Association of Virginia, *Annual Meeting Minutes, June 1865*, 21, VBHS.

49. "For the Moral and Religious Improvement of Young Men," *Religious Herald*, October 1865, 25, VBHS.

50. Kentuck Baptist Church Minutes, September 1865, June 1867 (quote), November 1867, May 1869, and August 1877, VBHS; Shockoe Baptist Church Minutes, September 1881, VBHS; Mt. Tabor Baptist Church Minutes, 1875–1880, VBHS.

51. Kentuck Baptist Church Minutes, July–August 1865, July 1866, and May 1874, VBHS; Shockoe Baptist Church Minutes, August 1870, October–November 1875, and January 1876, VBHS; Mt. Hermon Baptist Church Minutes, February 1870, VBHS.

52. Shockoe Baptist Church Minutes, August 1870, October–November 1875, and January 1876, VBHS; Kentuck Baptist Church Minutes, October–November 1878, and January 1879, VBHS.

53. Roanoke Baptist Association, *Minutes of the Annual Meeting*, 1865, 10–11; 1870, 13; 1875, 16; 1880, 19, VBHS. Southern religion, despite the physical and economic impact of the war on most churches, managed to survive and thrive in the late nineteenth century. See Harvey, "'Yankee Faith' and Southern Redemption," 175; Woodworth, *While God Is Marching On*, chap. 15; Hill, "Religion and the Results of the Civil War," 374; Ayers, *The Promise of the New South*, chap. 7; Schweiger, *The Gospel Working Up*, 109–205.

54. Dancing also resulted in expulsion for a number of members, including veteran Robert Yates. Straight Stone Baptist Church Minutes, January 1866, and February 1867, VBHS; Shockoe Baptist Church Minutes, April–May 1870, VBHS. On antebellum churches, see McCurry, *Masters of Small Worlds*, chap. 4.

55. Riceville Baptist Church Minutes, July 1866, VBHS; Chatham Baptist Church Minutes, February 1860, VBHS.

56. Riceville Baptist Church Minutes, 1845, VBHS; New Prospect Baptist Church Minutes, September 1873, VBHS.

57. *Religious Herald*, January 1866, 10, VBHS.

58. Roanoke Baptist Association, *Minutes of the Annual Meeting*, August 1867, 7, VBHS; Mt. Hermon Baptist Church Minutes, March 1872, VBHS; Kentuck Baptist Church Minutes, May 1869 and November 1871, VBHS; Shockoe Baptist Church Minutes, December 1879 and January 1880, VBHS; County Line Baptist Church Minutes, August 1870 and 1870–1885, VBHS.

59. Rorabaugh, *The Alcoholic Republic*, 233; Rosenburg, *Living Monuments*, 112–16.

60. Shockoe Baptist Church Minutes, September 1866 and June and August 1869, VBHS; Straight Stone Baptist Church Minutes, June 1867, VBHS; Kentuck Baptist Church Minutes, December 1866 and January 1867, VBHS. Adultery by veteran widows would have been further evidence for church leaders of the threats to postwar patriarchy.

61. Kentuck Baptist Church Minutes, September and October 1876, VBHS.

62. Riceville Baptist Church Minutes, January 1866 (first quote), VBHS; Mt. Tabor Baptist Church Minutes, May 1875, VBHS.

63. First Baptist Church of Danville Minutes, January and March 1866, VBHS.

4. Appeals for Local Elite Assistance: The Case of William T. Sutherlin

1. Charles Ball to WTS, July 26, 1865, WTS Papers, SHC.

2. Guide, WTS Papers, SHC, 1; Pollock, *Illustrated Sketchbook*, 120; Pittsylvania County Population Census, 1860, 1870; Siegel, *The Roots of Southern Distinctiveness*, 140–60; Dailey, *Before Jim Crow*, 103–31. See also McFall, *Danville in the Civil War*, 20–22; *Memorials of the Life, Public Services and Character of William T. Sutherlin*. For Sutherlin's potential generalship, see two letters from Abner Anderson to WTS, both dated April 28, 1862, WTS Papers, SHC. His worth in 1870, adjusted for inflation, would have equaled $3.1 million in 2005 ("The Inflation Calculator," www.westegg.com/inflation). See also the appendix for more on the population censuses.

3. French, "Sutherlin, Wm. Thomas, Major," LVA (quote); Danville Museum of Fine Arts and History, "History—Sutherlin Family," http://www.danvillemuseum.org/index.php?page_id=19; "William Thomas Sutherlin," *Virginia Magazine of History and Biography* 1 (January 1894): 339–40; G. Dame, *Historical Sketch of Roman Eagle Lodge*, 100–103; *Memorials of the Life, Public Service and Character of William T. Sutherlin*.

4. "Surviving members of the upper class" refers to the fact that not all members of the upper class did as well as Sutherlin in surviving the war and making the transition to the postwar economic world.

5. For a discussion of the antebellum "ligaments of community," including loans and gifts, between elites and non-elites in Georgia, see Harris, *Plain Folk and Gentry in a Slave Society*, 94–122. For a more Civil War–centered chronology, although not focused on veterans or their families, see Tripp, *Yankee Town, Southern City*, 25–37.

6. Database created by author from WTS Papers, SHC. Forty-one of the seventy-two appeals came from veteran families, and appeals from Pittsylvania-Danville people make up fifty-five of the seventy-two appeals, including nine appeals from veteran families who had lived in the area and fought with area units but then had moved after the war.

7. J. M. McCue to WTS, July 13, 1868, WTS Papers, SHC; "Augusta County, Virginia, Soldiers Records: Valley of the Shadow," Virginia Center for Digital History, http://valley.vcdh.virginia.edu/govdoc/soldiers_dossier.html; Henry Wise to WTS, April 8 and 27, 1867; William Robertson to WTS, May 9, 1868, both in WTS Papers, SHC.

8. WTS Papers, SHC. Unless otherwise noted, all statistics come from a database created from the appeal letters to Sutherlin from the WTS Papers, SHC. There are two gaps in the letters, 1863–64 and 1873–76. The final letters in the collection are from 1884, when Sutherlin had become fairly ill. The bulk of the appeal letters (thirty-nine) come from the critical period immediately after the war, 1865 to 1871.

9. For an example of an appeal as part of a larger letter, see J. M. McCue to WTS, July 13, 1868, WTS Papers, SHC.

10. Seven of fourteen requests made in 1860 and the first three months of 1861 asked Sutherlin for help getting a job.

11. A. E. Wiseman to WTS, March 1865; J. L. Masson to WTS, March 31, 1864, both in WTS Papers, SHC. Eleven out of twenty-one wartime petitioners asked for Sutherlin to use his influence for them.

12. James Redd to WTS, May 26, 1862; Joseph R. Cabell to WTS, August 16, 1861; William Rison to WTS, October 5, 1861; George Booker to WTS, February 23, 1862; W W. Edwards to WTS, February 1, 1865; Abner Anderson to WTS, April 28, 1862; A. E. Wiseman to WTS, March 1865; S. J. Henry to WTS, March 1865; C. R. Robertson to WTS, March 22, 1865, all in WTS Papers, SHC.

13. Thirty-four of fifty-one postwar requests were for money; eighteen of twenty-four postwar veteran family requests were for money; twenty of twenty-five requests for money in which it is possible to identify intent (as loan or gift) were for loans.

14. J. M. McCue to WTS, July 13, 1868; S. S. Saunder to WTS, March 1877; David Dyer to WTS, March 10, 1866, all in WTS Papers, SHC. Twenty-one people specified the amount of money they wanted from Sutherlin. Of those, the average amount was $430.58, and both the median and mode amounts were $100.

15. Henry Wise to WTS, April 27, 1867, WTS Papers, SHC.

16. William Harraway to WTS, October 27, 1867; Charles Redd to WTS, February 1, 1869; William A. Baugh to WTS, May 8, 1866; Lena (Peace) Hamblett to WTS, April 6, 1867, all in WTS Papers, SHC. Thirteen of all fifty-one postwar appeals and eight of twenty-four postwar appeals from veteran families were for jobs. There is some overlap because a few people asked for both money and help getting a job. For example, see Grief Lampkin to WTS, February 22, 1877, WTS Papers, SHC.

17. William Berryman to WTS, March 9, 1869; Agnes Burton to WTS, May 10, 1866; J. M. McCue to WTS, July 13, 1868; D. S. Graves to WTS, December 18, 1866, all in WTS Papers, SHC. Only five of fifty-one postwar petitions asked for Sutherlin to use his influence.

18. Henry Wise to WTS, April 8, 1867 (emphasis in original); William Baugh to WTS, May 8, 1866, both in WTS Papers, SHC.

19. David Dyer to WTS, March 10, 1866; Grief Lampkin to WTS, February 22, 1877; M. T. Lanier to WTS, September 1, 1869; Jessee Moore to WTS, June 28, 1869, all in WTS Papers, SHC.

20. Adie A. Ferguson to WTS, March 28, 1867; Charles Ball to WTS, July 11, 1865; M. M. Millner to WTS, October 1, 1877; S. S. Saunders to WTS, March 1877, all in WTS Papers, SHC.

21. David Dyer to WTS, March 10, 1866; Thomas S. Jones to WTS, April 26, 1867; Adie Ferguson to WTS, March 28, 1867; Robert Baugh to WTS, April 25, 1867, all in WTS Papers, SHC. Only twelve petitioners actually specified a length of time for repayment of the requested loan: half wanted one month or less, two wanted three months, one wanted six months, and one-fourth wanted a full year.

22. Trattner, *From Poor Law to Welfare State*, 53–57, 67, 182–83.

23. Edwin Redd to WTS, May 28, 1868; William Robertson to WTS, October 1, 1877, both in WTS Papers, SHC.

24. Robert Baugh to WTS, April 25, 1867; Thomas Jones to WTS, April 26, 1867; Edwin Redd to WTS, May 28, 1868, all in WTS Papers, SHC.

25. David Dyer to WTS, March 10, 1866; Henry Wise to WTS, April 8, 1867; Grief Lampkin to WTS, February 22, 1877, all in WTS Papers, SHC.

26. Charles Redd to WTS, February 1, 1869; George Linthicum to WTS, February 23, 1877, both in WTS Papers, SHC.

27. John McCain to WTS, August 8, 1867; William Harraway to WTS, October 27, 1867, both in WTS Papers, SHC.

28. David Dyer to WTS, March 10, 1866; Adie Ferguson to WTS, March 28, 1867; J. E. Joyner to WTS, March 28, 1867, all in WTS Papers, SHC.

29. Robert Baugh to WTS, April 25, 1867; William Baugh to WTS, May 8, 1866, both in WTS Papers, SHC.

30. M. M. Millner to WTS, October 1, 1877, WTS Papers, SHC.

31. M. T. Lanier to WTS, September 1, 1869, WTS Papers, SHC.

32. Edwin Redd to WTS, May 28, 1868, WTS Papers, SHC.

33. Loula Terry to WTS, October 29, 1877, WTS Papers, SHC.

34. Logue, *To Appomattox and Beyond*, 93–94, 117–19, 121–25. See also Piehler, *Remembering War the American Way*, 47–74.

35. Robert Baugh to WTS, April 25, 1867; J. M. McCue to WTS, July 13, 1868; Adie Ferguson to WTS, March 28, 1867, all in WTS Papers, SHC.

36. J. D. Blackwell to WTS, March 12, 1867; Adie Ferguson to WTS, March 28, 1867; William Robertson to WTS, May 9, 1868; Lena (Peace) Hamblett to WTS, April 6, 1867; M. T. Lanier to WTS, September 1, 1869, all in WTS Papers, SHC.

37. Thomas Jones to WTS, April 26, 1867 (emphasis in original); M. T. Lanier to WTS, September 1, 1869; J. E. Joyner to WTS, March 28, 1867, all in WTS Papers, SHC.

38. David Dyer to WTS, March 10, 1866; William Baugh to WTS, May 8, 1866; William Harraway to WTS, October 27, 1867; John W. McCain to WTS, August 8, 1867; Grief Lampkin to WTS, February 22, 1877, all in WTS Papers, SHC.

39. See also Harris, *Plain Folk and Gentry in a Slave Society*, 94–122; Tripp, *Yankee Town, Southern City*, 25–37. These relationships involving "personal capital" are distinct from those described by Crandall Shifflett as "patronage capitalism," because Shifflett focuses on the interactions between elite whites and non-elite African Americans and I argue that, despite power differences, the white-white relationships were not entirely based on elite domination but were also based on an obligation to help the needy and the families of Confederate veterans. Shifflett, *Patronage and Poverty in the Tobacco South*, xii–xvi.

40. S. S. Saunders to WTS, March 1877; Lena (Peace) Hamblett to WTS, April 6, 1867, both in WTS Papers, SHC.

41. J. M. McCue to WTS, July 13, 1868; J. E. Joyner to WTS, March 28, 1867; Edwin Redd to WTS, May 28, 1868; Charles Ball to WTS, September 14, 1865, all in WTS Papers, SHC.

42. J. A. S. Wooding to WTS, March 29, 1867; William Harraway to WTS, October 27, 1867; M. M. Millner to WTS, October 10, 1877, all in WTS Papers, SHC.

43. William Rison to WTS, October 5, 1861, WTS Papers, SHC.

44. S. J. Hopkins to WTS, April 20, 1862; William Berryman to WTS, March 9, 1869; George Linthicum to WTS, February 23, 1877, all in WTS Papers, SHC.

45. Adie Ferguson to WTS, March 28, 1867; J. A. S. Wooding to WTS, March 29, 1867, both in WTS Papers, SHC; Tripp, *Yankee Town, Southern City*, 28–31.

46. Lena (Peace) Hamblett to WTS, April 6, 1867; Adie Ferguson to WTS, March 28, 1867; Loula Terry to WTS, October 29, 1877, all in WTS Papers, SHC.

47. Charles Ball to WTS, July 26, 1865 (emphasis in original); J. M. McCue to WTS, July 13, 1868; Grief Lampkin to WTS, February 22, 1877, all in WTS Papers, SHC.

48. Only twenty-three of seventy-two applications (under 32 percent) had an outcome that could be determined. Seventeen of the twenty-three known outcomes were positive (about 74 percent). Thirteen of the seventeen approved applicants came from the Pittsylvania area (about 76 percent). Fourteen of the seventeen approved applicants were members of veteran families (over 82 percent).

49. Sutherlin Papers Database, WTS Papers, SHC. For job finding, see A. E. Wiseman to WTS, March 1865, WTS Papers, SHC. On yearly income, see Derks, ed., *The Value of a Dollar*, 10.

50. Alfred Barbour to WTS, May 13, 1862; Charles Ball to WTS, September 14, 1865, both in WTS Papers, SHC.

51. C. R. Robertson to WTS, March 22, 1865; Alfred Barbour to WTS, May 13, 1862; Joseph Cabell to WTS, August 16, 1861, all in WTS Papers, SHC. See also Harris, *Plain Folk and Gentry in a Slave Society*, 94–122.

52. On charity from postwar elites to lower-class whites, see Tripp, *Yankee Town, Southern City*, 193–94, 252–55. On the disconnect between elites and lower-class whites in the Readjusters in the late 1870s and early 1880s, see Dailey, *Before Jim Crow*, 15–47, 103–31.

53. If all those petitions whose result cannot be determined are assumed to be rejections—perhaps he just ignored some pleas—then Sutherlin would have turned down over three-quarters of the petitioners whose requests have survived (fifty-five of seventy-two).

54. S. R. Neal (for WTS) to Thomas S. Jones, May 1, 1867, WTS Papers, SHC.

55. D. A. Claiborne to WTS, January 15, 1867; J. M. McCue to WTS, July 13, 1868; J. A. S. Wooding to WTS, March 29, 1867; Thomas S. Neal to WTS, April 26, 1867, all in WTS Papers, SHC. Responses are indicated on the back of each letter.

56. For example, see George Linthicum to WTS, February 23, 1877; Charles Redd to WTS, February 1, 1869, both in WTS Papers, SHC.

57. Shifflett, *Patronage and Poverty in the Tobacco South*; Tripp, *Yankee Town, Southern City*, 163–250.

58. For religious support for aid to Virginia's Confederate veterans and their families, see the *Religious Herald*, October 1865, 25, VBHS; Baptist General Association of Virginia, *Annual Meeting Minutes, June 1864*, 5, VBHS; Schweiger, *The Gospel Working Up*, 122. For Virginia's commutations, see McDaid, "With Lame Legs and No Money," 17; Virginia, *Acts and Joint Resolutions* (1866–67): 575–76. For the support for pensions and homes, see chapter 6. For Confederate memorials, see Blight, *Race and Reunion*; Foster, *Ghosts of the Confederacy*, 11–75; Piehler, *Remembering War the American Way*, 47–91; Wilson, *Baptized in Blood*. On the different Union veteran experience, see Johnson, *Warriors into Workers*, 277–78; McConnell, *Glorious Contentment*, 18–24.

59. Pittsylvania County Population Census, 1860, 1870. These statistics are based on the top twenty in wealth in 1860 and the fourteen of those who could be located in the

1870 census. (One person had died in the intervening years, so the combined wealth of his children was used.) Although many of the richest residents of the county in 1860 may not have been as wealthy, it is logical that needy Pittsylvanians turned to the people who were the wealthiest at the time of their request. A similar approach to the 1870 county census reveals, however, that the county's richest residents in 1870 were not as well-off as those in 1860. The average total wealth of the top twenty in 1860 was nearly $200,000, whereas in 1870, the average total wealth for the top twenty was not quite $63,000.

5. Veteran Families, Mental Illness, and the State: Dealing with the "Blue Devils"

1. Grob, *The Mad among Us*, 79–85. See also Tomes, *The Art of Asylum-Keeping*, xviii–ix, xix–xx, 103–13; McCandless, *Moonlight, Magnolias, and Madness*.

2. Grob, *The Mad among Us*, 79–85; Tomes, *The Art of Asylum-Keeping*, xiv–xviii, 129–294; Dwyer, *Homes for the Mad*, 1–6. See also Dain, *Disordered Minds*.

3. Although Western Lunatic Asylum's patients were almost exclusively white in the antebellum period, Eastern Lunatic Asylum accepted free blacks and eventually slaves before the Civil War, though they were typically segregated from the white patients. Two other state asylums, Central and Southwestern, were built after the war, but neither seems to have had a significant number of veterans. Central Lunatic Asylum (later Central State Hospital) was built in the postwar period to house separately the state's African Americans with mental illnesses. In a confusion-causing act for historians and archivists, for a brief time (1861–65) the General Assembly changed the name of the Western Lunatic Asylum to the Central Lunatic Asylum. In the 1890s, Western Lunatic Asylum became Western State Hospital. Savitt, *Medicine and Slavery*, 247–79; Dain, *Disordered Minds*, 108–13; Randolph, "Central Lunatic Asylum for the Colored Insane"; Salmon, comp., *A Guide to State Records*, 34–35; Library of Virginia, "Agency History, Western State Hospital," http://ajax.lva.lib.va.us/.

4. On the shift away from curability, see Tomes, *The Art of Asylum-Keeping*, ix–xxvii; Grob, *The Mad among Us*, 103–28; McCandless, *Moonlight, Magnolias, and Madness*, 249–69. On the increasing focus on black mental illness after emancipation, see McCandless, *Moonlight, Magnolias, and Madness*, 213–96; Hughes, "Labeling and Treating Black Mental Illness in Alabama"; and especially Randolph, "Central Lunatic Asylum for the Colored Insane." On Georgia's asylum as a particularly Southern social-welfare institution, see Wallenstein, "Laissez Faire and the Lunatic Asylum." The two significant exceptions to the absence of material on the links between Civil War veterans and asylums focus on the Northern perspective: Dean, *Shook Over Hell*; Marten, "Exempt from the Ordinary Rules of Life."

5. The focus on Western State's records for this chapter is logical since the white residents of Pittsylvania County who went to an asylum would typically have been sent to the state mental hospital in Staunton. Open throughout the war, the asylum suffered from shortages, worsened by a March 1865 raid by Union troops, who seized a large quantity of food and other supplies. A. Wood, *Dr. Francis T. Stribling and Moral Medicine*, 159–69; Virginia, *Annual Report of the Board of Directors of Western State Hospital*, 1903–1904.

On the war in Staunton, see "Valley of the Shadow," Virginia Center for Digital History, UVA, http://valley.vcdh.virginia.edu/.

6. Patient Register, 1828–1895, WSH. Only one person overlaps between the two groups, Catherine Bailey, making a total of seventy-five people in the sample size. The Case Books and Patient Registers were originally consulted at Western State Hospital, but they have since been moved to the Library of Virginia.

7. John Reed, Male Case Book (MCB) #1, 520; Charles White, MCB #1, 108–9, both in WSH (as are all further references in this chapter to the Male Case Book and the Female Case Book).

8. Patient Register, 1828–1895, WSH. One study of the Union Army's policy toward enlisting the mentally ill found that as of 1863 only 0.66 percent of men who enlisted or were conscripted into the Northern military were "rejected for manifest imbecility or insanity," a figure much lower than the nearly 10 percent of men discharged "for mental or moral defects" from the World War II American forces. Dean, *Shook Over Hell*, 118. Unfortunately, no similar study has been done for the Confederacy (such a study may not be possible), but given the manpower needs of that military, it seems unlikely that any but the most violent or disturbed men were allowed to leave the Southern forces.

9. William Granville Gray, MCB #1, 583, 587; William A. Miller, MCB #1, 435; John Kerlin, MCB #1, 521.

10. Joseph Noel, MCB #1, 38–39.

11. James Langhorne, MCB #1, 588; Simon Hornsberger, MCB #1, 209; Richard Moran, MCB #1, 405.

12. Caleb Rector, MCB #1, 559; Catherine Bailey, Female Case Book (FCB) #1, 63–64.

13. Polly Shank, FCB #1, 530–31. Although interactions between Virginia women and Union soldiers were much less of a problem in Pittsylvania County and Danville (since Union armies did not arrive there until after Appomattox), many of Virginia's women who never went to the asylum experienced similar problems to those of Polly Shank, if perhaps without the same extreme psychological impact.

14. Catharine M. Nicholson, FCB #1, 471; Polly Shank, FCB #1, 530–31; Mary Calfee, FCB #1, 279; Elizabeth Ann Pittman, FCB #1, 215–16.

15. Richard Whitehead, MCB #1, 232–34.

16. Adam Thompson, MCB #1, 591; Maria Harris, FCB #1, 460. Out of seventy-five case files, eleven listed the death of a relative as a causative factor of insanity.

17. Mary Woodell, FCB #1, 125.

18. Rich B. Stratton, MCB #1, 582; Peter J. White, MCB #1, 427; Amos Pierce, MCB #1, 556.

19. William Granville Gray, MCB #1, 583, 587. Gray's symptoms are similar to those found in some veterans and others of traumatic stress disorders, a subject that is discussed later in this chapter.

20. James Elliott, MCB #2, 172; Christopher Columbus Hedrick File, Pittsylvania County, Act of 1900, Auditor of Public Accounts, Confederate Pension Applications, LVA.

21. William E. Herndon, MCB #1, 87; Edward Newcomb, MCB #1, 503; William Dix, MCB #2, 310. See also James Burruss, MCB #1, 500. Out of seventy-five case files, eleven

list poverty or financial difficulties as part of the patients' problems. It is probable that more people in the sample suffered financially in the postwar period, but that financial hardship was not connected to the patients' mental condition by the people giving background information to the physicians.

22. James C. McCue, MCB #1, 173; Benjamin S. Carder, MCB #1, 99–100.

23. Simeon J. Hernsberger (also "Hornsberger"), MCB #1, 209. Out of seventy-five patients in the group, nineteen entered after the war ended in 1865 or in 1866. If the 1867 admissions are included, 32 percent would have entered after the war ended (twenty-four of seventy-five). For a contemporary account, see Dennett, *The South as It Is*. See also Whites, *The Civil War as a Crisis in Gender*, 96–159; Logue, *To Appomattox and Beyond*, 105–6; Carter, *When the War Was Over*, 269–71.

24. Chamberlayne, ed., *Ham Chamberlayne—Virginian*, viii–ix; J. Hampden Chamberlayne, MCB #1, 82–84, 86, 88, 95.

25. The exceptions are William Dix and James Elliott, who were members of Pittsylvania veteran families.

26. Marcellus Cousins, MCB #2, 715. It is interesting that the staff of a Southern state institution in the 1880s considered violence toward African Americans a mental problem.

27. J. J. Nuckols, MCB #2, 308; William M. Tredway, Jr., MCB #2, 262; Logue, *To Appomattox and Beyond*, 124–25; Rosenburg, *Living Monuments*, 112–16. Out of fifteen Pittsylvania veterans admitted, seven had significant problems with "intemperate" use of these substances.

28. James C. McCue, MCB #1, 173; James P. Sykes, MCB #1, 477; Elizabeth A. Sykes file, Pittsylvania County, Act of 1900, Auditor of Public Accounts, Confederate Pension Applications, LVA; "Cerebro-spinal disease" probably meant that Sykes had meningitis.

29. William M. Tredway, Jr., MCB #2, 262. Three of fifteen Pittsylvania veterans were admitted with physical illnesses that contributed to their mental issues. "Debauchery" may have been code for sexually transmitted diseases. Grob, *The Mad among Us*, 124–25.

30. Samuel Davis, MCB #2, 142; Catherine M. Nicholson, FCB #1, 471. Asylum doctors explained four of the seventy-five cases in the sample by heredity.

31. James Burruss, MCB #1, 500; Catherine M. Nicholson, FCB #1, 471. See also John D. Price, MCB #1, 513. These three patients were the only ones in the overall sample to have recorded prewar problems.

32. Patient Register, 1828–1895, WSH; Cynthia Ann Gray (also listed as Ann Gray and Cinthia Gray), FCB #2, 215. Out of seventy-five patients in the sample, four had no recorded mental difficulties.

33. Mary Woodell, FCB #1, 125; Catherine M. Nicholson, FCB #1, 471.

34. Marcellus Cousins, MCB #2, 715; Simon Hornsberger, MCB #1, 209; Edward Newcomb, MCB #1, 503; Catherine Bailey, FCB #1, 63–64.

35. Polly Shank, FCB #1, 530–31; Samuel Davis, MCB #2, 142.

36. Elizabeth Ann Pittman, FCB #1, 215–16.

37. Marcellus Cousins, MCB #2, 715. See Grob, *The Mad among Us*, 103–28; Tomes, *The Art of Asylum-Keeping*, 44–321; Hughes, "Labeling and Treating Black Mental Illness," 436–60.

38. Dean, *Shook Over Hell*, 116–17; Grob, *The Mad among Us*, 58–59, 82; Tomes, *The Art of Asylum-Keeping*, xii–xiii.

39. These diagnoses were not mutually exclusive. Often patients were labeled as suffering from multiple disorders. For example, Marcellus Cousins was diagnosed as maniacal and delusional. See MCB #1, 715.

40. William Granville Gray, MCB #1, 583, 587; Polly Shank, FCB #1, 530–31; Charles W. White, MCB #1, 108–9. Out of forty-seven patients with designated mental disorders, thirty-four were classified with "mania."

41. Adam Thompson, MCB #1, 591.

42. Benjamin Carder, MCB #1, 99–100; Richard Y. Moran, MCB #1, 405; William E. Herndon, MCB #1, 87. Out of forty-seven patients with designated mental disorders, four were classified as "delusional."

43. J. Hampden Chamberlayne, MCB #1, 82–88, 95; William E. Herndon, MCB #1, 87.

44. William E. Herndon, MCB #1, 87. The exploration of this poisoning incident at Western State and its place in both contemporary mental-health practices and Virginia state politics is the subject of a separate project of mine, "Murder at the Asylum."

45. Louisa C. Powell, FCB #2, 562. See also Thomas Mathews (also "Matthews"), MCB #1, 590. Out of forty-seven patients with designated mental disorders, five were classified with "melancholia."

46. Mary Calfee, FCB #1, 279; William Granville Gray, MCB #1, 587. Out of forty-seven patients with designated mental disorders, four were classified with "dementia." Occasionally the staff eschewed a psychological diagnosis and simply described their patients as "Very insane." In most cases, this description covered patients with extreme symptoms of mania, dementia, and delusions. For example, see the file of veteran James R. Millner, MCB #2, 252.

47. Patient Register, 1828–1895, WSH; James C. McCue, MCB #1, 173.

48. See Dean, *Shook Over Hell*, 116–18; Grob, *The Mad Among Us*, 142–51, 191–221.

49. Dean, *Shook Over Hell*, 26–29.

50. Pitman and Orr, "Psychophysiologic Testing for PTSD," 38, quoted in Gorman, "When Johnny Came Marching Home Again," 194–96; Dean, *Shook Over Hell*, 101–8. See also American Psychiatric Association, *DSM-IV-TR*, 463–68.

51. James C. McCue, MCB #1, 173; William M. Tredway, Jr., MCB #2, 262; William H. White, MCB #3, 757.

52. Richard Y. Moran, MCB #1, 405; Mary Woodell, FCB #1, 125. Out of fifty-eight patients in the sample whose fate could be identified, eight attempted to escape the asylum.

53. John W. Kerlin, MCB #1, 521; Charles W. White, MCB #1, 108–9. Thirty-seven of the fifty-eight patients whose fate could be identified were eventually discharged.

54. Joseph Noel, MCB #1, 38–39; James Burruss, MCB #1, 501.

55. Maria Harris, FCB #1, 460.

56. Polly Shank, FCB #1, 530–31; Elizabeth Ann Pittman, FCB #1, 215–16.

57. Mary Bird, FCB #1, 506–8; Samuel Davis, MCB #2, 142.

58. Gertrude Handy, MCB #1, 524–26; James Millner, MCB #2, 252.

59. McCandless, *Moonlight, Magnolias, and Madness*, 232–33; Grob, *The Mad among Us*, 101–2, 126; Patient Register, 1828–1895, WSH. Only nine of thirty-seven patients dis-

charged returned to the asylum. McCandless's percentage is from 1870 to 1877. See Tomes, *The Art of Asylum-Keeping*, 324–26.

60. Mary Woodell, FCB #1, 125; Caleb Rector, MCB #1, 559.

61. James Langhorne, MCB #1, 588; Catherine Bailey, FCB #1, 63–64. Sixteen of the fifty-eight patients whose fate is known died.

62. William Granville Gray, MCB #1, 583, 587; James Millner, MCB #2, 252.

63. Martha J. Lewis, FCB #2, 160, and FCB #3, 315; Randolph Shelton, MCB #2, 467.

64. Grob, *The Mad among Us*, 103–28; McCandless, *Moonlight, Magnolias, and Madness*, 249–69; Gamwell and Tomes, *Madness in America*, 119–24, 134–41, 171–73. On Western Lunatic Asylum's becoming a caretaking, rather than curing, facility, see Virginia, *Annual Reports of the Board of Directors and of the Superintendent of the Western Lunatic Asylum of Virginia*, 1874–1875, table XI, in which the doctors noted that 332 of the 356 patients had an "Unfavorable Prospect of Recovery." By 1890, 63 percent of the residents (382 of 604) had been at the institution five years or more; over 38 percent (232 of 604) had been there ten years or more (Virginia, *Annual Reports of the Board of Directors and of the Superintendent of the Western Lunatic Asylum of Virginia*, 1889–1890, table 10).

65. Thomas Mathews (also "Matthews"), MCB #1, 590.

66. James Burruss, MCB #1, 501; Maria Harris, FCB #1, 460.

67. J. Hampden Chamberlayne, MCB #1, 82–88, 95; John W. Kerlin, MCB #1, 521.

68. James Elliott, MCB #2, 172; Benjamin Carder, MCB #1, 99–100.

69. Chapter 85, *Code of Virginia*, in *By-Laws, Regulations, Etc. of Western Lunatic Asylum* (1871), 38–39. Unfortunately, records indicating how many people paid and how many were released from payment have apparently not survived. See also Wallenstein, "Laissez Faire and the Lunatic Asylum," 9–19.

70. Chapter 85, *Code of Virginia*, in *By-Laws, Regulations, Etc. of Western Lunatic Asylum* (1871), 38–39; Virginia, *Acts and Joint Resolutions* (1900): 1258, (1902): 473, (1906): 215. For more on social stigma, see Tomes, *The Art of Asylum-Keeping*, xiv.

71. William A. Miller, MCB #1, 435.

72. William M. Tredway, Jr., MCB #2, 262; letter from Langhorne Scruggs, April 12, 1884, Langhorne Scruggs Papers, DU.

73. William Granville Gray, MCB #1, 583, 587.

74. Mary Bird, FCB #1, 506–8.

75. This is the claim that Burruss made about his wife (James Burruss, MCB #1, 500).

76. William M. Tredway, Jr., MCB #2, 262. Gerald Grob has noted that late-nineteenth-century mental institutions, in spite of their many limitations, "did provide *minimum* levels of care for individuals unable to survive by themselves." Nancy Tomes has pointed out, however, "how dangerous it is to generalize about 'the' patient experience of the asylum." Grob, *Mental Illness in American Society*, xi (emphasis in original); Tomes, *The Art of Asylum-Keeping*, xxi.

77. Polly Shank, FCB #1, 530–31; J. Hampden Chamberlayne, MCB #1, 82–88, 95; Chamberlayne, ed., *Ham Chamberlayne—Virginian*, viii–ix.

78. James McCue, MCB #1, 173. For other examples, see Whites, *The Civil War as a Crisis in Gender*, 96–159; Logue, *To Appomattox and Beyond*, 104–6; Carter, *When the War Was Over*, 269–71.

6. State Aid for Veteran Families: Artificial Limbs, Commutations, Pensions, and Confederate Homes

1. W. H. Power, Pittsylvania County, Act of 1888, Auditor of Public Accounts, Confederate Pension Applications, LVA (hereafter cited as Pension Applications, LVA).

2. Skocpol, *Protecting Soldiers and Mothers*; McConnell, *Glorious Contentment*; Kelly, *Creating a National Home*; Marten, "Exempt from the Ordinary Rules of Life."

3. Gorman, "Confederate Pensions as Southern Social Welfare"; Kenzer, "The Uncertainty of Life"; Gross, "'Good Angels': Confederate Widowhood and the Reassurance of Patriarchy"; Hamburger, "We Take Care of Our Womenfolk"; Green, *This Business of Relief*; Racer, "Wounded Women"; Dickens, "An Arm and a Leg for the Confederacy." See especially Green's sweeping work on social welfare in Richmond, *This Business of Relief*, 68–127.

4. For a discussion of the Readjusters, Conservative Democrats, the Lost Cause, and the politics of the post-Reconstruction years in Virginia, see Dailey, *Before Jim Crow*; Blair, *Cities of the Dead*. See also Green's study on a Reconstruction-era compromise among social-welfare providers that reinforced antebellum segregation of white and black relief efforts. Green, *This Business of Relief*, 101–2.

5. McDaid, "With Lame Legs and No Money," 17; Virginia, *Acts and Joint Resolutions* (1866–67): 575–76 (hereafter cited as Virginia, *Acts*). See also Dickens, "An Arm and a Leg for the Confederacy."

6. McDaid, "With Lame Legs and No Money," 17. The governor of Virginia, the Auditor of Public Accounts, and a physician made up the Board of Commissioners on Artificial Limbs. Virginia, *Acts* (1866–67): 575–76.

7. Morrison, "Increasing the Pensions of These Worthy Heroes," 5–11; Virginia, *Acts* (1867): 575; (1869–70): 533; (1871–72): 440–41; (1872–73): 14–15; (1874): 40–41; (1874–75): 98; (1875–76): 37–38; (1876–77): 238; (1877–78): 180–81; (1878–79): 73; (1881–82): 126, 488; (1883–84): 187–89; (1885–86): 71, 533; (1887): 433–34.

8. McDaid, "With Lame Legs and No Money," 18; Joseph A. Boyd, Pittsylvania County, Act of 1882, 1884, Auditor of Public Accounts, Confederate Pension Disability Applications and Receipts, LVA (hereafter cited as Artificial Limbs, LVA); Act of 1888, Pension Applications, LVA. McDaid's article indicates that commutations began in 1882, but the March 1872 artificial-limb act contained a provision that allowed a former soldier to get "an amount in money equivalent to the cost of such leg" if he could not "use said artificial leg, or . . . it is unfit for use." See also January 1873 Act, in Virginia, *Acts* (1872–73): 14–15.

9. Virginia, *Acts* (1875–76): 37–38; (1881–82): 126.

10. Virginia, *Acts* (1879–80): 154–55; (1885–86): 71. See McClintock, "Civil War Pensions," 463.

11. Virginia, *Acts* (1866–67): 575–76; (1883–84): 187–89; quote from instructions to court in Joseph T. Miller, Act of 1884, Artificial Limbs, LVA; Virginia, *Acts* (1887): 483–84; U.S. Census Office, *Statistics of the Population of the United States at the Tenth Census*, 850. See McClintock, "Binding Up the Nation's Wounds."

12. Virginia, *Acts* (1871–72): 440–41; (1874–75): 98; (1875–76): 37–38; (1881–82): 126.

13. Virginia, *Acts* (1883–84): 187–89; table 14, "List of Disabled Soldiers and Marines Paid," in Virginia, *Annual Report of the Auditor of Public Accounts* (1884–85), 1–23; Virginia, *Acts* (1885–86): 71; (1887): 483–84. See Thomas Cook, John C. Davis, and Joseph T. Miller, Act of 1884, Artificial Limbs, LVA.

14. Skocpol, *Protecting Soldiers and Mothers*, 139–42; Green, *This Business of Relief*, 104–5, 118–27, tables 5–8; Resch, *Suffering Soldiers*; Dailey, *Before Jim Crow*; Blair, *Cities of the Dead*, 4, 9, 115–34; Gorman, "Confederate Pensions as Southern Social Welfare," 24–39.

15. Virginia, *Acts* (1887–88): 469–74 (quotes on 469); Green, *This Business of Relief*, 124–25.

16. Virginia, *Acts* (1887–88): 469–74.

17. Ibid. (quotes on 472).

18. Ibid. See McClintock, "Binding Up the Nation's Wounds."

19. Holmes, "Such Is the Price We Pay," 172. For more on the state as a surrogate husband, see Gross, "'Good Angels': Confederate Widowhood in Virginia."

20. Compiled from Pittsylvania County and Danville, Act of 1888, Pension Applications, LVA.

21. David Shields, Pittsylvania County, Act of 1888, Pension Applications, LVA.

22. For the sake of comparison, pension amounts in table 6.1 can be adjusted for inflation. The approximate equivalents in 2005 dollars adjusted for inflation since 1888 are $6,100 ($300), $20,500 ($1,000), $1,200 ($60), $600 ($30), and $300 ($15). The approximate equivalents in 2005 dollars adjusted for inflation since 1900 are $2,200 ($100), $1,100 ($50), and $900 ($40). The approximate equivalents in 2005 dollars adjusted for inflation since 1902 are $3,300 ($150) and $11,000 ($500). The approximate pension equivalents in 2005 dollars adjusted for inflation since 1912 are $3,000 ($150), $1,300 ($65), $700 ($36), and $475 ($24). See "The Inflation Calculator," www.westegg.com/inflation.

23. *Senate Journal* (1898): 96, 274, 637, 677; *Journal of the House* (1898): 161, 418, 594, both cited in Morrison, "Increasing the Pensions of These Worthy Heroes," 13–14; Virginia, *Acts* (1899–1900): 1477–81.

24. Elizabeth Hagood (also "Hagwood"), Pittsylvania County, Act of 1888, Pension Applications, LVA; Green, *This Business of Relief*, 119–20; Virginia, *Acts* (1899–1900): 1257, 1261.

25. Virginia, *Acts* (1899–1900): 1257–62; Rueben F. Hankins, Pittsylvania County, Act of 1888, Act of 1900, Pension Applications, LVA. See also John Bennett, G. H. Edwards, Obediah Hogan, and W. W. Adams, Pittsylvania County, Act of 1900, Pension Applications, LVA.

26. Virginia, *Acts* (1899–1900): 1257–59; Harriet G. Hodnett, Pittsylvania County, Act of 1900, Pension Applications, LVA.

27. Virginia, *Acts* (1901–2): 472–97 (quotes from 473). On loyalty as a factor in Georgia's pensions, see Gorman, "Confederate Pensions as Southern Social Welfare," 24–39.

28. Virginia, *Acts* (1901–2): 488.

29. Ibid., 496–97; Virginia, *Annual Report of the Auditor of Public Accounts*, 1899, 1900, 1905.

30. Virginia, *Acts* (1912): 385; Cassandra Burch, Mary Davis, Pittsylvania County, Act of 1888, Pension Applications, LVA.

31. Virginia, *Acts* (1912): 385–86.

32. Ibid., 385–87.

33. Virginia, *Acts* (1915): 58; (1916): 2–11; (1918): 143–53; (1922): 253–54; (1924): 294–303; (1926): 138–39, 836–37; (1927): 202–3.

34. E. Williams, "A Home . . . for the Old Boys," 40–42. Out of $600,000 given to the home before 1904, $475,000 came from the state. See also Green, *This Business of Relief*, 121–22, table 6.

35. Rosenburg, *Living Monuments*, esp. 3–12; A. Anderson, *Address on the Opening of Lee Camp Soldiers' Home*, 7–9.

36. The definitive work on the Richmond Home for Needy Confederate Women is Susan Hamburger's "We Take Care of Our Womenfolk," 61–77. See also Green, *This Business of Relief*, 121–22, table 6. In discussions of the Southern state homes for Confederate women, Karen Cox and Jennifer Gross stress the key role played by the women of the United Daughters of the Confederacy in creating these institutions and convincing the states to subsidize them. Cox, *Dixie's Daughters*, 76–82; Gross, "'Good Angels': Confederate Widowhood and the Reassurance of Patriarchy," 208–19.

37. McDaid, "With Lame Legs and No Money," 15; U.S. Census Office, *Abstract of the Eleventh Census*, 85; Virginia, *Annual Report of the Auditor of Public Accounts*, 1888, 1900. The percentage of veterans receiving pensions in 1900 was almost certainly higher since the 1890 census count of veterans in the state was used. Undoubtedly, some of those veterans had died in the intervening ten years. Unfortunately, counts of the total number of Confederate veterans in the state at various times are lacking, making more accurate rates of state veteran pension usage near impossible. Similar percentages are not possible for widows since there are no similar state-level counts for them in the 1890 census.

38. E. Williams, "A Home . . . for the Old Boys," 40–46; Rosenburg, *Living Monuments*, 161, 165, 171; Hamburger, "We Take Care of Our Womenfolk," 72. The percentage is calculated from the 1890 census count of Virginia's Confederate veterans (48,713) and the number of people admitted to the home from Virginia (2,694) as reported in the home's 1931 annual report. U.S. Census Office, *Abstract of the Eleventh Census*, 85; Virginia, *Report of the Board of Visitors* (1932), 9–11.

39. Compiled from Pittsylvania County and Danville, Artificial Limbs and Pension Applications, LVA; Robert E. Lee Camp Confederate Soldiers' Home Applications for Admission, LVA. Of the 3,283 men from Pittsylvania who fought in front-line units, 2,452 survived the war. The numbers given here underestimate the percentage of living Pittsylvania veterans who applied for commutations, pensions, or admission to the home because a lot of them died by the time full pensions or beds in the home were available. As for the Home for Needy Confederate Women, it seems unlikely, based on the extant records, that any female relatives of Pittsylvania or Danville veterans stayed at the home. Home for Needy Confederate Women Records, LVA.

40. Rodgers, *Tracing the Civil War Veteran Pension System in the State of Virginia*, 2; McClintock, "Civil War Pensions and the Reconstruction of Union Families," 463.

41. Logue, *To Appomattox and Beyond*, 89–90; McConnell, *Glorious Contentment*, 143–53.

42. McClintock, "Civil War Pensions and the Reconstruction of Union Families," 464; McConnell, *Glorious Contentment*, 153; Glasson, *Federal Military Pensions in the United States*, 272; Virginia, *Annual Report of the Auditor of Public Accounts*, 1888–1927, Morrison, "Increasing the Pensions of These Worthy Heroes," table 1; Skocpol, *Protecting Soldiers and Mothers*, 109. The percentage of Virginia's veterans who received pensions was probably higher than 17 percent, but it certainly was not anywhere near three-fourths of all surviving veterans.

43. Skocpol, *Protecting Soldiers and Mothers*, 139–43; Logue, *To Appomattox and Beyond*, 90–93. See also Kelly, *Creating a National Home*; Marten, "Exempt from the Ordinary Rules of Life."

44. Skocpol, *Protecting Soldiers and Mothers*, 139–40; Logue, *To Appomattox and Beyond*, 108–46; Morton, "Federal and Confederate Pensions Contrasted," 68–74; Glasson, "The South's Pension and Relief Provisions for the Soldiers of the Confederacy," 61–71; Rosenburg, *Living Monuments*; Cox, *Dixie's Daughters*, 76–82; Gross, "'Good Angels': Confederate Widowhood and the Reassurance of Patriarchy," 208–19; Green, *This Business of Relief*, 123–26, tables 6–8. On Georgia's exceptionally generous pensions, see Morton, "Federal and Confederate Pensions Contrasted," 69; Young, "Confederate Pensions in Georgia," 47–52; Glasson, "The South's Pension and Relief Provisions for the Soldiers of the Confederacy," 64; Rosenburg, *Living Monuments*, 161; Gorman, "Confederate Pensions as Southern Social Welfare."

45. D. P. Marshall, Pittsylvania County, Act of 1886, Artificial Limbs, LVA; John Henry Riddle and John H. Tower, Pittsylvania County, Act of 1888, Pension Applications, LVA; Pittsylvania County Population Census, 1870. For more on the census, see the appendix.

46. Reuben Powell, Pittsylvania County, Act of 1888, Pension Applications, LVA.

47. Isaac A. Keesee and Henry W. Davis, Pittsylvania County, Act of 1900, Pension Applications, LVA; Pittsylvania County Population Census, 1900.

48. Pittsylvania County Population Census, 1860, 1870 (72 percent of white men and 76 percent of veterans worked in agriculture in 1870); Thomas R. Cook, A. N. Crews, and B. H. Lewis, Pittsylvania County, Act of 1888, Pension Applications, LVA.

49. John Douglas and Nannie (Nancy) Douglas, Pittsylvania County, Act of 1900, Pension Applications, LVA; James C. Wilson, Pittsylvania County, Act of 1884, Artificial Limbs, LVA.

50. Samuel A. Robertson, Pittsylvania County, Act of 1900, Pension Applications, LVA; Pittsylvania County Population Census, 1900.

51. Amelia Riddle, Pittsylvania County, Act of 1888; Mary Hubbard and Nancy Mullins, Danville, Act of 1888, Pension Applications, LVA.

52. Enoch H. Farmer, Danville, Act of 1882; John S. Robertson, Pittsylvania County, Act of 1884, Artificial Limbs, LVA.

53. Martha Yeatts and James M. Banks, Pittsylvania County, Act of 1888; David N. Adkinson (also Atkinson and Adkins), Pittsylvania County, Act of 1900, all in Pension Applications, LVA; Pittsylvania County Population Census, 1870.

54. John T. Mann and Martha Dodson, Pittsylvania County, Act of 1888, Pension Applications, LVA.

55. Richard K. Pugh, John T. Gatewood, Francis H. Gibson, and Gabriella Ricketts, Pittsylvania County, Act of 1900, Pension Applications, LVA.

56. Thomas J. Tucker and Robert T. Biggs, Pittsylvania County, Act of 1900, Pension Applications, LVA.

57. John H. Milam, John A. Ferguson, and James J. Shelton, Jr., Act of 1888; J. J. Shelton, Pittsylvania County, Act of 1900, all in Pension Applications, LVA.

58. Joshua Towler, Pittsylvania County; James W. Gosney, Danville, Act of 1900, both in Pension Applications, LVA.

59. Joseph R. Green, Pittsylvania County, Act of 1900, Pension Applications, LVA.

60. Gorman, "Confederate Pensions as Southern Social Welfare," 36–37; Green, *This Business of Relief*, 118–27; Rosenburg, *Living Monuments*.

61. Gregory, *38th Virginia Infantry*, 111; Joseph T. Miller, Danville, Act of 1884, Artificial Limbs, LVA; Act of 1888, Pension Applications, LVA. Quotes from Artificial Limbs file.

62. Pittsylvania County Population Census, 1880.

63. McDaid, "With Lame Legs and No Money," 16–17. See also Herschbach, "Fragmentation and Reunion."

64. Pittsylvania County Population Census, 1860, 1870; Joseph T. Miller, Danville, Act of 1884, Artificial Limbs, and Act of 1888, Pension Applications, LVA; McDaid, "With Lame Legs and No Money," 18–19; John S. Robertson, Pittsylvania County, Act of 1884, Artificial Limbs, LVA.

65. John S. Robertson, Pittsylvania County, Act of 1884, Artificial Limbs, LVA. See also Dickens, "An Arm and a Leg for the Confederacy," 53–88.

66. C. Long, *Wages and Earning*, 151.

67. Derks, ed., *The Value of a Dollar*, 10; Hall et al., *Like a Family*, 79–80. Spinners' annual salary calculated from weekly salary multiplied by an estimate of fifty work weeks per year. Most pensioners under the 1888 act received $15 to $30 each year, and most pensioners under the 1900 to 1912 acts received $15 to $50.

68. Pittsylvania County Population Census, 1870, 1880, 1900; Martha Yeatts, Pittsylvania County, Act of 1888, Pension Applications, LVA.

69. John W. Douglas and Nannie (Nanncy) V. Douglas, Pittsylvania County, Act of 1900, Pension Applications, LVA.

70. S. M. Garrett, Pittsylvania County, Act of 1888; Nannie J. Mullins, Danville, Act of 1900, both in Pension Applications, LVA.

71. Rawley W. Martin, Act of 1883, Artificial Limbs, LVA.

72. McClintock, "Civil War Pensions and the Reconstruction of Union Families," 471–79; Gross, "'Good Angels' or Dangerous Women," 11–13; Nancy C. East, Bettie S. Galloway, Maria O. Simpson, Martha Thomas, and Mary Worley, Pittsylvania County, Act of 1888, Pension Applications, LVA. At least one of the cases that McClintock cites indicates that some women probably did live with, rather than marry, new love interests. See also Holmes, "Such Is the Price We Pay," 171–95.

73. Compiled from Pittsylvania County and Danville, Act of 1888, Pension Applications, LVA. This percentage consists of 42 completely disallowed pension applicants under

the 1888 act and 21 who were initially disallowed but who were eventually successful before 1900, out of 313 total Pittsylvania County and Danville applicants under the 1888 act. See also Gorman, "Confederate Pensions as Southern Social Welfare," 31; Racer, "Wounded Women."

74. George C. Lynch and Charles H. Owen, Pittsylvania County, Act of 1888, Pension Applications, LVA.

75. Charles H. Owen, Pittsylvania County, Act of 1888, Pension Applications, LVA; compiled from Pittsylvania County and Danville, Act of 1888, Pension Applications, LVA. Of those forty-two, twenty-three reapplied under the 1900 Pension Act, almost all of them successfully.

76. Compiled from Pittsylvania County and Danville, Act of 1888, Pension Applications, LVA. Under the 1888 act, 123 out of 129 widow applicants and 57 out of 191 veteran applicants from Pittsylvania-Danville first filed in 1888 or 1889.

77. Compiled from Pittsylvania County and Danville, Act of 1888, Pension Applications, LVA; John T. Gunnell, Pittsylvania County, Act of 1888, Pension Applications, LVA. Under the 1888 act, 114 out of 191 veteran applicants from Pittsylvania-Danville first filed in 1894 or after.

78. Robert K. Turner, Act of 1888, Pittsylvania County; Robert H. Evans, Act of 1900, Pittsylvania County, both in Pension Applications, LVA.

79. Compiled from Pittsylvania County and Danville, Act of 1900, Pension Applications, LVA. Both veterans and widows applied under the 1900 Pension Act at similar times: 87.5 percent of veterans (175 of 200) first applied in April or May 1900, compared to 85.5 percent of widows (65 of 76) who applied during that same period.

80. Robert E. Lee Camp Confederate Soldiers' Home Applications for Admission, LVA; Rosenburg, *Living Monuments*, 3–12.

81. E. Williams, "A Home . . . for the Old Boys," 42–45; Logue, *To Appomattox and Beyond*, 124–25; Rosenburg, *Living Monuments*, 72.

82. E. Williams, "A Home . . . for the Old Boys," 43; Logue, *To Appomattox and Beyond*, 124–25; James S. Redd, Robert E. Lee Camp Confederate Soldiers' Home Applications for Admission, LVA.

83. E. Williams, "A Home . . . for the Old Boys," 43; Logue, *To Appomattox and Beyond*, 124–25. See also Rosenburg, *Living Monuments*, 93–110.

84. Quoted in E. Williams, "A Home . . . for the Old Boys," 45–46.

85. Ibid.

86. Rosenburg, *Living Monuments*, 5; Hamburger, "We Take Care of Our Womenfolk."

Appendix: A Note on Sources

1. In *Danville in the Civil War*, Lawrence McFall lists 4,324 names of men from the county and town who served in Confederate forces. McFall notes in his introduction, however, that this list includes hundreds of duplicate names of individuals who served in multiple units. McFall, *Danville in the Civil War*, ix, 116–46.

2. Data points included house and family numbers (assigned by the census taker), name, age, occupation, birthplace, sex, race, real and personal estate owned, literacy, school

attendance, if married in the last year, and so on. The 1870 census numbers nearly doubled because ex-slaves were then being included in the population census.

3. As discussed in more detail in chapter 2, this difficulty in finding widows and orphans results in some underrepresentation of the widows and families of soldiers who died during the war or in the postwar period before 1870.

4. Blake, "First in the Path of the Firemen."

Bibliography

ARCHIVAL COLLECTIONS

Duke University, Durham, NC
  William B. G. Andrews Papers
  E. J. Bell Papers
  Jedediah Carter Papers
  Jacob B. Click Papers
  J. F. Cobbs Papers
  Walter Coles Papers
  John Warwick Daniel Papers
  George W. Dickenson Papers
  Thomas J. Elliott Papers
  William A. J. Finney Papers
  James C. Franklin Papers
  William Clark Grasty and John F. Rison Collection
  George W. Jones Papers
  Richard Jones Papers
  Elisha Ford Keen Papers
  Williamson Kelly Papers
  James Leach Papers
  Rawley White Martin Papers
  Thomas Miley Papers
  Robert Edward Nelson Papers
  Pittsylvania Masonic Lodge No. 24 Papers
  John R. Raine Papers
  Roane Family Papers
  Langhorne Scruggs Papers
  Olivia E. Spencer Papers
  William T. Sutherlin Papers
  Henry E. Taurman Papers
  Nannie Tunstall Papers
  James M. Whittle Papers
  Womack Family Papers

LIBRARY OF VIRGINIA, RICHMOND
Auditor of Public Accounts, Confederate Pension Disability Applications and Receipts, Acts of 1882, 1883, 1884, 1886–1887
Auditor of Public Accounts, Confederate Pension Applications, Acts of 1888, 1900, 1902
S. Bassett French Biographical Sketches
Home for Needy Confederate Women (Richmond, VA)
Robert E. Lee Camp Confederate Soldiers' Home Applications for Admission
Western Lunatic Asylum Female Case Book #1, #2 (formerly at Western State Hospital, Staunton, VA)
Western Lunatic Asylum Male Case Book #1, #2, #3 (formerly at Western State Hospital, Staunton, VA)
Western Lunatic Asylum Patient Register, 1828–1895 (formerly at Western State Hospital, Staunton, VA)

NATIONAL ARCHIVES, WASHINGTON, DC
Compiled Service Records of Confederate Soldiers Who Served in Organizations from the State of Virginia, microfilm copy
U.S. Census Office. Pittsylvania County, Virginia Population Schedules, 1860, 1870, 1880, and 1900, microfilm copy
———. Pittsylvania County, Virginia Slave Schedules, 1860, microfilm copy

SOUTHERN HISTORICAL COLLECTION, UNIVERSITY OF NORTH CAROLINA, CHAPEL HILL, NC
Benson Papers
Elias Davis Papers
Robert D. Ferguson Collection
Elizabeth Seawell Hairston Papers
George Hairston Papers
Peter Wilson Hairston Papers
Robert Hairston Papers
Hairston-Wilson Family Papers
Lewis Edwin Harvie Papers
Charles Fenton James Papers
Charles Edward Lippitt Papers
Rawley W. Martin Papers
R. S. Phifer Papers
William Thomas Sutherlin Papers
Zebulon B. Vance Papers
Richard Woolfolk Waldrop Papers
Lewis Neale Whittle Papers
Wilson and Hairston Family Papers
Robert B. Wilson Papers

UNIVERSITY OF VIRGINIA, CHARLOTTESVILLE
  Pittsylvania Central Alliance Trade Union Records
  Pittsylvania County Public Schools, Financial Accounts
  Pittsylvania County School Records
  Pittsylvania Ladies' Soldiers' Aid Society Papers
  Records of the Pittsylvania County School Commissioners

VIRGINIA BAPTIST HISTORICAL SOCIETY, UNIVERSITY OF RICHMOND
  Baptist General Association of Virginia, *Annual Meeting Minutes*, 1860–1900
  Jones, F. H., Rev. "Historical Sketch of Kentuck Church from May 1788 to May 1888."

  Pittsylvania County Church Records
    Cascade Primitive Baptist Church Minutes
    Chatham Baptist Church Minutes
    Chestnut Level Baptist Church Minutes
    County Line Church Minutes
    Edge Hill Baptist Church Minutes
    First Baptist Church of Danville Minutes
    Greenfield Baptist Church Minutes
    Kentuck Baptist Church Minutes
    Mill Creek Baptist Church Minutes
    Mt. Hermon Baptist Church Minutes
    Mt. Tabor Baptist Church
    New Prospect (Mt. Pleasant) Baptist Church
    Riceville Baptist Church
    Shockoe Baptist Church Minutes
    Straight Stone Baptist Church Minutes
    Vandola Baptist Church Minutes

  Religious Herald, 1860–1900

  Roanoke Baptist Association, *Minutes of the Annual Meeting*, 1860–1900

VIRGINIA HISTORICAL SOCIETY, RICHMOND
  Bailey Papers
  Carrington Papers
  Catherine M. P. Cochran Diary
  Dame Family Papers
  Douthat Family Papers
  Emily Howe Dupuy Papers
  Benjamin Lyons Farinholt Papers
  Achilles Whitlocke Hoge Diary
  Katherine Spiller Graves Moses Papers
  Saunders Family Papers
  David Harris Watson Papers

NEWSPAPERS

Daily Danville News
Daily Post (Danville, VA)
Daily Register (Danville, VA)
Danville Appeal
Danville Bee
Danville Daily New Era
Danville Daily Post
Danville Daily Register
Danville Evening Star
Danville Register
Danville Reporter
Danville Republican
Danville Times
Danville Weekly News
Danville Weekly Register
Pittsylvania Tribune
The Sixth Corps (Danville, VA)
Solid Facts (Spring Garden, VA)

OTHER SOURCES

Alderman, John Perry. *29th Virginia Infantry*. 1st ed. Virginia Regimental Histories Series. Lynchburg, VA: Howard, 1989.

American Psychiatric Association. *Diagnostic and Statistical Manual of Mental Disorders: DSM-IV-TR*. 4th ed., Text Revision. Washington, DC: American Psychiatric Association, 2000.

Anderson, Archer. *Address on the Opening of Lee Camp Soldiers' Home*. Richmond, VA: R. E. Lee Camp, No. 1, 1885.

Anderson, Eric, and Alfred Moss. *The Facts of Reconstruction: Essays in Honor Of John Hope Franklin*. Baton Rouge: Louisiana State University Press, 1991.

Anderson, James D. *The Education of Blacks in the South, 1860–1935*. Chapel Hill: University of North Carolina Press, 1988.

Andrus, Michael J. *The Brooke, Fauquier, Loudoun and Alexandria Artillery*. 1st ed. Virginia Regimental Histories Series. Lynchburg, VA: Howard, 1990.

Ash, Stephen V. *Middle Tennessee Society Transformed, 1860–1870: War and Peace in the Upper South*. Baton Rouge: Louisiana State University Press, 1988.

———. *When the Yankees Came: Conflict and Chaos in the Occupied South, 1861–1865*. Chapel Hill: University of North Carolina Press, 1995.

Axinn, June, and Mark J. Stern. *Social Welfare: A History of the American Response to Need*. Boston: Allyn and Bacon, 2001.

BIBLIOGRAPHY

Ayers, Edward L. *The Promise of the New South: Life after Reconstruction.* New York: Oxford University Press, 1992.

———. *Vengeance and Justice: Crime and Punishment in the 19th Century American South.* New York: Oxford University Press, 1984.

Ayers, Edward L., and John C. Willis. *The Edge of the South: Life in Nineteenth-Century Virginia.* Charlottesville: University Press of Virginia, 1991.

Bailey, Fred A. *Class and Tennessee's Confederate Generation.* Chapel Hill: University of North Carolina Press, 1987.

Barber, E. Susan. "'Sisters of the Capital': White Women in Richmond, Virginia, 1860–1880." Ph.D. diss., University of Maryland at College Park, 1997.

———. "'The White Wings of Eros': Courtship and Marriage in Confederate Richmond." In *Southern Families at War: Loyalty and Conflict in the Civil War South*, edited by Catherine Clinton, 119–32. New York: Oxford University Press, 2000.

Bardaglio, Peter. *Reconstructing the Household: Families, Sex, and the Law in the Nineteenth Century South.* Chapel Hill: University of North Carolina Press, 1995.

Barton, Michael, and Larry M. Logue, eds. *The Civil War Soldier: A Historical Reader.* New York: New York University Press, 2002.

Bell, Robert T. *11th Virginia Infantry.* 1st ed. Virginia Regimental Histories Series. Lynchburg, VA: Howard, 1985.

Berry, Stephen. *All That Makes a Man: Love and Ambition in the Civil War South.* New York: Oxford University Press, 2003.

Black, Robert C. *The Railroads of the Confederacy.* Chapel Hill: University of North Carolina Press, 1952; reprint, with a foreword by Gary W. Gallagher, Chapel Hill: University of North Carolina Press, 1998.

Blair, William. *Cities of the Dead: Contesting the Memory of the Civil War in the South, 1865–1914.* Chapel Hill: University of North Carolina Press, 2004.

———. *Virginia's Private War: Feeding Body and Soul in the Confederacy, 1861–1865.* New York: Oxford University Press, 1998.

Blake, Kellee. "First in the Path of the Firemen." *Prologue* 28, no. 1 (Spring 1996). http://www.archives.gov/publications/prologue/index/.

Blanck, Peter. "Civil War Pensions and Disability." *Ohio State Law Journal* 62, no. 1 (2001): 109–238.

Bleser, Carol, ed. *In Joy and in Sorrow: Women, Family, and Marriage in the Victorian South, 1830–1900.* New York: Oxford University Press, 1991.

Blight, David W. *Race and Reunion: The Civil War in American Memory.* Cambridge, MA: Harvard University Press, 2001.

Bode, Frederick A., and Donald E. Ginter. *Farm Tenancy and the Census in Antebellum Georgia.* Athens: University of Georgia Press, 1986.

Boney, F. N. *John Letcher of Virginia: The Story of Virginia's Civil War Governor.* Tuscaloosa: University of Alabama Press, 1966.

Bremner, Robert H. *American Philanthropy.* Chicago: University of Chicago Press, 1960.

———. *The Public Good: Philanthropy and Welfare in the Civil War Era.* New York: Knopf, 1980.

Brown, Edward M., and Harold Merskey. "Post-traumatic Stress Disorder and Shell

Shock." In *A History of Clinical Psychiatry: The Origin and History of Psychiatric Disorders*, edited by German E. Berrios and Roy Porter, 490–508. London: Athlone, 1999.

Brubaker, John H., III. *The Last Capital, Danville, Virginia, and the Final Days of the Confederacy*. Danville, VA: Danville Museum of Fine Arts and History, 1979.

Bryant, Jonathan M. *How Curious a Land: Conflict and Change in Greene County, Georgia, 1850–1885*. Chapel Hill: University of North Carolina Press, 1996.

Burr, Virginia Ingraham, ed. *The Secret Eye: The Journal of Ella Gertrude Clanton Thomas, 1848–1889*. Chapel Hill: University of North Carolina Press, 1990.

Burton, Matthew Wade. "The River of Blood and the Valley of Death: The Lives of Two Cousins for the Cause, Robert Selden Garnett and Richard Brooke Garnett, C.S.A." Master's thesis, Bowling Green State University, 1996.

Burton, Orville Vernon. *In My Father's House Are Many Mansions: Family and Community in Edgefield, SC*. Chapel Hill: University of North Carolina Press, 1985.

Busey, John W., and David G. Martin. *Regimental Strengths and Losses at Gettysburg*. 3rd ed. Hightstown, NJ: Longstreet House, 1994.

By-Laws, Regulations, Etc. of Western Lunatic Asylum, Virginia. Revised and Approved. Staunton, VA: Valley Virginian Job Office, 1871.

Bynum, Victoria. *Unruly Women: The Politics of Social and Sexual Control in the Old South*. Chapel Hill: University of North Carolina Press, 1992.

Campbell, Randolph. "Planters and Plain Folk: The Social Structure of the Antebellum South." In *Interpreting Southern History*, edited by John Boles and Evelyn Nolen, 48–77. Baton Rouge: Louisiana State University Press, 1987.

Carmichael, Peter. *The Last Generation: Young Virginians in Peace, War, and Reunion*. Chapel Hill: University of North Carolina Press, 2005.

Carter, Dan T. *When the War Was Over: The Failure of Self-Reconstruction in the South, 1865–67*. Baton Rouge: Louisiana State University Press, 1985.

Cashin, Joan E., ed. *The War Was You and Me: Civilians in the American Civil War*. Princeton, NJ: Princeton University Press, 2002.

Cavanaugh, Michael A. *The Otey, Ringgold and Davidson Virginia Artillery*. Virginia Regimental Histories Series. Lynchburg, VA: Howard, 1993.

Censer, Jane Turner. *The Reconstruction of White Southern Womanhood, 1865–1895*. Baton Rouge: Louisiana State University Press, 2003.

Chamberlayne, J. Hampden. *Ham Chamberlayne—Virginian: Letters and Papers of an Artillery Officer in the War for Southern Independence, 1861–1865*, edited by C. G. Chamberlayne. Richmond, VA: Dietz, 1932.

Clement, Maud Carter. *The History of Pittsylvania County, Virginia*. Lynchburg, VA: J. P. Bell, 1929.

———, ed. *Recollections of the Confederate Veterans of Pittsylvania County, Virginia*. Danville, VA: United Daughters of the Confederacy, Rawley Martin Chapter, 1960.

Clinton, Catherine. *Civil War Stories*. Athens: University of Georgia Press, 1998.

———. *The Other Civil War: American Women in the 19th Century*. New York: Hill and Wang, 1984.

———. *The Plantation Mistress: Woman's World in the Old South*. New York: Pantheon, 1982.

———. *Southern Families at War: Loyalty and Conflict in the Civil War South*. New York: Oxford University Press, 2000.

———. *Tara Revisited: Women, War and the Plantation Legend*. New York: Abbeville, 1995.

Clinton, Catherine, and Nina Silber, eds. *Battle Scars: Gender and Sexuality in the American Civil War*. New York: Oxford University Press, 2006.

———, eds. *Divided Houses: Gender and the Civil War*. New York: Oxford University Press, 1992.

Cohen, Lizabeth. *Making a New Deal: Industrial Workers in Chicago, 1919–1939*. Cambridge: Cambridge University Press, 1990.

Collins, Darrell. *46th Virginia Infantry*. 1st ed. Virginia Regimental Histories Series. Lynchburg, VA: Howard, 1992.

Cox, Karen. *Dixie's Daughters: The United Daughters of the Confederacy and the Preservation of Confederate Culture*. Gainesville: University Press of Florida, 2003.

Craven, Avery O. *Soil Exhaustion as a Factor in the Agricultural History of Virginia and Maryland, 1606–1860*. Urbana: University of Illinois Press, 1925.

Crews, Edward R., and Timothy A. Parrish. *14th Virginia Infantry*. 1st ed. Virginia Regimental Histories Series. Lynchburg, VA: Howard, 1995.

Crofts, Daniel W. *Reluctant Confederates: Upper South Unionists in the Secession Crisis*. Chapel Hill: University of North Carolina Press, 1989.

Culpepper, Marilyn M. *All Things Altered: Women in the Wake of Civil War and Reconstruction*. Jefferson, NC: McFarland, 2002.

———. *Trials and Triumphs: Women of the American Civil War*. East Lansing: Michigan State University Press, 1991.

Dailey, Jane. *Before Jim Crow: The Politics of Race in Postemancipation Virginia*. Chapel Hill: University of North Carolina Press, 2000.

———. "Deference and Violence in the Postbellum Urban South: Manners and Massacres in Danville, Virginia." *Journal of Southern History* 63 (August 1997): 553–90.

Dain, Norman. *Disordered Minds: The First Century of Eastern State Hospital in Williamsburg, Virginia, 1766–1866*. Charlottesville: University Press of Virginia, 1971.

Dame, George W. *Historical Sketch of Roman Eagle Lodge, 1820–1895*. Danville, VA: J. T. Townes, 1895.

Dame, William M. *From the Rapidan to Richmond and the Spotsylvania Campaign: A Sketch in Personal Narrative of the Scenes a Soldier Saw*. Baltimore: Green-Lucas, 1920.

Daniel, Pete. *Breaking the Land: The Transformation of Cotton, Tobacco, and Rice Cultures since 1880*. Urbana: University of Illinois Press, 1985.

Danville Museum of Fine Arts and History. "History—Sutherlin Family." http://www.danvillemuseum.org/index.php?page_id=19 (accessed August 2, 2007).

Dean, Eric T. *Shook Over Hell: Post-Traumatic Stress, Vietnam, and the Civil War*. Cambridge, MA: Harvard University Press, 1997.

———. "'We Will All Be Lost and Destroyed': Post-Traumatic Stress Disorder and the Civil War." *Civil War History* 37 (June 1991): 138–53.

DeCredico, Mary A. "'Hardships Most Bitter': The Impact of War on Urban Families, Richmond, 1861–1865." Paper presented at the Douglas Southall Freeman Symposium, "Families at War: Loyalty and Conflict in the Civil War South." University of Richmond, April 1998.

Degler, Carl. *The Other South: Southern Dissenters in the Nineteenth Century*. New York: Harper and Row, 1974.

Dennett, John R. *The South as It Is: 1865–1866*, edited by Henry M. Christman. New York: Viking, 1965.

Derks, Scott, ed. *The Value of a Dollar: Prices and Incomes in the United States, 1860–1999*. Lakeville, CT: Grey House, 1999.

Dickens, W. Jackson. "An Arm and a Leg for the Confederacy: Virginia's Disabled Veteran Legislation, 1865–1888." Master's thesis, University of Richmond, 1997.

Divine, John E. *8th Virginia Infantry*. 2d ed. Virginia Regimental Histories Series. Lynchburg, VA: Howard, 1984.

Donald, David Herbert. "A Generation of Defeat." In *From the Old South to the New: Essays on the Transitional South*, edited by Walter J. Fraser, Jr., and Winifred B. Moore, 3–20. Westport, CT: Greenwood, 1981.

Douglas, Ann. *The Feminization of American Culture*. New York: Knopf, 1977.

Driver, Robert J. *5th Virginia Cavalry*. 1st ed. Virginia Regimental Histories Series. Lynchburg, VA: Howard, 1997.

Durrill, Wayne. *War of Another Kind: A Southern Community in the Great Rebellion*. New York: Oxford University Press, 1990.

Dwyer, Ellen. *Homes for the Mad: Life inside Two Nineteenth-Century Asylums*. New Brunswick, NJ: Rutgers University Press, 1987.

Easterlin, Richard A. *Population, Labor Force, and Long Swings in Economic Growth: The American Experience*. New York: Columbia University Press, 1968.

Edwards, Laura. *Gendered Strife and Confusion: The Political Culture of Reconstruction*. Urbana: University of Illinois Press, 1997.

Escott, Paul. *After Secession: Jefferson Davis and the Failure of Confederate Nationalism*. Baton Rouge: Louisiana State University Press, 1978.

———. *Many Excellent People: Power and Privilege in North Carolina, 1850–1900*. Chapel Hill: University of North Carolina Press, 1985.

Evans, Sara. *Born for Liberty: A History of Women in America*. Rev. ed. New York: Free Press, 1997.

Evans, William McKee. *Ballots and Fence Rails: Reconstruction on the Lower Cape Fear*. Chapel Hill: University of North Carolina Press, 1966.

Faust, Drew Gilpin. "Christian Soldiers: The Meaning of Revivalism in the Confederate Army." In *The Civil War Soldier: A Historical Reader*, edited by Michael Barton and Larry M. Logue, 327–53. New York: New York University Press, 2002.

———. *Mothers of Invention: Women of the Slaveholding South in the American Civil War*. Chapel Hill: University of North Carolina Press, 1996.

———. "The Peculiar South Revisited: White Society, Culture, and Politics in the Antebellum Period, 1800–1860." In *Interpreting Southern History*, edited by John Boles and Evelyn Nolen, 78–119. Baton Rouge: Louisiana State University Press, 1987.

———. "'Without Pilot or Compass': Elite Women and Religion in the Civil War South."

In *Religion and the American Civil War*, edited by Randall M. Miller, Harry S. Stout, and Charles Reagan Wilson, 250–60. New York: Oxford University Press, 1998.
Fields, Frank E., Jr. *28th Virginia Infantry*. 1st ed. Virginia Regimental Histories Series. Lynchburg, VA: Howard, 1985.
First Baptist Church, Danville. *Centennial Celebration, 1834–1934*. N.p., 1934.
———. *First Baptist Church, Danville, Virginia, 1834–1959*. Danville, VA: First Baptist Church, 1959.
Foner, Eric. *Reconstruction: America's Unfinished Revolution, 1863–1877*. New York: Harper and Row, 1988.
Foster, Gaines. *Ghosts of the Confederacy: Defeat, the Lost Cause and the Emergence of the New South, 1865 to 1913*. New York: Oxford University Press, 1987.
Fox-Genovese, Elizabeth. *Within the Plantation Household: Black and White Women of the Old South*. Chapel Hill: University of North Carolina Press, 1988.
Frank, Joseph Allan. *With Ballot and Bayonet: The Political Socialization of American Civil War Soldiers*. Athens: University of Georgia Press, 1998.
Gamwell, Lynn, and Nancy Tomes. *Madness in America: Cultural and Medical Perceptions of Mental Illness before 1914*. Ithaca, NY: Cornell University Press, 1995.
Garnett, Mary Brumfield. *Bright Leaf: An Account of a Virginia Farm*. N.p., 1971.
Gilmour, Robert A. "The Other Emancipation: Studies in the Society and Economy of Alabama Whites During Reconstruction." Ph.D. diss., Johns Hopkins University, 1972.
Glasson, William H. *Federal Military Pensions in the United States*. New York: Oxford University Press, 1918.
———. "The South's Care for Her Confederate Veterans." *American Monthly Review of Reviews* 36 (1907): 40–47.
———. "The South's Pension and Relief Provisions for the Soldiers of the Confederacy." *North Carolina Historical Commission Bulletin* 23 (1918): 61–71.
Goldberg, Rebecca. "Last of the Johnny Rebs." *Richmond Quarterly* 5, no. 4 (Spring 1983): 43–46.
Goodheart, Lawrence B. *Mad Yankees: The Hartford Retreat for the Insane and Nineteenth-Century Psychiatry*. Amherst: University of Massachusetts Press, 2003.
Gorman, Kathleen L. "Confederate Pensions as Southern Social Welfare." In *Before the New Deal: Social Welfare in the South, 1830–1930*, edited by Elna C. Green, 24–39. Athens: University of Georgia Press, 1999.
———. "When Johnny Came Marching Home Again: Confederate Veterans in the New South." Ph.D. diss., University of California, Riverside, 1994.
Green, Elna C., ed. *Before the New Deal: Social Welfare in the South, 1830–1930*. Athens: University of Georgia Press, 1999.
———, ed. *The New Deal and Beyond: Social Welfare in the South since 1930*. Athens: University of Georgia Press, 2003.
———. *This Business of Relief: Confronting Poverty in a Southern City, 1740–1940*. Athens: University of Georgia Press, 2003.
Gregory, G. Howard. *53rd Virginia Infantry and 5th Battalion Virginia Infantry*. Virginia Regimental Histories Series. Lynchburg, VA: Howard, 1999.

———. *38th Virginia Infantry*. Lynchburg, VA: Howard, 1988.
Griffin, William E., Jr. *The Atlantic and Danville Railway Company: The Railroad of Southside Virginia*. N.p.: Carter, 1987.
Grimsley, Mark. *The Hard Hand of War: Union Military Policy toward Southern Civilians, 1861–1865*. Cambridge: Cambridge University Press, 1995.
Grob, Gerald N. *The Mad among Us: A History of the Care of America's Mentally Ill*. New York: Free Press, 1994.
———. *Mental Illness in American Society, 1875–1940*. Princeton, NJ: Princeton University Press, 1983.
Gross, Jennifer L. "'Good Angels': Confederate Widowhood and the Reassurance of Patriarchy in the Postbellum South." Ph.D. diss., Emory University, 2001.
———. "'Good Angels': Confederate Widowhood in Virginia." In *Southern Families at War: Loyalty and Conflict in the Civil War South*, edited by Catherine Clinton, 133–53. New York: Oxford University, 2000.
———. "'Good Angels' or Dangerous Women: Confederate Widows in Virginia." Paper presented at the Douglas Southall Freeman Symposium, "Families at War: Loyalty and Conflict in the Civil War South." University of Richmond, April 1998.
Gunn, Ralph White. *24th Virginia Infantry*. 1st ed. Virginia Regimental Histories Series. Lynchburg, VA: Howard, 1987.
Hahn, Steven. *The Roots of Southern Populism: Yeoman Farmers and the Transformation of the Georgia Upcountry, 1850–1890*. New York: Oxford University Press, 1983.
Hall, Jacquelyn Dowd, James Leloudis, Robert Korstad, Mary Murphy, Lu Ann Jones, and Christopher B. Daly. *Like a Family: The Making of A Southern Cotton Mill World*. New York: Norton, 1987.
Hall, Jacquelyn Dowd, and Anne Firor Scott. "Women in the South." In *Interpreting Southern History*, edited by John Boles and Evelyn Nolen, 454–509. Baton Rouge: Louisiana State University Press, 1987.
Hall, Matthew Glenn. "'Old Flu's' Artillerymen in War and Peacetime." Master's thesis, University of Richmond, 1996.
Hamburger, Susan. "We Take Care of Our Womenfolk: The Home for Needy Confederate Women in Richmond, Virginia." In *Before the New Deal: Social Welfare in the South, 1830–1930*, edited by Elna C. Green, 61–77. Athens: University of Georgia Press, 1999.
Harris, J. William. *Plain Folk and Gentry in a Slave Society: White Liberty and Black Slavery in Augusta's Hinterlands*. Middletown, CT: Wesleyan University Press, 1985.
Harrison, Kathy Georg, and John W. Busey. *Nothing but Glory: Pickett's Division at Gettysburg*. Gettysburg, PA: Thomas, 1993.
Harvey, Paul. "'Yankee Faith' and Southern Redemption: White Southern Baptist Ministers, 1850–1890." In *Religion and the American Civil War*, edited by Randall M. Miller, Harry S. Stout, and Charles Reagan Wilson, 167–86. New York: Oxford University Press, 1998.
Heimann, Robert K. *Tobacco and Americans*. New York: McGraw-Hill, 1960.
Herschbach, Lisa Marie. "Fragmentation and Reunion: Medicine, Memory and Body in the American Civil War." Ph.D. diss., Harvard University, 1997.

Heyrman, Christine Leigh. *Southern Cross: The Beginnings of the Bible Belt.* New York: Knopf, 1997.
Hill, Samuel S. "Religion and the Results of the Civil War." In *Religion and the American Civil War,* edited by Randall M. Miller, Harry S. Stout, and Charles Reagan Wilson, 360–75. New York: Oxford University Press, 1998.
Historical Census Browser. Geospatial and Statistical Data Center, University of Virginia, 2004. http://fisher.lib.virginia.edu/collections/stats/histcensus/.
Holmes, Amy E. "'Such Is the Price We Pay': American Widows and the Civil War Pension System." In *Toward a Social History of the Civil War: Exploratory Essays,* edited by Maris Vinovskis, 171–96. Cambridge: Cambridge University Press, 1990.
Hughes, John S. "Labeling and Treating Black Mental Illness in Alabama, 1861–1910." *Journal of Southern History* 58 (August 1992): 435–60.
Inter-University Consortium for Political and Social Research. Study 00003: *Historical Demographic, Economic, and Social Data: U.S., 1790–1970.* Ann Arbor, MI: ICPSR, 1970–1979.
Isaac, Rhys. *The Transformation of Virginia, 1740–1790.* New York: Norton, 1982.
James, Arthur W. *Virginia's Social Awakening: The Contribution of Dr. Mastin and the Board of Charities and Corrections.* Richmond, VA: Garrett and Massie, 1939.
Janney, Caroline E. *Burying the Dead but Not the Past: Ladies' Memorial Associations and the Lost Cause.* Chapel Hill: University of North Carolina Press, 2008.
Johnson, Russell L. "The Civil War Generation: Military Service and Mobility in Dubuque, Iowa." *Journal of Social History* 32 (Summer 1999): 791–820.
———. *Warriors into Workers: The Civil War and the Formation of Urban-Industrial Society in a Northern City.* New York: Fordham University Press, 2003.
Johnston, Angus James. *Virginia Railroads in the Civil War.* Chapel Hill: University of North Carolina Press, 1961.
Jordan, Ervin L., Jr., and Herbert A. Thomas. *19th Virginia Infantry.* 1st ed. Virginia Regimental Histories Series. Lynchburg, VA: Howard, 1987.
Katz, Michael B. *In the Shadow of the Poorhouse: A Social History of Welfare in America,* rev. and updated ed. New York: Basic Books, 1996.
Kelly, Patrick J. *Creating a National Home: Building the Veterans' Welfare State, 1860–1900.* Cambridge, MA: Harvard University Press, 1997.
Kenzer, Robert. *Kinship and Neighborhood in a Southern Community: Orange County, North Carolina, 1849–1881.* Knoxville: University of Tennessee Press, 1987.
———. "The Uncertainty of Life: A Profile of Virginia's Civil War Widows." In *The War Was You and Me: Civilians in the American Civil War,* edited by Joan E. Cashin, 112–35. Princeton, NJ: Princeton University Press, 2002.
Kerr-Ritchie, Jeffrey R. *Freedpeople in the Tobacco South: Virginia, 1860–1900.* Chapel Hill: University of North Carolina Press, 1999.
———. "Free Labor in the Virginia Tobacco Piedmont, 1865–1900." Ph.D. diss., University of Pennsylvania, 1993.
Kousser, J. Morgan, and James M. McPherson, eds. *Region, Race and Reconstruction: Essays in Honor of C. Vann Woodward.* New York: Oxford University Press, 1982.

Krick, Robert K. *The Gettysburg Death Roster: The Confederate Dead at Gettysburg*. Dayton, OH: Morningside Bookshop, 1981.

———. *Lee's Colonels: A Biographical Register of the Field Officers of the Army of Northern Virginia*. Dayton, OH: Morningside Bookshop, 1979.

———. *30th Virginia Infantry*. 4th ed. Virginia Regimental Histories Series. Lynchburg, VA: Howard, 1991.

Langhorne, Orra Henderson. *Southern Sketches from Virginia, 1881–1901*. Charlottesville: University Press of Virginia, 1964.

Lebsock, Suzanne. *The Free Women of Petersburg: Status and Culture in a Southern Town, 1784–1860*. New York: Norton, 1984.

Levin, Kevin M. "William Mahone, the Lost Cause, and Civil War History." *Virginia Magazine of History and Biography* 113, no. 4 (2005): 379–412.

Lightner, David L. *Asylum, Prison, and Poorhouse: The Writings and Reform Work of Dorothea Dix in Illinois*. Carbondale: Southern Illinois University Press, 1999.

Linderman, Gerald. *Embattled Courage: The Experience of Combat in the American Civil War*. New York: Free Press, 1987.

Link, William A. *A Hard Country and a Lonely Place: Schooling, Society and Reform in Rural Virginia, 1870–1920*. Chapel Hill: University of North Carolina Press, 1986.

———. *The Paradox of Southern Progressivism, 1880–1930*. Chapel Hill: University of North Carolina Press, 1992.

Logue, Larry. *To Appomattox and Beyond: The Civil War Soldier in War and Peace*. Chicago: Ivan R. Dee, 1996.

———. "Who Joined the Confederate Army? Soldiers, Civilians, and Communities in Mississippi." In *The Civil War Soldier: A Historical Reader*, edited by Michael Barton and Larry M. Logue, 44–56. New York: New York University Press, 2002.

Long, Clarence D. *Wages and Earning in the United States, 1860–1890*. Princeton, NJ: Princeton University Press, 1960.

Long, Lisa A. *Rehabilitating Bodies: Health, History, and the American Civil War*. Philadelphia: University of Pennsylvania Press, 2004.

Longacre, Edward G. *Pickett, Leader of the Charge: A Biography of General George E. Pickett, C.S.A*. Shippensburg, PA: White Mane, 1995.

Lowe, Richard G. *Republicans and Reconstruction in Virginia, 1856–1870*. Charlottesville: University Press of Virginia, 1991.

Mainwaring, W. Thomas. "Community in Danville, Virginia, 1880–1963." Ph.D. diss., University of North Carolina, Chapel Hill, 1988.

Manarin, Louis H. *15th Virginia Infantry*. 1st ed. Virginia Regimental Histories Series. Lynchburg, VA: Howard, 1990.

Mann, Charles Kellogg. *Tobacco: The Ants and the Elephants*. Salt Lake City, UT: Olympus, 1975.

Marten, James. *The Children's Civil War*. Chapel Hill: University of North Carolina Press, 1998.

———. "Exempt from the Ordinary Rules of Life: Researching Postwar Adjustment Problems of Union Veterans." *Civil War History* 47, no. 1 (2001): 57–70.

———. "'The War Was Continually Rising in Front of Me': Southern Children as Civil

War Dissenters." Paper presented at the Douglas Southall Freeman Symposium, "Families at War: Loyalty and Conflict in the Civil War South," University of Richmond, April 1998.

Martin, Edgar. *The Standard of Living in 1860: American Consumption Levels on the Eve of the Civil War*. Chicago: University of Chicago Press, 1942.

McCandless, Peter. *Moonlight, Magnolias, and Madness: Insanity in South Carolina from the Colonial Period to the Progressive Era*. Chapel Hill: University of North Carolina Press, 1996.

McClintock, Megan J. "Binding Up the Nation's Wounds: Nationalism, Civil War Pensions, and American Families, 1861–1890." Ph.D. diss., Rutgers University, 1994.

———. "Civil War Pensions and the Reconstruction of Union Families." *Journal of American History* 83 (September 1996): 456–80.

McConnell, Stuart. *Glorious Contentment: The Grand Army of the Republic, 1865–1900*. Chapel Hill: University of North Carolina Press, 1992.

McCurry, Stephanie. *Masters of Small Worlds: Yeoman Households, Gender Relations, and the Political Culture of the Antebellum South Carolina Lowcountry*. New York: Oxford University Press, 1995.

McCusker, John J. *How Much Is That in Real Money? A Historical Price Index for Use as a Deflator of Money Values in the Economy of the United States*. Worcester, MA: American Antiquarian Society, 1992.

McDaid, Jennifer Davis. "'With Lame Legs and No Money': Virginia's Disabled Confederate Veterans." *Virginia Cavalcade* 47 (Winter 1998): 14–25.

McFall, F. Lawrence. *Danville in the Civil War*. Virginia Regimental Histories Series. Lynchburg, VA: Howard, 2001.

McKenzie, Robert Tracy. *One South or Many? Plantation Belt and Upcountry in Civil War–Era Tennessee*. Cambridge: Cambridge University Press, 1994.

McPherson, James M. *Battle Cry of Freedom: The Civil War Era*. New York: Oxford University Press, 1988.

———. *Drawn with the Sword: Reflections on the American Civil War*. New York: Oxford University Press, 1996.

———. *For Cause and Comrades: Why Men Fought in the Civil War*. New York: Oxford University Press, 1997.

McPherson, James M., and William J. Cooper, Jr. *Writing the Civil War: The Quest to Understand*. Columbia: University of South Carolina Press, 1998.

Melton, Will. "Virginia Carbines of Danville and Pittsylvania Court House." *Pittsylvania Packet*, no. 23 (Winter 1997): 14–16.

Memorials of the Life, Public Services and Character of William T. Sutherlin. Danville, VA: Dance Bros., 1894.

Mitchell, Reid. "Christian Soldiers? Perfecting the Confederacy." In *Religion and the American Civil War*, edited by Randall M. Miller, Harry S. Stout, and Charles Reagan Wilson, 297–309. New York: Oxford University Press, 1998.

———. *Civil War Soldiers*. New York: Viking, 1988.

———. "'Not the General but the Soldier': The Study of Civil War Soldiers." In *Writing* the Civil War: The Quest to Understand, edited by James M. McPherson and William J. Cooper, 81–95. Columbia: University of South Carolina Press, 1998.

———. The Vacant Chair: The Northern Soldier Leaves Home. New York: Oxford University Press, 1993.

Montgomery, William H. Under Their Own Vine and Fig Tree: The African-American Church in the South, 1865–1900. Baton Rouge: Louisiana State University Press, 1992.

Moore, Robert H. The Danville, Eighth Star New Market and Dixie Artillery. 1st ed. Virginia Regimental Histories Series. Lynchburg, VA: Howard, 1989.

———. The Richmond Fayette, Hampden, Thomas, and Blount's Lynchburg Artillery. 1st ed. Virginia Regimental Histories Series. Lynchburg, VA: Howard, 1991.

Morrison, Jeffrey. "'Increasing the Pensions of These Worthy Heroes': Virginia's Confederate Pensions, 1888 to 1927." Master's thesis, University of Richmond, 1996.

Morton, M. B. "Federal and Confederate Pensions Contrasted." Forum 16 (September 1893): 68–74.

Murrell, Amy E. "'Of Necessity and Public Benefit': Southern Families and Their Appeals for Protection." In Southern Families at War: Loyalty and Conflict in the Civil War South, edited by Catherine Clinton, 77–99. New York: Oxford University Press, 2000.

Musick, Michael P. 6th Virginia Cavalry. 1st ed. Virginia Regimental Histories Series. Lynchburg, VA: Howard, 1990.

Oates, Stephen B. A Woman of Valor: Clara Barton and the Civil War. New York: Free Press, 1994.

O'Connor, Adrian. River City: Stories of Danville. N.p.: N.p., 1994.

Otto, John S. Southern Agriculture during the Civil War Era, 1860–1880. Westport, CT: Greenwood, 1994.

Ownby, Ted. Subduing Satan: Religion, Recreation and Manhood in the Rural South, 1865–1920. Chapel Hill: University of North Carolina Press, 1990.

Owsley, Frank. Plain Folk of the Old South. Baton Rouge: Louisiana State University Press, 1949.

Piehler, G. Kurt. Remembering War the American Way. Washington, DC: Smithsonian Institution Press, 1995.

Pitman, Roger, and Scott Orr. "Psychophysiologic Testing for Post-Traumatic Stress Disorder: Forensic Psychiatric Application." Bulletin of American Academy Psychiatry and Law 21 (1993): 37–52.

Pollock, Edward. Illustrated Sketchbook: Danville, Virginia, Its Manufactures, and Commerce. Danville, VA: E. R. Waddill and Bro., 1885; reprint, Danville, VA: Womack, 1976. Page cites refer to reprint edition.

Potter, David. The Impending Crisis, 1848–1861. New York: Harper and Row, 1976.

Powell, Lawrence. New Masters: Northern Planters during the Civil War and Reconstruction. New Haven, CT: Yale University Press, 1980.

Quist, John W. Restless Visionaries: The Social Roots of Antebellum Reform in Alabama and Michigan. Baton Rouge: Louisiana State University Press, 1998.

Rable, George. Civil Wars: Women and the Crisis of Southern Nationalism. Urbana: University of Illinois Press, 1989.

Racer, Heather A. "Wounded Women: A Study of Central Virginia's Civil War Pension Widows." Master's thesis, University of Richmond, 2001.

Randolph, Kirby Ann. "Central Lunatic Asylum for the Colored Insane: A History of African Americans with Mental Disabilities, 1844–1885." Ph.D. diss., University of Pennsylvania, 2003.

Ransom, Roger, and Richard Sutch. *One Kind of Freedom: The Economic Consequences of Emancipation*. Cambridge: Cambridge University Press, 1977.

Reardon, Carol Ann. "The Image of 'Pickett's Charge,' 1863–1913: Virginia's Gift to American Martial Tradition." Master's thesis, University of South Carolina, 1980.

———. *Pickett's Charge in History and Memory*. Chapel Hill: University of North Carolina Press, 1997.

Rees, Albert. *Real Wages in Manufacturing, 1890–1914*. Princeton, NJ: Princeton University Press, 1961.

Reidy, Joseph P. *From Slavery to Agrarian Capitalism in the Cotton Plantation South: Central Georgia, 1800–1880*. Chapel Hill: University of North Carolina Press, 1992.

Resch, John. *Suffering Soldiers: Revolutionary War Veterans, Moral Sentiment, and Political Culture in the Early Republic*. Amherst: University of Massachusetts Press, 1999.

Riggs, David. *7th Virginia Infantry*. 2d ed. Virginia Regimental Histories Series. Lynchburg, VA: Howard, 1991.

Riggs, Susan. *21st Virginia Infantry*. 1st ed. Virginia Regimental Histories Series. Lynchburg, VA: Howard, 1991.

Roark, James. *Masters without Slaves: Southern Planters in the Civil War and Reconstruction*. New York: Norton, 1977.

Robert, Joseph C. *The Story of Tobacco in America*. New York: Knopf, 1949.

———. *The Tobacco Kingdom: Plantation, Market, and Factory in Virginia and North Carolina, 1800–1860*. Durham, NC: Duke University Press, 1938.

Robertson, James I. *Civil War Virginia: Battleground for a Nation*. Charlottesville: University Press of Virginia, 1991.

———. "Danville under Military Occupation." *Virginia Magazine of History and Biography* 75, no. 3 (1967): 331–48.

———. *18th Virginia Infantry*. 2d ed. Virginia Regimental Histories Series. Lynchburg, VA: Howard, 1984.

———. "Houses of Horror: Danville's Civil War Prisons." *Virginia Magazine of History and Biography* 69 (July 1961): 329–45.

———. *Soldiers Blue and Gray*. Columbia: University of South Carolina Press, 1988.

Rodgers, Mark E. *Tracing the Civil War Veteran Pension System in the State of Virginia: Entitlement or Privilege*. Lewiston, NY: Edwin Mellen, 1999.

Rogers, Benjamin. "Life in the Camp Lee Soldiers' Home." *Virginia Magazine of History and Biography* 70 (1962): 468–70.

Rollins, Richard, ed. *Pickett's Charge: Eyewitness Accounts*. Redondo Beach, CA: Rank and File, 1994.

Romero, Sidney J. *Religion in the Rebel Ranks*. Lanham, MD: University Press of America, 1983.

Rorabaugh, W. J. *The Alcoholic Republic: An American Tradition.* New York: Oxford University Press, 1979.
Rosenburg, R. B. *Living Monuments: Confederate Soldiers' Homes in the New South.* Chapel Hill: University of North Carolina Press, 1993.
Rothman, David J. *Conscience and Convenience: The Asylum and Its Alternatives in Progressive America.* Boston: Little, Brown, 1980.
Rouse, Parke, Jr. *Below the James Lies Dixie: Smithfield and Southside Virginia.* Richmond, VA: Dietz, 1968.
Salmon, John S., comp. *A Guide to State Records in the Archives Branch of the Virginia Branch of the Virginia State Library and Archives.* Richmond: Virginia State Library, 1985.
Saum, Lewis O. *The Popular Mood of America, 1860–1890.* Lincoln: University of Nebraska Press, 1990.
Saville, Julie. *The Work of Reconstruction: From Slave to Wage Laborer in South Carolina, 1860–1870.* Cambridge: Cambridge University Press, 1994.
Savitt, Todd. *Medicine and Slavery: The Diseases and Health Care of Blacks in Antebellum Virginia.* Urbana: University of Illinois Press, 1978.
Schweiger, Beth Barton. *The Gospel Working Up: Progress and the Pulpit in Nineteenth-Century Virginia.* New York: Oxford University Press, 2000.
Severo, Richard, and Lewis Milford. *The Wages of War: When America's Soldiers Came Home—From Valley Forge to Vietnam.* New York: Simon and Schuster, 1989.
Shattuck, Gardiner. *A Shield and Hiding Place: The Religious Life of the Civil War Armies.* Macon, GA: Mercer University Press, 1999.
Sheehan-Dean, Aaron C. *Why Confederates Fought: Family and Nation in Civil War Virginia.* Chapel Hill: University of North Carolina Press, 2007.
Shifflett, Crandall. *Patronage and Poverty in the Tobacco South: Louisa County, Virginia, 1860–1900.* Knoxville: University of Tennessee Press, 1982.
Siegel, Frederick F. *The Roots of Southern Distinctiveness: Tobacco and Society in Danville, Virginia, 1780–1865.* Chapel Hill: University of North Carolina Press, 1987.
Silber, Nina. *The Romance of Reunion: Northerners and the South, 1865–1900.* Chapel Hill: University of North Carolina Press, 1993.
Sitton, Sarah C. *Life at the Texas State Lunatic Asylum, 1857–1997.* College Station: Texas A&M University Press, 1999.
Skarstedt, Vance R. "The Confederate Veteran Movement and National Reunification." Ph.D. diss., Florida State University, 1993.
Skocpol, Theda. *Protecting Soldiers and Mothers: The Political Origins of Social Policy in the United States.* Cambridge, MA: Belknap, 1992.
Smith, Robert Sidney. *Mill on the Dan: A History of Dan River Mills, 1882–1950.* Durham, NC: Duke University Press, 1960.
Steiner, Paul E. *Disease in the Civil War: Natural Biological Warfare in 1861–1865.* Springfield, IL: Charles C. Thomas, 1968.
Stevenson, Brenda. *Life in Black and White: Family and Community in the Slave South.* New York: Oxford University Press, 1996.

Sublett, Charles W. *57th Virginia Infantry*. 1st ed. Virginia Regimental Histories Series. Lynchburg, VA: Howard, 1985.
Sutherland, Daniel. *Seasons of War: The Ordeal of a Confederate Community, 1861–1865*. New York: Free Press, 1995.
Swem, Earl G., and John W. Williams. *A Register of the General Assembly of Virginia, 1776–1918, and of the Constitutional Conventions*. Richmond, VA: n.p., 1917.
Taylor, Amy Murrell. *The Divided Family in Civil War America*. Chapel Hill: University of North Carolina Press, 2005.
Taylor, Joe Gray. "The White South from Secession to Redemption." In *Interpreting Southern History*, edited by John Boles and Evelyn Nolen, 162–98. Baton Rouge: Louisiana State University Press, 1987.
Thielman, Samuel Barnett. "Madness and Medicine: The Medical Approach to Madness in Antebellum America, with Particular Reference to the Eastern Lunatic Asylum of Virginia and the South Carolina Lunatic Asylum." Ph.D. diss., Duke University, 1986.
Thomas, Emory. *The Confederacy as a Revolutionary Experience*. Englewood Cliffs, NJ: Prentice-Hall, 1971.
Thomas, Emory, Harry P. Owens, and James J. Cooke. *The Old South in the Crucible of War: Essays*. Jackson: University Press of Mississippi, 1983.
Tilley, Nannie M. *The Bright-Tobacco Industry*. Chapel Hill: University of North Carolina Press, 1948.
Tomes, Nancy. *The Art of Asylum-Keeping: Thomas Story Kirkbride and the Origins of American Psychiatry*. Cambridge: Cambridge University Press, 1984. Reprint, with a new introduction, Philadelphia: University of Pennsylvania Press, 1994. Page cites refer to reprint edition.
Trask, Benjamin. *9th Virginia Infantry*. 2d ed. Virginia Regimental Histories Series. Lynchburg, VA: Howard, 1984.
Trattner, Walter I. *From Poor Law to Welfare State: A History of Social Welfare in America*, 6th ed. New York: Free Press, 1999.
Trelease, Allen. *White Terror: The Ku Klux Klan Conspiracy and Southern Reconstruction*. New York: Harper and Row, 1971.
Tripp, Stephen Elliott. *Yankee Town, Southern City: Race and Class Relations in Civil War Lynchburg*. New York: New York University Press, 1997.
Truslow, Marion A. "Peasants into Patriots: The New York Irish Brigade Recruits and Their Families in the Civil War Era, 1850–1900." Ph.D. diss., New York University, 1994.
U.S. Census Office. *Statistics of the Population of the United States at the Ninth Census*. Washington, DC: Government Printing Office, 1872.
———. *Statistics of the Population of the United States at the Tenth Census*. Washington, DC: Government Printing Office, 1883.
———. *Abstract of the Eleventh Census: 1890*. 2nd ed., rev. and enl. Washington, DC: Government Printing Office, 1896.
"Valley of the Shadow: Two Communities in the American Civil War." Virginia Center for Digital History, University of Virginia, http://jefferson.village.virginia.edu/vshadow2/.

Vinovskis, Maris A. "Have Social Historians Lost the Civil War? Some Preliminary Demographic Speculations." Chap. 1 in *Toward a Social History of the American Civil War*. Cambridge: Cambridge University Press, 1990.

Virginia. *Acts and Joint Resolutions Passed by the General Assembly of the State of Virginia*, 1860–1920.

———. *Annual Report of the Auditor of Public Accounts to the General Assembly of Virginia*, 1860–1920.

———. *Annual Reports of the Board of Directors and of the Superintendent of the Western Lunatic Asylum of Virginia*, 1868–1920.

———. *Annual Reports of Officers, Boards and Institutions of the Commonwealth of Virginia*, 1871–1941.

———. *Report of the Board of Visitors: R. E. Lee Camp Soldiers' Home*, 1896–1932.

Wallace, Lee A., Jr. *1st Virginia Infantry*. 3d ed. Virginia Regimental Histories Series. Lynchburg, VA: Howard, 1985.

———. *A Guide to Virginia Military Organizations, 1861–1865*. Rev. ed. Virginia Regimental Histories Series. Lynchburg, VA: Howard, 1986.

———. *17th Virginia Infantry*. 1st ed. Virginia Regimental Histories Series. Lynchburg, VA: Howard, 1990.

———. *3rd Virginia Infantry*. 1st ed. Virginia Regimental Histories Series. Lynchburg, VA: Howard, 1986.

Wallenstein, Peter. *From Slave South to New South: Public Policy in Nineteenth-Century Georgia*. Chapel Hill: University of North Carolina Press, 1987.

———. "Laissez Faire and the Lunatic Asylum: State Welfare Institutions in Georgia—The First Half-Century, 1830s–1880s." In *Before the New Deal: Social Welfare in the South, 1830–1930*, edited by Elna C. Green, 3–23. Athens: University of Georgia Press, 1999.

Watkins, Sam R. *"Co. Aytch": A Side Show of the Big Show*. New York: Touchstone, 1990.

Watkinson, James D. "Rogues, Vagabonds, and Fit Objects: The Treatment of the Poor in Antebellum Virginia." *Virginia Cavalcade* 49 (Winter 2000): 16–29.

Wayne, Michael. *The Reshaping of Plantation Society: The Natchez District, 1860–1880*. Baton Rouge: Louisiana State University Press, 1983.

Weaver, J. C. *Virginia Home Guards*. 1st ed. Virginia Regimental Histories Series. Lynchburg, VA: Howard, 1996.

Wecter, Dixon. *When Johnny Comes Marching Home*. Cambridge, MA: Riverside, 1944.

Weitz, Mark A. *More Damning than Slaughter: Desertion in the Confederate Army*. Lincoln: University of Nebraska Press, 2005.

Whites, LeeAnn. *The Civil War as a Crisis in Gender: Augusta, Georgia, 1860–1890*. Athens: University of Georgia Press, 1995.

———. *Gender Matters: Civil War, Reconstruction, and the Making of the New South*. New York: Palgrave, 2005.

Wiener, Jonathan M. *Social Origins of the New South, Alabama, 1860–1885*. Baton Rouge: Louisiana State University Press, 1978.

Wiley, Bell I. *The Life of Billy Yank*. Baton Rouge: Louisiana State University Press, 1951.

———. *The Life of Johnny Reb*. Baton Rouge: Louisiana State University Press, 1943.

Williams, Emily J. "'A Home . . . for the Old Boys': The Robert E. Lee Camp Confederate Soldiers' Home." *Virginia Cavalcade* 28 (Summer 1979): 40–47.
Williams, Kathleen, comp. "Pittsylvania County, Virginia Wills, 1800–1870." N.p., n.d.
Williams, Mike. *Confederate Soldiers of Pittsylvania County and Danville*. Signal Mountain, TN: Mountain, 1988.
"William Thomas Sutherlin." *Virginia Magazine of History and Biography* 1 (January 1894): 339–40.
Wilson, Charles Reagan. *Baptized in Blood: The Religion of the Lost Cause, 1865–1920*. Athens: University of Georgia Press, 1980.
Wisner, Elizabeth. *Social Welfare in the South from Colonial Times to World War I*. Baton Rouge: Louisiana State University Press, 1970.
Withers, Robert Enoch. *Autobiography of an Octogenarian*. Roanoke, VA: Stone, 1907.
Wood, Alice Davis. *Dr. Francis T. Stribling and Moral Medicine: Curing the Insane at Virginia's Western State Hospital, 1836–1874*. Waynesboro, VA: GallileoGianniny, 2004.
Wood, Kirsten. *Masterful Women: Slaveholding Widows from the American Revolution through the Civil War*. Chapel Hill: University of North Carolina Press, 2004.
Woodman, Harold. "Economic Reconstruction and the Rise of the New South, 1865–1900." In *Interpreting Southern History*, edited by John Boles and Evelyn Nolen, 254–307. Baton Rouge: Louisiana State University Press, 1987.
Woodward, C. Vann. *The Burden of Southern History*. Baton Rouge: Louisiana State University Press, 1968.
———. *Origins of the New South, 1877–1913*. Baton Rouge: Louisiana State University Press, 1951.
Woodworth, Steven E. *While God Is Marching On: The Religious World of Civil War Soldiers*. Lawrence: University Press of Kansas, 2001.
Wright, Gavin. *Old South, New South: Revolutions in the Southern Economy since the Civil War*. New York: Basic Books, 1986.
———. *The Political Economy of the Cotton South: Households, Markets and Wealth in the 19th Century*. New York: Norton, 1978.
Wyatt-Brown, Bertram. *The Shaping of Southern Culture: Honor, Grace, and War, 1760s–1890s*. Chapel Hill: University of North Carolina Press, 2001.
———. *Southern Honor: Ethics and Behavior in the Old South*. New York: Oxford University Press, 1982.
Young, James R. "Confederate Pensions in Georgia, 1886–1929," *Georgia Historical Quarterly* 66 (1982): 47–52.
Young, William A., Jr., and Patricia C. Young. *56th Virginia Infantry*. 1st ed. Virginia Regimental Histories Series. Lynchburg, VA: Howard, 1990.

Index

adultery, 67, 96, 97
age, pensions and, 151–52, 159, 162–63
agriculture. *See* farming
alcohol, 66, 95–96, 125–26, 205n27
amputations, 24, 25
amputees, aid for, 143, 152, 158
Appomattox, surrender at, 41
armies. *See* Confederate Army
artificial limbs, 144, 145–48, 156, 164–65, 208n8
artillery fire, 21–23
Ash, Stephen, 28, 74
asylums, 43, 203n3; caretaking role of, 137, 207n64; chronic patients in, 136–37; commitments to, 127–29, 141; costs of care at, 139; deaths and, 135–36, 207n61; discharges from, 206n53; escapes from, 133, 134, 206n52; experiences in, 141–42; goals of, 118–19, 133; patients returning to, 127, 206n59; trends in, 119. *See also* Western State Hospital
attendance at Baptist churches, 94–95

Baptist churches, 72, 194n1, 195n14; alcohol and, 95–96; behavioral expectations of, 94–98; blacks and, 195n15; Civil War and, 73–78; disputes among members in, 78, 95; dissatisfaction with, 93; financial support and, 73–74, 79–87, 196n32; First Baptist Church of Danville, 73, 81–82, 85, 88; Greenfield Baptist Church, 78; Kentuck Baptist Church, 79–81, 83, 86–87; membership growth of, 42, 76, 77, 92, 93–94; post–Civil War, 78–98; Shockoe Baptist Church, 30–31, 73–74
Baptist General Association of Virginia, 74–75, 77, 85–86, 88, 90
Bardaglio, Peter, 181n19
Bell, John, 12

blacks, 119, 180n6, 195n15
boarders, taking in, 54, 190n27

casualties and death rates, 23, 24, 188n2
celebrations for departing soldiers, 14–15
Chatham (Va.), 9–12
child-father relationships, 50–51
children, occupations for, 63–64
church charities, 82–84, 87. *See also* Baptist churches
Civil War: Baptist churches and, 73–78; death rates, 23, 24, 188n2; defeat of Confederacy, 51, 68, 90–91, 124–25, 130; demographic impact of, 45; economic impact of, 31–32, 47, 158; emotional impact of, 49–52; end of, 40–41; families' experiences of, 28–34; mental illness and, 119, 120–29; preparations for, 12–15; psychological impact on veterans, 181n18; rebuilding after, 42–43; separation and, 49–51; soldiers' experiences of, 15–28
clothing, lack of, 16
combat stress. *See* PTSD (Post-Traumatic Stress Disorder)
commitment to asylums, 127–29; benefits of, 141
"Committee of Forty," 100
commutations, 144, 146–48, 156, 164–65; ability to work and, 146, 161, 163; economic hardship and, 160; widows and, 147
Confederate Army: celebrations for, 14–15; defeat of, 51, 68, 90–91, 124–25, 130; formation of, 13–14, 39; percentage of white male population in, 14–15, 183n13, 188n2; soldiers' experiences in, 15–28
Confederate Arsenal, 41
Confederate government, aid from, 42–43
"Confederate Interior," 28, 79
Confederate veterans organizations, 108

235

conscription, 13; mental illness and, 120, 127, 204n8

Danville (Va.), 9–12, 57; as Confederate center, 28–29
Danville Female College, 100, 102
Danville Riot, 100
Davis, Jefferson, 41, 68
deacons, 81–82
Dean, Eric, 132
deaths, 18, 25, 26, 51–52; in asylums, 135–36, 207n61; Civil War, 23, 24, 188n2; dealing with, 39–40; funeral expenses and, 154; impact on household wealth, 48; impact on mental illness, 122; vs. mental illness, 139
defeat of Confederacy, 51, 68, 90–91, 124–25, 130
delusional, diagnosis of, 130–31, 206n42
dementia, diagnosis of, 131, 206n46
demographic impact of Civil war, 45
Dependent Pension Act of 1890, 157
depression, economic, 65
depression, emotional, 66, 131
desertions, 37–38
disability, mental illness and, 205n29
discharges: asylum, 133–34, 133–35, 206n53; medical, 25
diseases, 17–20, 67, 184n25; deaths from, 18; inability to work and, 158–59; pension amounts and, 152–53
domestic labor, 54, 63
domestic servants, 62, 192n56
domestic violence, 66–67, 69, 96–97
dysentery, 18

Eastern Lunatic Asylum, 119
economic depression, 65
economic hardship, mental illness and, 124–25, 204n21
economic help. *See* financial support
economic impact of Civil War, 31–32, 47, 158
education, 64, 87–90, 193n61, 197n46
Edwards, Laura, 69
elites, 42, 60, 99, 102–3, 202n57; noblesse oblige, 116. *See also* Sutherlin, William T.
emancipation, 68, 190n23
emotional effects of Civil War, 49–52
emotional support, Baptist churches and, 74, 79, 90–94
employment, 104, 190n27; artificial limbs and, 165; Baptist churches and, 73–74, 84, 87; elites and, 60, 102; farming, 54, 59, 60, 62, 192n43; injuries and, 59–60; Sutherlin and, 102, 103–4, 106–7, 113, 199n10, 200n16; wartime injuries and, 59–60, 158–59; women and, 61–63, 192n56
escapes from asylums, 133, 134, 206n52
exposure, 15–16, 17, 162
expulsions, church, 78, 94, 97
extended-family households, 53–54, 190n25; stressors in, 65–66
extra-family households, 54, 190n28

families: child-father relationships, 50–51; Civil War and, 28–34, 34–40, 46–52; extended, 53–54, 65–66, 190n25; strategies of, 52–71
families, veteran, 2–3; appeals to Sutherlin by, 113, 114; elites and aid to, 116; employment of women in, 61–63, 192n56; farming and, 29–30, 36, 62; impact of Civil War on, 123–25; impact of mental illness on, 121–23, 137–41; impact of state aid on, 160, 163–71; stressors and, 65–70
farming, 29–30, 60, 191n38; families and, 29–30, 36, 62; in Pittsylvania County, 57–59; tenant, 58–59, 62; tobacco, 29–30, 57–58; women and, 61–62, 192n53, 192n55
farm laborers, 54, 59, 62, 190n27, 192n43
fasting days, 75, 91
father-child relationships, 50–51
Faust, Drew Gilpin, 69
federal government, pensions and, 157
finances, household, 36–37; impact of mental illness on, 138–39, 140–41; short-term impact of Civil War, 46
financial support: appeals for loans, 105, 200n21; Baptist churches and, 73–74, 79–87, 196n32; from elites, 99, 101, 102, 111; extra-household networks and, 40. *See also* pensions; state aid; Sutherlin, William T.
First Baptist Church of Danville, 73, 81–82, 85, 88
food, 17, 31–33, 41, 63
Fort Sumter, 13
funeral expenses, 154
furloughs, 35–36, 134–35

gardening, 61
gender roles, 67–68; asylums and, 133; church charities and, 82–84
Gettysburg, Battle of, 22

Green, Elna, 2
Greenfield Baptist Church, 78
Grob, Gerald, 135
Gross, Jennifer, 55, 56, 168
guilt, sense of, 110

Hamburger, Susan, 156
heredity, mental illness and, 126–27, 205n30
Home for Needy Confederate Women, 155–56, 171, 210n39
homes, veteran, 144, 155–56, 157–58, 170–71, 210n39. *See also* Robert E. Lee Camp Confederate Soldiers' Home
homesickness, 20–21
hospitals, Confederate, 23–24, 36, 184n24
hospitals, mental. *See* asylums; Western State Hospital
households, 2–3; combining, 40; emancipation and, 190n23; extended-family, 53–54, 65–66, 190n25; extra-family, 54, 190n28; female-headed, 62; restructuring of, 53–57; single-family, 53, 190n24; veteran, 188n4. *See also* finances, household
household wealth, 46, 47–49
housekeeping, 62–63, 73–74, 84, 193n57

illness, 17–20
infections, nosocomial, 24
inflation, 31–32
injuries, employment and, 59–60

Jeter, J. B., 61
Johnston, Joseph, 41

Kentuck Baptist Church, 79–81, 83, 86–87
Kenzer, Robert, 70

Lake, J. B., 81
land ownership, 11, 58, 188n5; property taxes, 154
laws, artificial-limb, 145–46, 208n8
Lebsock, Suzanne, 55, 56
Lee Camp Home. *See* Robert E. Lee Camp Confederate Soldiers' Home
letters, 21, 33–34, 34–35, 38–39, 101
Lincoln, Abraham, 12, 13
"living monuments," 170
loans, appeals for, 105, 200n21

malaria, 18
mania, diagnosis of, 129–30, 131, 206n40

marriage, 55, 56, 65; impact of Civil War on, 49–50; impact of mental illness on, 137–38; pensions and, 150, 153, 168; remarriage, 56, 191n34. *See also* widows
Marten, James, 50–51
martial law, 41
masculinity, 68–70; Baptist church and, 93–94
McCandless, Peter, 135
McClintock, Megan, 168
McDaid, Jennifer Davis, 146, 156
measles, 18
melancholia, diagnosis of, 131, 206n45
men: membership in Baptist churches, 94; shortage of, 55, 56, 191n30; single, 54, 191n29
mental illness, 118; alcohol and, 125–26, 205n27; battle and, 120–21; blacks and, 119; care of by family members, 127, 128, 134–35; Civil War and, 119, 120–29, 131; conscription and, 120, 127, 204n8; death and, 122, 204n16; diagnoses of, 129–37, 206n39; economic hardship and, 124–25, 204n21; financial impact of, 138–39; heredity and, 126–27, 205n30; POWs and, 121, 124; race relations and, 125; social stigma of, 139–40; vs. wartime death, 139; wounded veterans and, 123, 205n29
mental patients: experience of asylums, 141–42; returning to asylums, 127, 206n59
military draft, 13
Ministers' Relief Fund, 85–86, 87
moving, 64–65, 193n62

National Soldiers' Home, 157
networks, social, 34, 38–40, 52, 70–71
newspapers, 33–34
noblesse oblige, 116

occupations: multiple, 60–61, 63; non-agricultural, 59–61, 62; postwar, 57–64. *See also* employment
officers, resignation of, 38, 187n77

"partial disability," 150
patriarchy, 55, 66, 67–70, 133, 181n19. *See also* white male superiority
patron-client relationships, 116
pension acts: of 1888, 147, 149–52, 161; of 1900, 152–53, 161; of 1902, 153–54; of 1912, 154; disbursement amounts for, 151; exceptions to, 152; number of veterans helped by, 156

pensions, 145, 148–54, 210n37, 211n42; amputees and, 152; disease and, 152–53; federal government vs. Virginia, 157; financial impact of, 166–67; funeral expenses and, 154; growth in requests for, 153–54; impact on veteran families by, 166–70; inability to work requirements for, 151, 161, 163; old age and, 151–52, 159, 162–63; payment amounts, 154; Pittsylvania County and, 158–63; political context of, 149; poverty qualifications of, 149, 153, 160; POWs and, 162; property taxes and, 154; as recognition of sacrifice, 167–68; re-widowed women and, 154; timing of applications for, 169–70, 213n76, 213n77, 213n79; unsuccessful applications for, 150–51, 168–69; veterans and, 169–70, 210n37, 213n77; widows and, 149, 150, 153, 167, 168, 169, 213n76
persistence rate, 64–65, 193n62
"personal capital," 109, 110, 114, 201n39
personal estate, 46, 188n4
physicians, pension applications and, 163
Pickett's Charge, 22–23
Piedmont Railroad, 185n50
Pierpont, Francis, 145
Pittsylvania County (Va.), 9–12, 10, 180n11; Baptist churches in, 79; casualty and death rates, 23, 24; deaths of soldiers, 25; elites of, 99, 202n57; employment in postwar, 104; experiences of families in, during Civil War, 28–34; moving out of by veteran families, 64–65; pensions and, 158–63; postwar occupations in, 57–64; state aid and, 156; total wealth of, 46–47; wartime deaths from, 26
Pittsylvania Court House (Va.). *See* Chatham (Va.)
Pittsylvania Ladies' Soldiers' Aid Society, 42
planters, 11
pneumonia, 18
poisoning, 130–31
poorhouses, 57, 70–71, 191n37; veteran homes as, 170
poor-relief systems, church-based, 79–84
postal service, 36
Post-Traumatic Stress Disorder (PTSD). *See* PTSD (Post-Traumatic Stress Disorder)
POWs, 25, 27, 185n45, 185n47, 188n3; mental illness and, 121, 124; pensions and, 162
prayer days, 75
prayer meetings, 91

prisoners of war. *See* POWs
prisons, 25–27, 29, 162, 185n45, 189n10
PTSD (Post-Traumatic Stress Disorder), 51, 132–33
public schools, 88, 89

railroads, 9, 41, 111–12, 185n50
Randolph Macon College, 100
real estate, 46, 188n4
reciprocity, offers of, 110
remarriage, 56, 191n34
resections, 146
resignation of officers, 38, 187n77
revivals, religious, 77
rheumatism, 20
Richmond and Danville Railroad, 9, 41, 111–12
Roanoke Baptist Association, 76, 77, 86, 88, 92; alcohol and, 95–96
Robert E. Lee Camp Confederate Soldiers' Home, 155, 156, 210n34, 210n38; experiences of, 170–71; Pittsylvania County veterans and, 210n39
Robert E. Lee Camp of Confederate Veterans, 155
Rosenburg, R. B., 170

salaries of soldiers, 31, 32, 36
schools, public, 88, 89
Schweiger, Beth Barton, 87–88
secession, 12–13
sense of loss, 51, 68, 90–91, 124–25, 130
separation, wartime, 49–51
servants, domestic, 62, 192n56
services, religious, 74
sextons, 73–74, 84
shame, articulations of, 108–9
sharecropping, 58–59, 62
Sherman, William T., 41
Shifflett, Crandall, 116, 201n39
Shockoe Baptist Church, 30–31, 73–74
Shook Over Hell (Dean), 132
single-family households, 53, 190n24
Skocpol, Theda, 157
slavery, 11, 29–31
smallpox, 18
social networks, 34, 38–40, 52, 70–71
social-welfare system, 144–45
soldiers, salaries of, 31, 32, 36
Soldiers' Children Fund, 85, 88–90
spiritual support, 75, 77; Baptist churches and, 74, 90–94

state aid, 43, 143–44, 144–56; application process for, 147–48, 149; asylums as, 118–19, 142; federal government vs. Virginia, 157; impact on veteran families by, 163–71; Pittsylvania County and, 156; Southern states vs. Virginia, 157–58; as surrogate husband, 150, 153, 181n19; taking advantage of, 145–46, 155–58; veteran families and, 160

State Asylum of South Carolina, 135

Staunton River Bridge, Battle of, 183n14

stigma, social, 139–40

Straight Stone Church, 77

stressors, 65–70

support. *See* financial support; spiritual support

Sutherlin, William T., 13, 99–102; Civil War and appeals for help to, 102–3; common elements in requests to, 102, 105–11; impact of aid from, 113–14; reasons for/against helping, 114–15, 202n53; reasons for requests for help, 111–12; requests for employment and, 102, 103–4, 106–7, 113, 199n10, 200n16; requests for loans, 105, 200n21; requests for money, 200n13; results of petitions to, 113–17, 202n48; use of influence, 104, 111–12, 200n11, 200n17; veteran applicants and, 108, 199n6

taxes, property, 154

tenant farming, 58–59, 62. *See also* farming

tobacco, 11–12, 182n5; shortage of, 30

tobacco farming, 29–30, 57–58. *See also* farming

"total disability," 150, 157

Tripp, Steven, 116

"20 Negro" exemption, 30

typhoid fever, 18, 20

United Daughters of the Confederacy, 69, 155–56

veteran homes, 144, 155–56, 157–58, 170–71. *See also* Home for Needy Confederate Women; Robert E. Lee Camp Confederate Soldiers' Home

veterans: economic impact of war on, 189n7, 189n8; household wealth of, 47–49; impact of veteran homes on, 170–71; as "living monuments," 170; pensions and, 169–70, 210n37, 213n77

veterans, wounded, 188n3, 189n8; ability to work and, 158; masculinity and, 68–69; mental illness and, 123; recovery of, 24–25; state aid and, 144–45

Vinovskis, Maris, 45

violence, domestic, 66–67, 69, 96–97

Virginia Baptist Association, 74–75, 77, 85–86, 88, 90

Virginia General Assembly, 143, 148–49

volunteers, army, 13

warehousing of patients, 119

wealth: elite, 116, 202n57; household, 46, 47–49

Western Lunatic Asylum. *See* Western State Hospital

Western State Hospital, 118, 119, 203n3, 203n5; attempted escapes from, 133, 134; discharges of patients from, 133–34; growth in size of, 137, 138; poisoning and, 130–31; reasons for commitment to, 127–29; symptoms of PTSD at, 132–33

white male superiority, 68–70, 114; church charities and, 83–84. *See also* patriarchy

Whites, LeeAnn, 63, 65, 69

widows: Baptist churches and, 80–81; farming and, 192n53, 192n55; households of, 55–57, 191n35, 191n36; marriage and, 56, 150, 191n34; pensions and, 149, 150, 153, 154, 167, 168, 169, 213n76

Withers, Robert, 41

women: elite white, 69; employment for, 61–63; membership in Baptist churches, 77; mental illness and, 122

Wood, Kirsten, 56

Woodward, C. Vann, 51

A NATION DIVIDED:
STUDIES IN THE CIVIL WAR ERA

Neither Ballots nor Bullets: Women Abolitionists and the Civil War
Wendy Hamand Venet

Black Confederates and Afro-Yankees in Civil War Virginia
Ervin L. Jordan Jr.

Longstreet's Aide: The Civil War Letters of Major Thomas J. Goree
Thomas W. Cutrer

Lee's Young Artillerist: William R. J. Pegram
Peter S. Carmichael

Yankee Correspondence: Civil War Letters between New England Soldiers and the Homefront
Nina Silber and Mary Beth Sievens, editors

Southern Rights: Political Prisoners and the Myth of Confederate Constitutionalism
Mark E. Neely Jr.

Apostles of Disunion: Southern Secession Commissioners and the Causes of the Civil War
Charles B. Dew

Exile in Richmond: The Confederate Journal of Henri Garidel
Michael Bedout Chesson and Leslie Jean Roberts, editors

Ashe County's Civil War: Community and Society in the Appalachian South
Martin Crawford

The War Hits Home: The Civil War in Southeastern Virginia
Brian Steel Wills

Lincoln's Tragic Admiral: The Life of Samuel Francis Du Pont
Kevin John Weddle

A Separate Civil War: Communities in Conflict in the Mountain South
Jonathan Dean Sarris

Petersburg, Virginia, 1861–1865: Confederate City in the Crucible of War
A. Wilson Greene

Take Care of the Living: Reconstructing Confederate Veteran Families in Virginia
Jeffrey W. McClurken